AQA Mathematics

Book 2

Foundation (Linear)

Yeovil College
English & Maths

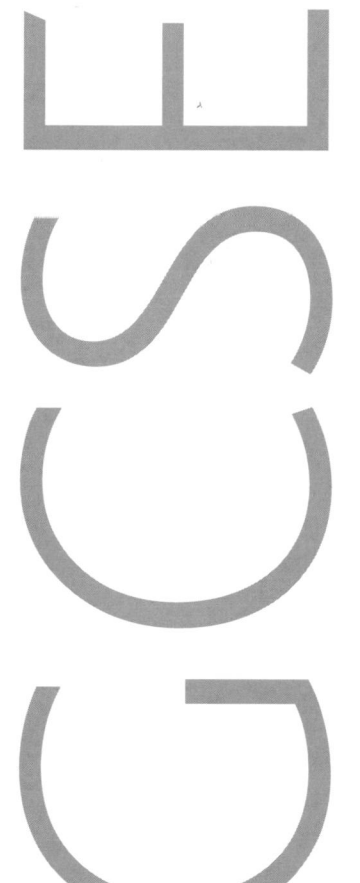
GCSE

Series Editor
Paul Metcalf

Series Advisor
Andy Darbourne

Lead Authors
Sandra Burns
Shaun Procter-Green
Margaret Thornton

Authors
Tony Fisher
June Haighton
Anne Haworth
Gill Hewlett
Steve Lomax
Jan Lucas
Andrew Manning
Ginette McManus
Howard Prior
David Pritchard
Dave Ridgway
Kathryn Scott
Paul Winters

Nelson Thornes

This edition published in 2013 by:
Nelson Thornes Ltd
Delta Place
27 Bath Road
CHELTENHAM
GL53 7TH
United Kingdom

13 14 15 16 / 10 9 8 7 6 5 4 3 2

A catalogue record for this book is available from the British Library

ISBN 978 1 4085 2147 2

Cover photograph: Purestock/Getty Images

Illustrations by Rupert Besley, Roger Penwill, Angela Knowles and Tech-Set Limited

Page make-up by Tech-Set Limited, Gateshead

Printed and bound in Spain by GraphyCems

Photo acknowledgements
Alamy: p17, p105, p141
Fotolia: p28 p44 p49 p77 p88 p88a p88b p137 p156 p168
iStockphoto: p51 p76 p79 p91 p97 p115 p132 p180 p184
Science Photo Library: p24

Contents

Introduction

Nelson Thornes has developed these resources to ensure that the book and the accompanying online resources offer you the best support for your GCSE course.

All resources have been reviewed by subject experts so you can feel assured that they closely match the specification for this subject.

The print and online resources together unlock blended learning; this means that the links between the activities in the book and the activities online blend together to maximise your understanding of a topic and help you achieve your potential.

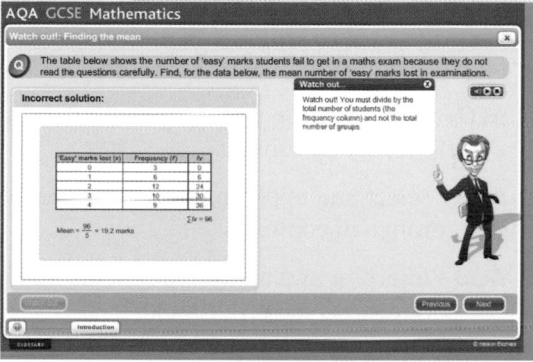

These online resources are available on  which can be accessed via the internet at **www.kerboodle.com/live**, anytime, anywhere.

If your school or college subscribes to kerboodle you will be provided with your own personal login details. Once logged in, access your course and locate the required activity.

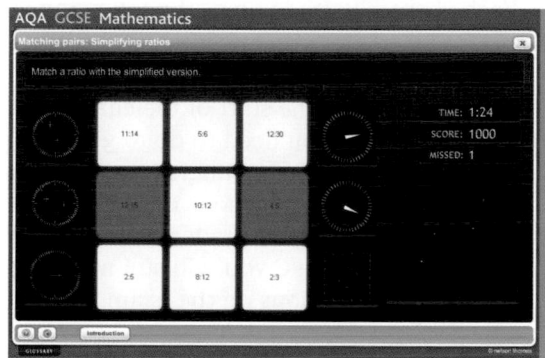

For more information and help on how to use kerboodle visit **www.kerboodle.com**.

How to use this book

To help you unlock blended learning, we have referenced the activities in this book that have additional online coverage in Kerboodle by using this icon:

The icons in this book show you the online resources available from the start of the new specification and will always be relevant.

In addition, to keep the blend up-to-date and engaging, we review customer feedback and may add new content onto Kerboodle after publication!

Welcome to GCSE Mathematics

This book has been written by teachers who not only want you to get the best grade you can in your GCSE exam, but also to enjoy maths. Together with Book 1 it covers all the material you will need to know for AQA GCSE Mathematics Foundation (Linear). Look out for calculator or non-calculator symbols (shown below) which tell you whether to use a calculator or not.

In the exam, you will be tested on the Assessment Objectives (AOs) below. Ask your teacher if you need help to understand what these mean.

AO1 recall and use your knowledge of the prescribed content

AO2 select and apply mathematical methods in a range of contexts

AO3 interpret and analyse problems and generate strategies to solve them.

Each chapter is made up of the following features:

Objectives

The objectives at the start of the chapter give you an idea of what you need to do to get each grade. Remember that the examiners expect you to do well at the lower grade questions on the exam paper in order to get the higher grades. So, even if you are aiming for a Grade C you will still need to do well on the Grade G questions on the exam paper.

On the first page of every chapter, there are also words that you will need to know or understand, called Key Terms. The box called 'You should already know' describes the maths that you will have learned before studying this chapter. There is also an interesting fact at the beginning of each chapter which tells you about maths in real life.

Learn...

The Learn sections give you the key information and examples to show how to do each topic. There are several Learn sections in each chapter.

Practise...

Questions that allow you to practise what you have just learned.

E The bars that run alongside questions in the exercises show you what grade the question is aimed at. This will give you an idea of what grade you're working at. Don't forget, even if you are aiming at a Grade C, you will still need to do well on the Grades G–D questions.

These questions are Functional Maths type questions, which show how maths can be used in real life.

These questions are problem solving questions, which will require you to think carefully about how best to answer.

These questions are harder questions.

These questions should be attempted **with** a calculator.

These questions should be attempted **without** using a calculator.

Assess

End of chapter questions test your skills. Some chapters feature additional questions taken from real past papers to further your understanding.

Hint

These are tips for you to remember whilst learning the maths or answering questions.

Study tip

Hints to help you with your study and exam preparation.

1 Representing data

Objectives

Examiners would normally expect students who get these grades to be able to:

G

construct and interpret a pictogram

construct and interpret a bar chart

F

construct and interpret a dual bar chart

interpret a pie chart

E

construct a pie chart

interpret a stem-and-leaf diagram

D

construct a stem-and-leaf diagram (ordered)

construct a histogram for data with equal class intervals

interpret a line graph

C

construct a frequency polygon.

Key terms

pictogram	back-to-back stem-and-leaf diagram
bar chart	line graph
pie chart	frequency polygon
key	frequency diagram
dual bar chart	histogram
composite bar chart	
stem-and-leaf diagram	

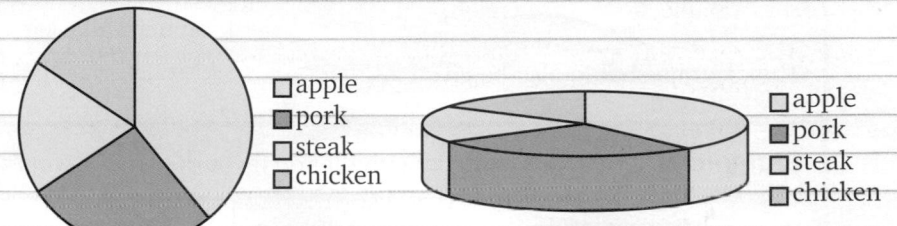

A. Favourite pies   B. Favourite pies

Did you know?

Favourite pie chart!

Charts and diagrams can sometimes be misleading. Look at the two pie charts above.

Which is the most popular pie shown in Chart A?

Which is the most popular pie shown in Chart B?

Is chicken pie more popular in Chart A or Chart B?

Without knowing the underlying data, it can be difficult to interpret the charts.

In fact, each of the two charts represents exactly the same set of data.

Apple pie is the favourite pie.

The proportions only look different because of the way the pie charts have been drawn.

3-D charts can misrepresent data.

Beware when representing data. Not every picture tells the same story!

You should already know:

✔ the measures of average: mean, mode and median

✔ how to find and work with the range

✔ how to measure and draw angles

✔ types of data, e.g. discrete and continuous, qualitative and quantitative

✔ the meaning of inequality signs

✔ how to construct and interpret a tally chart

✔ how to work with percentages and fractions.

Learn... 1.1 Pictograms, bar charts and pie charts

Pictograms, **bar charts** and **pie charts** are used to display either qualitative data or discrete quantitative data.

Qualitative data involve a description or feature, and are not numerical (a quality).

Quantitative data involve numbers of some kind (a quantity).

Pictograms

A symbol is used to represent a certain number of items.

A **key** shows the number of items each symbol stands for.

For example: Key: ▽ = 2 ice creams.

You can use part symbols for fewer items.

For example, ▽ = 1 ice cream.

The diagram should also be given a title.

> **Study tip**
>
> Remember to draw symbols the same size and line them up.

Example: Here are some data on the top favourite crisp flavours for a class of students in Year 10.

Flavour	Salt and vinegar	Cheese and onion	Ready salted
Number of students (frequency)	6	7	10

Draw a pictogram to show these data.

Solution: First you must decide on a symbol and how many it will represent. As the data only go up to 10, a symbol representing 2 students will be fine.

Often you can use a symbol connected to the situation.

> **Study tip**
>
> You may be asked to draw a pictogram in the exam. You will save time if your symbol represents more than one item.

Salt and vinegar	🧍 🧍 🧍
Cheese and onion	🧍 🧍 🧍 🧍
Ready salted	🧍 🧍 🧍 🧍 🧍

Key: 🧍 = 2 students

One symbol represents 2 students.

Six students preferred salt and vinegar so they need 3 symbols (6 ÷ 2).

Seven students preferred cheese and onion so they need $3\frac{1}{2}$ symbols (7 ÷ 2) and so on.

Bar charts

In all bar charts:

The length of each bar shows the number of items. Bars are the same width.

There must be an equal gap between the bars as they are separate items.

The vertical axis is labelled frequency and given an appropriate scale.

The horizontal axis is labelled appropriately.

The chart needs to be given a title.

Example: Draw a bar chart for the data on favourite crisps for all 30 students in a Year 10 class.

Flavour	Salt and vinegar	Cheese and onion	Ready salted	Steak and onion	Prawn cocktail
Number of students (frequency)	6	7	10	5	2

Solution:

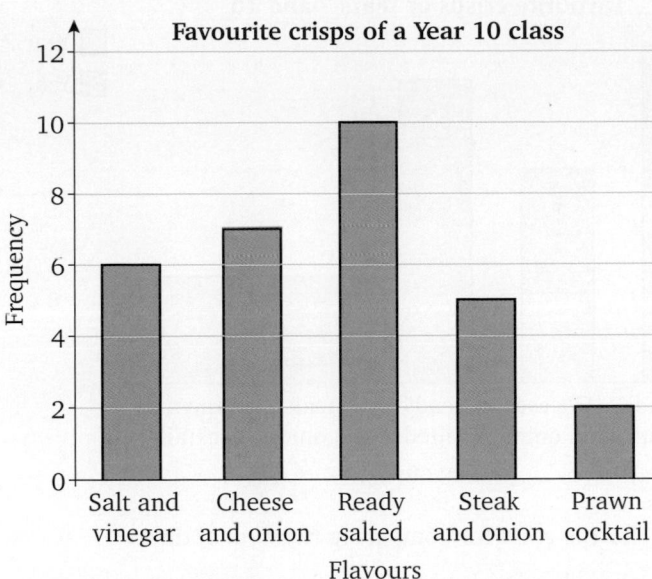

Bar charts can also be used to compare two sets of data.

A **dual bar chart** has pairs of bars separated by gaps.

A **composite bar chart** has single bars with two parts.

Example: Here are some data on the favourite crisp flavours for a class of 30 students in Year 7.

Flavour	Salt and vinegar	Cheese and onion	Ready salted	Steak and onion	Prawn cocktail
Number of students	13	5	7	1	4

  a Draw a dual bar chart to show these data and the data from Year 10 given above.

  b Draw a composite bar chart to show these data.

  c Give one advantage of using the dual bar chart.

  d Give one advantage of using the composite bar chart.

  e Compare the students' favourite crisps. What conclusions do you reach?

Solution: **a**

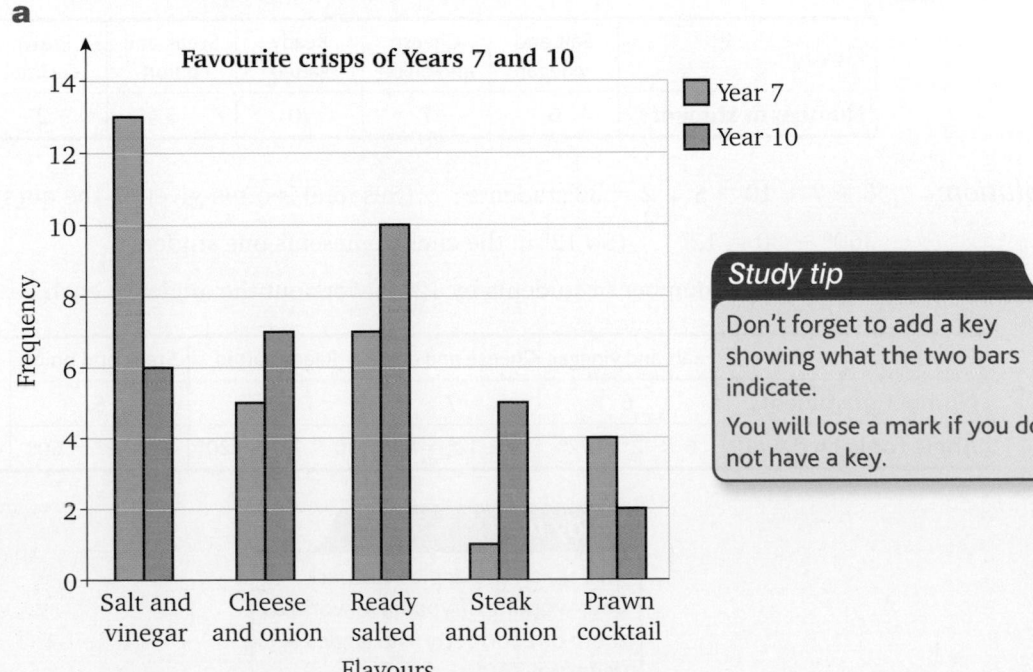

b

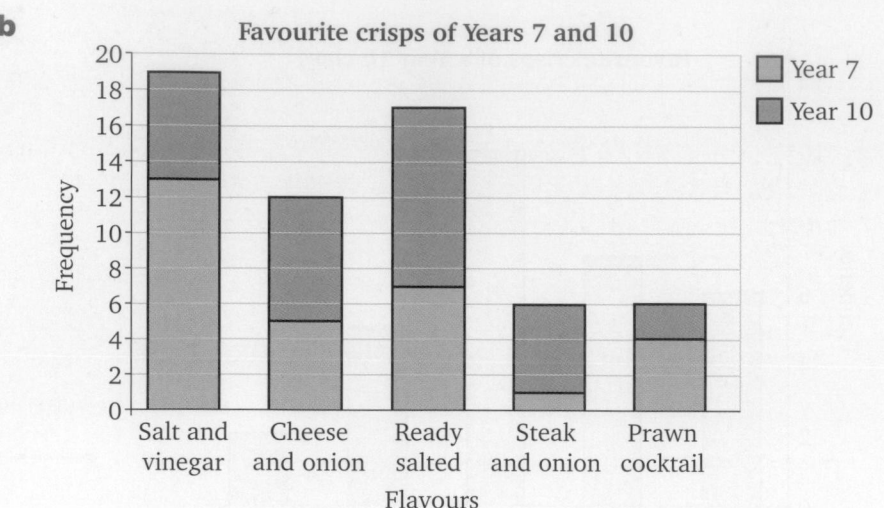

Favourite crisps of Years 7 and 10

c   The dual bar chart is good for comparing two sets of data.

d   The composite bar chart is good for looking at combined data.

e   Possible conclusions might include:

- Salt and vinegar is the most popular for Year 7 and Ready salted is the most popular for Year 10.
- Steak and onion is the least popular for Year 7 and Prawn cocktail is the least popular for Year 10.
- Both years only named five different flavours in their answers (you don't know if it was a closed question or an open question).

Pie charts

In a pie chart, the frequency is represented by the angle (or area) of a sector of a circle.

Use the fact that the angles in a circle add up to 360°.
Pie charts either need a key or each factor must be labelled.

Don't forget the title.

> **Study tip**
>
> You will lose marks if you do not have a key or forget to label your pie chart.

Example: **k** Draw a pie chart to show the data for the favourite crisps of Year 10.

Flavour	Salt and vinegar	Cheese and onion	Ready salted	Steak and onion	Prawn cocktail
Number of students	6	7	10	5	2

Solution: $6 + 7 + 10 + 5 + 2 = 30$ students   (this total is often given in the question)

$360° \div 30 = 12°$ (So 12° in the circle represents one student)

Multiply each number of students by 12° to work out the angle for each flavour.

Flavour	Salt and vinegar	Cheese and onion	Ready salted	Steak and onion	Prawn cocktail
Number of students	6	7	10	5	2
Angle for each flavour	$6 \times 12° = 72°$	$7 \times 12° = 84°$	$10 \times 12° = 120°$	$5 \times 12° = 60°$	$2 \times 12° = 24°$

> **Study tip**
>
> Add up all the angles to check your working. If you have worked them out correctly, the angles will total 360°.

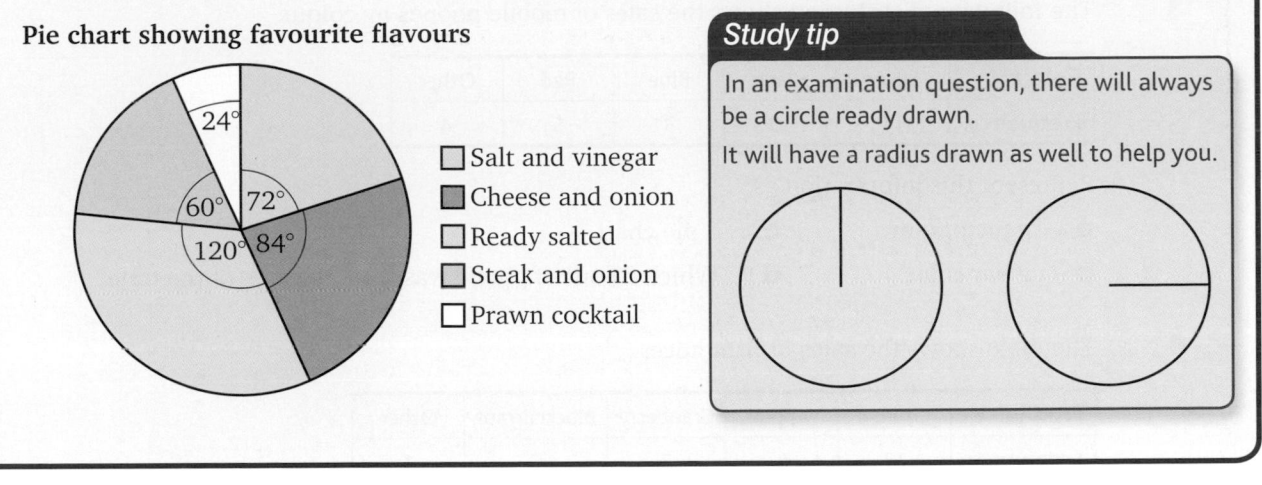

Pie chart showing favourite flavours

24°
60° 72°
120° 84°

☐ Salt and vinegar
☐ Cheese and onion
☐ Ready salted
☐ Steak and onion
☐ Prawn cocktail

Study tip

In an examination question, there will always be a circle ready drawn.
It will have a radius drawn as well to help you.

Practise... 1.1 Pictograms, bar charts and pie charts Ⓚ Ⓖ Ⓕ Ⓔ Ⓓ Ⓒ

G

1   The pictogram shows the number of cars owned by families in one street.

	Number of families
No cars	🚗 🚗 🚗
One car	🚗 🚗 🚗 🚗 🚗 🚗
Two cars	🚗 🚗 🚗
Three cars	🚗

Key: 🚗 represents 10 families

a   How many families did not own a car?

b   How many families owned two or more cars?

2   The pictogram shows the number of ice creams sold over five days.

Day	Number of ice creams sold
Monday	🍦 🍦 🍦 🍦 🍦
Tuesday	🍦 🍦 🍦 🍦 🍦 🍦 🍦 🍦
Wednesday	
Thursday	🍦 🍦 🍦 🍦
Friday	🍦 🍦 🍦 🍦 🍦 🍦

Key: 🍦 = 4 ice creams

a   How many ice creams were sold on Monday?

b   How many ice creams were sold on Friday?

c   On what day were most ice creams sold?

G
D

3 The following distribution shows the sales of mobile phones by colour.

Colour	Silver	Black	Blue	Red	Other
Frequency	14	10	3	5	4

Represent this information as:

a a pictogram   **c** a pie chart

b a bar chart   **d** Which colour of phone was sold about $\frac{1}{12}$ of the time?

4 The table shows the sales of fruit juices.

Fruit juice	Orange	Apple	Cranberry	Blackcurrant	Other
Frequency	18	8	3	6	1

a Represent this information as:

i a pictogram

ii a bar chart

iii a pie chart.

b Which diagram is best for comparing the different fruit juices sold? Give a reason for your answer.

c Which fruit juice has sales that are just over 20% of the total sales?

F
D

5 Ian has to track emails and faxes over one week at the office.

The graph shows a dual bar chart for the number of emails and faxes received on five days of a week.

a Copy and complete the following table for the number of emails and faxes received.

Day	Emails	Faxes
Monday		
Tuesday		
Wednesday		
Thursday		
Friday		

Emails and faxes received

☐ Email
▨ Fax

b What is the modal number of emails?

c What is the modal number of faxes?

d Calculate the range for the number of emails.

e Which day had the least number of faxes?

6 The table shows the gas and electricity bills (in pounds to the nearest pound) for the quarters in one year.

a Show these data in a dual bar chart.

b Show these data in a composite bar chart.

c Give one advantage of each of your charts in part **a** and part **b**.

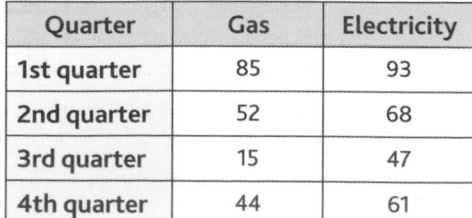

Quarter	Gas	Electricity
1st quarter	85	93
2nd quarter	52	68
3rd quarter	15	47
4th quarter	44	61

d What percentage of gas costs for the year are billed in the 1st quarter?

e Compare the costs of gas and electricity throughout the year.

7 The table shows how 180 students travelled to college.

Travel	Car	Bus	Taxi	Walk	Cycle
Frequency	88	22	7	40	23

Use a suitable diagram to represent these data.

 8 Some students are asked to choose their favourite type of film.

Their choices are shown in the pie chart.

A total of 135 students choose horror films.

a How many students choose thrillers?

Twice as many students choose 'Comedy' as choose 'Romance'.

b How many students chose 'Comedy'?

c Carry out a similar survey in your school.
Draw a pie chart of the results and make comparisons of the results.

Favourite film

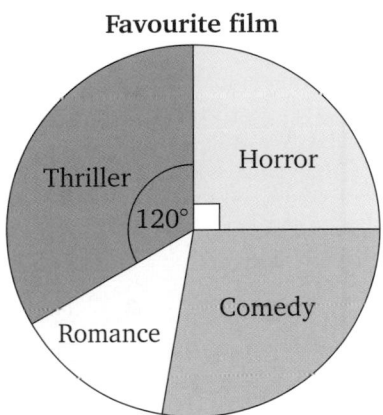

 Learn... **1.2 Stem-and-leaf diagrams**

Stem-and-leaf diagrams are a useful way of representing data. They are used to show discrete data, or continuous data that have been rounded.
Stem-and-leaf diagrams need a key to show the 'stem' and 'leaf'.

For two-digit numbers the first digit (tens) is the stem and the 2nd digit (units) is the leaf.

Stem (tens)	Leaf (units)
1	6 8 1 9 7
2	7 8 2 7 7 2 9
3	4 1 6

In this case the number 6 stands for 16 (1 ten and 6 units).

In this case the number 6 stands for 36 (3 tens and 6 units).

It is often useful to provide **an ordered stem-and-leaf diagram** where the items are placed in order.

Stem (tens)	Leaf (units)
1	1 6 7 8 9
2	2 2 7 7 7 8 9
3	1 4 6

Here the leaves (units) are arranged numerically.

Key: 3 | 1 represents 31

For three-digit numbers the first digit (hundreds) is often used as the stem and the other digits are the leaves.

For example 5 | 67 might represent 567.

Hint

Stem-and-leaf diagrams are useful because they show all the actual data values in a set of data. It is the only diagram that does this.

Study tip

Remember to include a key for a stem-and-leaf diagram. If you don't include a key you will lose marks.

Example: A sample of 25 children in a primary school record how many portions of fruit and vegetables they eat from Monday to Friday.

23	37	14	32	42	38	15	33	27	20	31	19	18
26	25	38	31	32	28	34	25	22	17	12	22	

a Draw an ordered stem-and-leaf diagram for the data.

b Work out the range of the results.

c Work out the median number of portions eaten.

d The Government advises that you should eat at least five portions of fruit and vegetables a day.

    i What fraction of children have followed this advice?

    ii What percentage of children have followed this advice?

    iii What assumption did you make in answering these questions?

Solution: **a** The data run from 12 to 42 so the stem will represent the tens.

The stem will be 1, 2, 3 and 4 placed in a vertical line.

The leaves will represent the units.

For example, the first value recorded is 23 so write a 3 alongside the stem value of 2.

You will now have an unordered stem-and-leaf diagram. The diagram is unordered as the leaves are not in order.

> **Study tip**
>
> Always complete an unordered diagram first. It is then far easier to complete the ordered one. There will always be space to do this on the exam paper.

Unordered stem-and-leaf showing portions of fruit and vegetables eaten

Now write the leaves in order to give an ordered stem-and-leaf diagram.

Remember to include a key.

```
1 | 4 5 9 8 7 2
2 | 3 7 0 6 5 8 5 2 2
3 | 7 2 8 3 1 8 1 2 4
4 | 2
```

Ordered stem-and-leaf showing portions of fruit and vegetables eaten

Notice how the diagram looks a little like a bar chart or pictogram in that it is easy to see where most data lie.

```
1 | 2 4 5 7 8 9
2 | 0 2 2 3 5 5 6 7 8
3 | 1 1 2 2 3 4 7 8 8
4 | 2
```

Key: 3 | 1 represents 31 portions of fruit and vegetables

b Range = highest value minus lowest value

$= 42 - 12$

$= 30$

c The median is the middle value when values are put in order.

In an ordered stem-and-leaf diagram the data are in order.

There are 25 values so the median is the $\left(\dfrac{25 + 1}{2}\right)$th value or the 13th value.

Counting along this gives 26 portions.

> **Study tip**
>
> Don't forget to include the stem number in your answer. For example, here you must say that the median is 26, not 6.

In 5 days, you should eat $5 \times 5 = 25$ portions.

d **i** Looking at the diagrams, 15 out of 25 have eaten 25 or more portions.

Fraction is $\dfrac{15}{25} = \dfrac{3}{5}$

ii Percentage is $\dfrac{3}{5} \times 100 = 60\%$

iii The number of portions of fruit and vegetables is spread evenly over the days.

Two data sets can be shown at the same time on a **back-to-back stem-and-leaf diagram**.

This example of a back-to-back stem-and-leaf diagram compares the portions of frut eaten by boys and girls. Each side of the diagram then needs a stem label.

```
7 7 6 5 4 2 2 | 1 | 1 6 7 8 9
    7 6 4 3 2 1 | 2 | 2 2 7 7 7 8 9
            7 0 | 3 | 1 4 6
```

Key: 7 | 1 represents 17   Key: 1 | 7 represents 17

Notice the leaves run from right to left in order of size on the left side of the diagram.

This also means you need a key for **each side** of the diagram.

Practise...   1.2 Stem-and-leaf diagrams

1   The prices paid for a selection of items from a supermarket are as follows.

45p   32p   38p   21p   66p   54p   60p   44p   35p   42p   44p

Show the data in an ordered stem-and-leaf diagram.

2   The marks obtained by some students in a test were recorded as follows.

    8   20   9   21   18   22   19   13   22   24
   14   9   25   10   19   20   17   14   12

   a   Show this information in an ordered stem-and-leaf diagram.
   b   What was the highest mark in the test?
   c   Write down the median of the marks in the test.
   d   Write down the range of the marks in the test.
   e   The pass mark for the test was 15 marks.
           What fraction of the students passed the test?

3   The times taken to complete an exam paper were recorded as follows.

   2 h 12 min,   1 h 53 min,   1 h 26 min,   2 h 26 min,   1 h 50 min,
   1 h 46 min,   2 h 05 min,   1 h 43 min,   1 h 49 min,   2 h 10 min,
   1 h 49 min,   1 h 55 min,   2 h 06 min,   1 h 57 min.

   a   Convert all the times to minutes.
   b   Show the converted data in an ordered stem-and-leaf diagram.

4   A set of 31 pieces of data has the following:

       Minimum value of 23
       Maximum value of 65
       Median of 44
       Mode of 42 and 55

   Draw a possible stem-and-leaf diagram making up data values which satisfy these conditions.

5 Emma is investigating this hypothesis: Girls take longer to complete an exercise than boys.

She collects the data shown in this back-to-back stem-and-leaf diagram.

Number of minutes to complete a task

Leaf (units) Girls	Stem (tens)	Leaf (units) Boys
7 7 6 5 4 2 2	1	1 6 7 8 9
7 6 4 3 2 1	2	2 2 7 7 7 8 9
7 0	3	1 4 6

Key: 3 | 2 represents 23 minutes   Key: 3 | 4 represents 34 minutes

Write some conclusions that Emma might make about her hypothesis. You must show your working to justify your answer.

Hint

Emma needs to work out values of average and spread to help make her conclusions.

 6 Declan is investigating reaction times for Year 7 and Year 11 students.

In an experiment he obtains these results.

Year	Times (tenths of a second)													
7	18	19	09	28	10	04	11	14	15	18	09	27	28	06	05
11	07	20	09	12	21	17	11	12	15	08	09	12	08	16	19

a Show this information in a back-to-back stem-and-leaf diagram.

b Declan thinks Year 7 have quicker reaction times than Year 11.
Use your diagram to show whether he is correct.

  7 A village football team played 32 games during one season.

The number of spectators for the first 31 games is shown in the stem-and-leaf diagram.

a The number of spectators at the 32nd game increases the range by 14.
Work out two possible values for the number of spectators at the 32nd game.

b Do either of these possible values affect the median of the number of spectators after 31 games?
Explain your answer.

c Do either of the possible values found in part **a** affect the modal number of spectators after 31 games.
Explain your answer.

18	4 6
19	0 2 3 5
20	3 3 7 9 9 9 9
21	0 1 5 5 6 7 8 8 9
22	3 4 4 6 9
23	2 5
24	7 8

Key: 18 | 4 represents 184 spectators

 Learn... **1.3 Line graphs, frequency polygons and histograms**

Line graphs

A **line graph** is a series of points joined with straight lines.

Line graphs show how data change over a period of time.

Example: The table shows the temperature of a patient at different times during the day.

Time	10.00	11.00	12.00	13.00	14.00
Temperature (°F)	102.5	101.3	102	99.1	99.2

Draw a line graph to show this information.

Solution: Plot the points and join them up with straight lines.

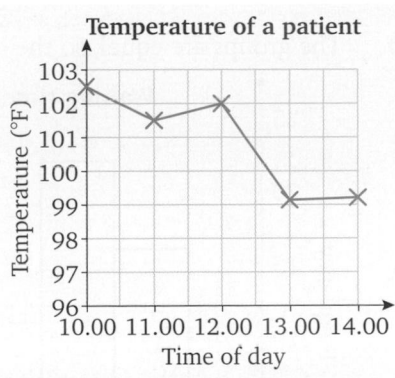

Temperature of a patient

Frequency polygons

A **frequency polygon** is a way of showing continuous grouped data in a diagram.

Points are plotted at the midpoint of each class interval. The groups may have equal or unequal widths.

The frequency polygon is an example of a **frequency diagram**.

Another type of frequency diagram is a **histogram**.

Histograms

A histogram is a way of showing continuous grouped data in a diagram. The area of the bar represents the frequency.

The groups may have equal or unequal widths. At Foundation Tier all histograms will have equal width groups.

Histograms with equal group widths

If the group widths are equal, bars are drawn to the height of the frequency.

Example: 50 people were asked how long they had to wait for a train.
The table below shows the results.

Time, t (minutes)	Frequency
$5 \leqslant t < 10$	16
$10 \leqslant t < 15$	22
$15 \leqslant t < 20$	11
$20 \leqslant t < 25$	1

a   Draw a frequency polygon to represent the data.

b   Draw a histogram to represent the same data.

Study tip

Make sure that the axes are labelled properly and not in terms of class intervals.

Solution: **a**   For a frequency polygon, the points are plotted at the midpoint of each class interval.

E.g. the midpoint for $5 \leqslant t < 10$ is $\dfrac{5 + 10}{2} = 7.5$

Study tip

There is no need to draw lines beyond the first and last plots.

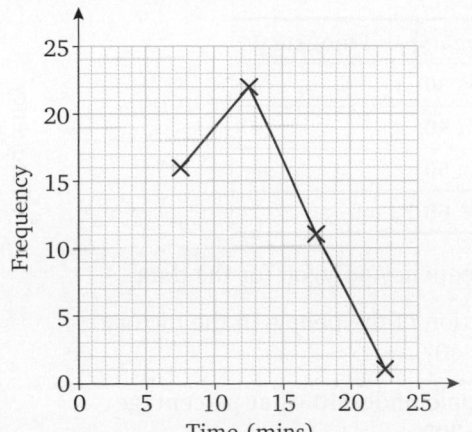

Frequency polygon to show waiting times

b   The groups are equal, so the bars are drawn to the height of the frequency.

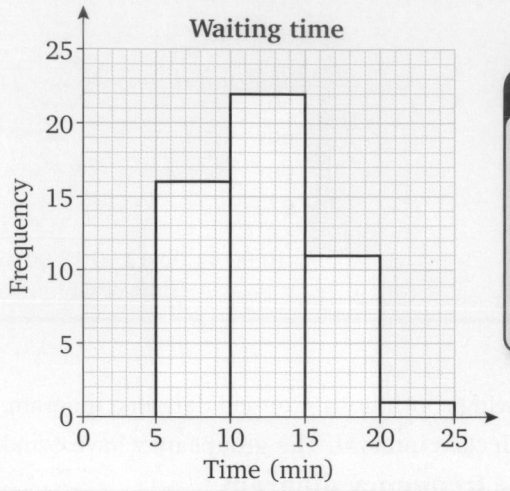

> **Study tip**
>
> You may be asked to draw a frequency diagram. You have a choice of drawing a histogram or a frequency polygon. If the classes are of equal width it is usually easier to draw a histogram – if you draw a frequency polygon you will have to the get the midpoints correct.

1.3 Line graphs, frequency polygons and histograms

Practise...

1   The table shows the times of runners in a fun run.

Time, t (minutes)	Frequency
5 up to 10	40
10 up to 15	125
15 up to 20	100
20 up to 25	55
25 up to 30	15

Draw a histogram for the data.

2   The table shows the time spent in a local shop by 60 customers.

a   Draw one type of frequency diagram for the data.

b   Draw a different type of frequency diagram for the data.

Time, t (minutes)	Frequency
$5 \leqslant t < 10$	8
$10 \leqslant t < 15$	30
$15 \leqslant t < 20$	16
$20 \leqslant t < 25$	6

3   The frequency diagram shows the ages of 81 people in a factory.

a   Copy and complete the table to show this information.

Age, y (years)	Frequency
$20 \leqslant y < 30$	
$30 \leqslant y < 40$	
$40 \leqslant y < 50$	
$50 \leqslant y < 60$	

b   Draw a frequency polygon for the data.

c   What fraction of the people in the factory are under 40?

d   Of the people under 40 what percentage are under 30?

4   The table shows the pressure in millibars (mb) over five days at a seaside resort.

Day	Pressure (mb)
Monday	1018
Tuesday	1022
Wednesday	1028
Thursday	1023
Friday	1019

a   Draw a line graph to show the pressure each day.

b   What do you assume when drawing this line graph?

5   The table shows the minimum and maximum temperatures at a seaside resort.

Day	Minimum temperature (°C)	Maximum temperature (°C)
Monday	15	19
Tuesday	11	21
Wednesday	13	22
Thursday	14	23
Friday	17	23

Draw a line graph to show:

a   the minimum temperatures

b   the maximum temperatures.

Use your graph to find:

c   the day on which the lowest temperature was recorded

d   the day on which the highest temperature was recorded

e   the biggest difference between the daily minimum and maximum temperatures.

f   Collect data about minimum and maximum temperatures for different parts of the world over one week. You should find data in most daily newspapers or on the internet.

Draw suitable graphs to compare different places.

! 6   The head teacher of a college thinks that attendance becomes worse as the week progresses.

The table shows the number of students at college present during morning and afternoon registration.

Day	Mon	Mon	Tue	Tue	Wed	Wed	Thu	Thu	Fri	Fri
Session	am	pm	am	pm	am	pm	am	pm	am	pm
Number	220	210	243	215	254	218	251	201	185	152

a   Show this information on a graph.

b   There are 260 students in the college.
Work out the percentage attending each registration session.
Give your answers to the nearest whole number.

c   Do your answers to parts **a** and **b** support the head teacher?
Explain your answer.

7   The table shows the cost of electricity bills at the end of every three months.

Year	2006	2006	2006	2006	2007	2007	2007	2007
Quarter	1st	2nd	3rd	4th	1st	2nd	3rd	4th
Cost	£230	£120	£50	£80	£215	£120	£25	£55

a   Show this information on a graph.

b   Describe any patterns in the data.

G F

1 Assess

1 The graph shows the number of people in a library each day at noon.

a Write down the number of people in the library each day at noon.

b On which of these days is the library closed at noon?

c Give two reasons why the graph does **not** show that more people visit on a Saturday than any other day.

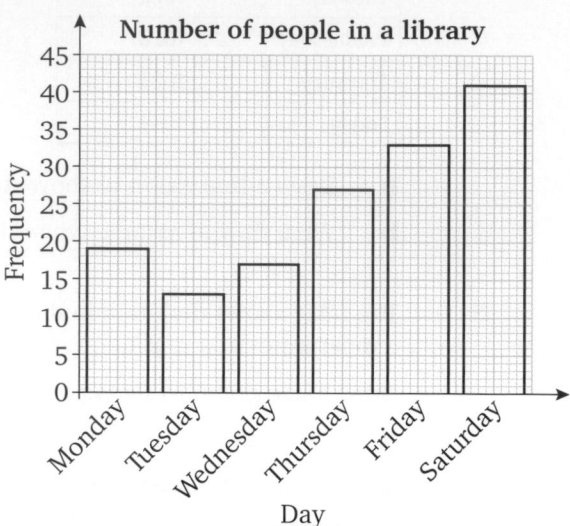

Number of people in a library

2 The pictogram shows the number of DVDs sold in a shop during Monday morning.

a What time do you think the shop opens? Give a reason for your answer.

b How many DVDs were sold between 9 am and 9.30 am?

c What proportion of the morning sales is made before 10 am?

d The mean profit on a DVD sold is £2.56.
The cost of running the shop is £12.04 per hour.
Does the shop make an overall profit on Monday morning?

You **must** show your working.

Time period	Number of DVDs sold
9.00 – 9.30	◎ ◎
9.30 – 10.00	◖
10.00 – 10.30	◎ ◎ ◎ ◎ ◖
10.30 – 11.00	◎ ◎
11.00 – 11.30	◎
11.30 – 12.00	◎ ◎ ◖

Key: ◎ = 2 DVDs sold

E D C

3 The pie charts below show how 200 students travel to college one day during winter and one day during summer.

Fraction of students in winter

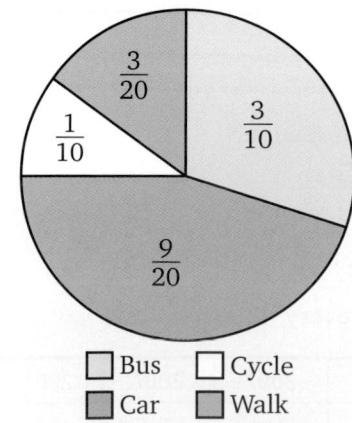

Number of students in summer

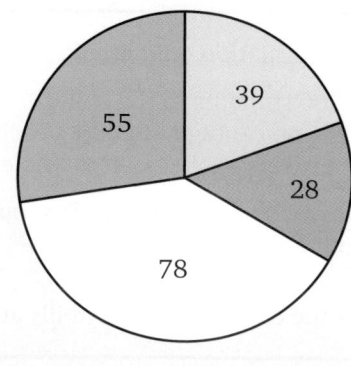

☐ Bus ☐ Cycle
■ Car ■ Walk

a Work out the angles for each method of travel for each chart.

b Compare the methods of travel for the different times of the year.

c Sandy said 'This proves more people walk to college in summer'.
Is Sandy correct? Give a reason for your answer.

4   The heights of the 40 workers in a factory are given in the diagram below.

Females												Males					
									9	14							
						9	8	2	15								
9	9	8	7	6	6	6	4	4	3	1	16	2	4	7	9	9	
	8	7	5	3	3	2	2	1	17	2	2	4	5	5	8		
								2	18	3	3	6	9				
									19	1							

Key: 7 | 16 represents 167 cm   Key: 18 | 3 represents 183 cm

a   Explain why the median male height is 174.5 cm.

b   Show that only about 19% of males are shorter than the median female height.

c   Compare the ranges of the male and female heights.

d   Produce a similar diagram for data from your class.

5   For each of these tables of data, draw an appropriate graph.

Table A

Five coins were thrown together 100 times and the number of tails showing uppermost was recorded as shown below.

Number of tails	Frequency
0	2
1	17
2	29
3	34
4	15
5	3

Table B

Four different airlines make the following number of flights from a regional airport.

Airline	Number of flights
Big Wing	12
Fly Maybe	9
Squeezyjet	4
Fly on Air	7

Table C

Vinoj and Ling went fishing every month for six years.

They keep the following record of the number of fish caught each month.

One number needs to be filled in before you can draw a graph.

Number caught	Frequency
$0 \leqslant n \leqslant 10$	3
$10 < n \leqslant 20$	17
$20 < n \leqslant 30$	31
$30 < n \leqslant 40$	19
$40 < n \leqslant 50$	?

D

6   The number of workers in the staff restaurant in a hospital is shown in the line graph.

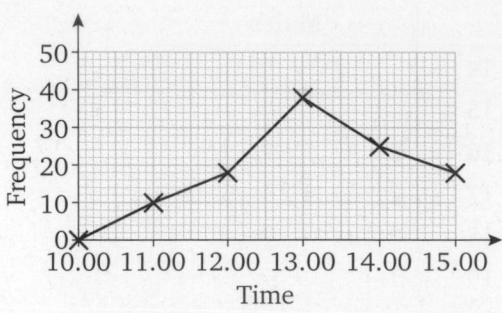

a   At what time is the restaurant busiest?

b   What time do you think the restaurant opens?
Give a reason for your answer.

c   Complete this table.

Time	10.00	11.00	12.00	13.00	14.00	15.00
Number of workers in restaurant						

d   Is a line graph a suitable diagram for these data?

e   Display the data in a suitable diagram of your choice.

7   Draw a suitable ordered stem-and-leaf diagram for the following data.

The distance travelled by 15 motorists alone and by 15 motorists with passengers.

Distance travelled alone	22	3	12	31	6	10	19	25	9	4	11	16	14	26	8
Distance travelled with passengers	25	10	7	27	37	37	21	48	23	4	13	33	37	25	33

For your diagram, write down three features you notice.

Practice questions Ⓚ

1   The bar chart shows the number of men and women visiting a dentist in one week.
The bar for women on Friday is missing.

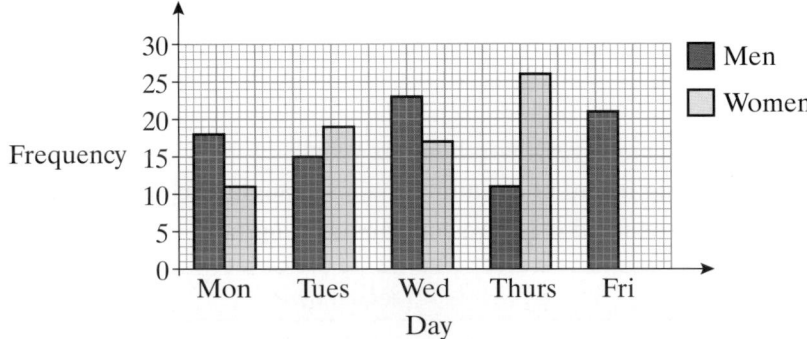

a   How many women visited the dentist on Tuesday?   *(1 mark)*

b   How many men and women in total visited the dentist on Monday?   *(2 marks)*

c   During that week an equal number of men and women visited the dentist.
How many women visited the dentist on Friday?   *(4 marks)*

AQA 2008

2 Area and volume

Objectives

Examiners would normally expect students who get these grades to be able to:

G

find the volume of a shape by counting cubes

E

find the volume of a cuboid

D

convert between square units such as changing 2.6 m² to cm²

C

convert between cube units such as changing 3.7 m³ to cm³

find the volume of prisms including cylinders

find the surface area of simple prisms.

Key terms

dimension
solid
cross-section
prism
cube
cuboid
volume
surface area
face
net

Did you know?

Optical prisms

An optical prism is transparent with flat, polished surfaces that separate a beam of white light into its spectrum of colours.

Before Isaac Newton's experiments, it was thought that white light was colourless, and it was the prism producing the colour. Newton did experiments that made him think that all the colours were already in light, and that particles of light were spread out because different coloured particles went through the prism at different speeds, making a rainbow-like effect.

The traditional geometrical shape is that of a triangular prism with a triangular base and rectangular sides, but there are other shapes that are known as prisms.

You should already know:

✔ how to find the area of rectangles, triangles, parallelograms and circles

✔ how to convert between metric units, e.g. centimetres to metres

✔ how to draw nets of solids.

Learn... 2.1 Volume of a cuboid

Shapes such as rectangles have two **dimensions**: length and width.

Shapes that have a third dimension such as thickness or height are called **solids**.

Solids which have the same **cross-section** all the way through the shape are called **prisms**.

Two of the most commonly known prisms are **cube** and **cuboid**.

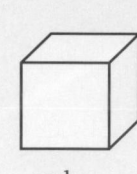 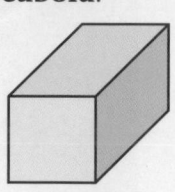

cube
(cross-section
is a square)

cuboid
(cross-section
is a square)

The **volume** of a shape is the amount of space it occupies.
It is measured in cubic units.

For example, this cube is 1 cm long, 1 cm wide and 1 cm high.

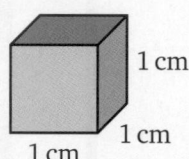

The amount of space it takes up is 1 cm × 1 cm × 1 cm, which is 1 cubic centimetre, written 1 cm³.

Volume can be measured by counting the number of 1 centimetre cubes in a three-dimensional shape.

Counting the number of 1 centimetre cubes in this shape gives a volume of 16 cubes or 16 cm³.

Counting cubes can take a long time.

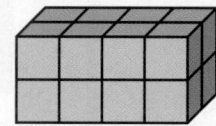

In this cuboid each layer has 4 × 2 = 8 cubes (the length × the width of the cuboid), and there are 2 layers (the height of the cuboid).

The total number of cubes is 4 × 2 × 2 = 16

So

volume of a cuboid = length × width × height

As the length × width gives the area of the base, the formula can also be written:

volume = area of base × height

Units of volume and area

Volume is always measured in cubic units such as cubic millimetres (written mm³), cubic centimetres (written cm³) or cubic metres (written m³).

Sometimes it is necessary to convert between these units.

There are 100 centimetres in 1 metre.

How many cubic centimetres (cm³) are there in 1 cubic metre (m³)?

This cube has sides of 1 metre. Its volume is 1 m × 1 m × 1 m = 1 m³

If the dimensions of the cube were given in centimetres then each side would measure 100 cm.

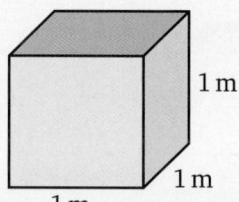

The volume would be 100 cm × 100 cm × 100 cm = 1 000 000 cm³

So 1 m³ = 1 000 000 cm³

In the same way the area of the base can be found in square metres or square centimetres.

The area of the base of this cube is 1 m × 1 m = 1 m²

Working in centimetres the area of the base is 100 cm × 100 cm = 10 000 cm²

So 1 m² = 10 000 cm²

Example: Work out the volume of this cuboid.

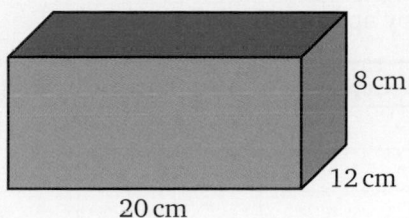

8 cm

12 cm

20 cm

Solution: Using the formula, volume = length × width × height

= 20 cm × 12 cm × 8 cm

Volume = 1920 cm³

Example: A cuboid has a volume of 260 m³.

The area of the base of the cuboid is 65 m².

Work out the height of the cuboid.

Solution: Using the formula,   volume = length × width × height

and the formula,   area of base = length × width

gives: volume = area of base × height

260 = 65 × height

$\frac{260}{65}$ = height   Divide both sides by 65.

Height = 4 m

Example: **a**   Convert 24 500 cm² to square metres.

b   Convert 5 m² to square centimetres.

c   Convert 7 250 000 cm³ to cubic metres.

Solution: 1 m² = 1 m × 1 m = 100 cm × 100 cm = 10 000 cm²

a   To convert cm² to m² divide by 10 000.

24 500 ÷ 10 000 = 2.45 m²

b   To convert m² to cm² multiply by 10 000.

5 × 10 000 = 50 000 cm²

c   1 m³ = 1 m × 1 m × 1 m = 100 cm × 100 cm × 100 cm = 1 000 000 cm³

To convert cm³ to m³ divide by 1 000 000.

7 250 000 ÷ 1 000 000 = 7.25 m³

Practise...   2.1 Volume of a cuboid   **G F E D C**

1   These solid shapes are made from 1 cm cubes.
Find the volume of each shape.

G

a 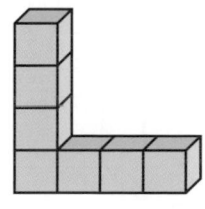   **b**    **c** 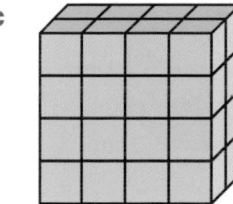   **d**

E

2 The table gives the measurements of some cuboids.

Copy and complete the table.

Cuboid	Length (cm)	Width (cm)	Height (cm)	Volume (cm³)
a	6	5	3	
b	15	8	7	
c	9.6	4.8	5	
d	42.2	25	4.5	

3 Find the volume of each of the following cuboids.

State the units of each answer.

a

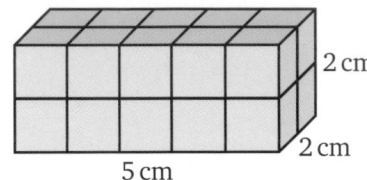

2 cm
2 cm
5 cm

c

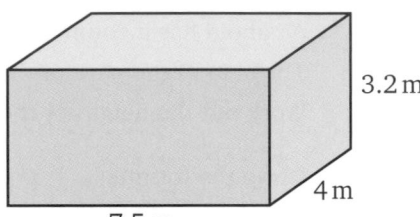

3.2 m
4 m
7.5 m

b

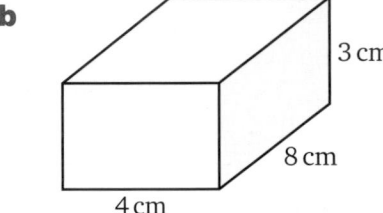

3 cm
8 cm
4 cm

Hint
Remember to change all lengths to the same units.

d

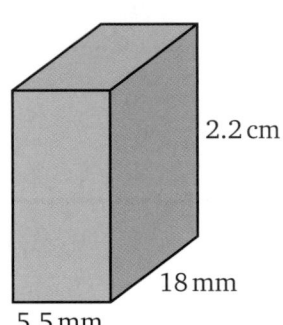

2.2 cm
18 mm
5.5 mm

4 Which has the larger volume: a cuboid measuring 5 cm by 7 cm by 3 cm, or a cube of side 5 cm?

Show your working.

D

5 **a** Convert the following areas to square centimetres.

   i 4.6 m²   **ii** 23 m²   **iii** 9 m²   **iv** 0.5 m²

b Convert the following areas to square metres.

   i 300 000 cm²   **ii** 75 000 cm²   **iii** 57 600 cm²   **iv** 8 500 cm²

6 Find the volume of these solids.

a

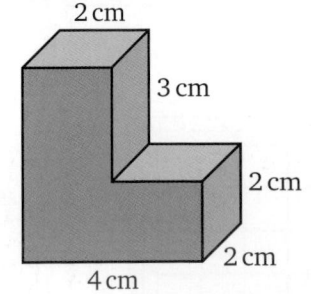

2 cm
3 cm
2 cm
2 cm
4 cm

b

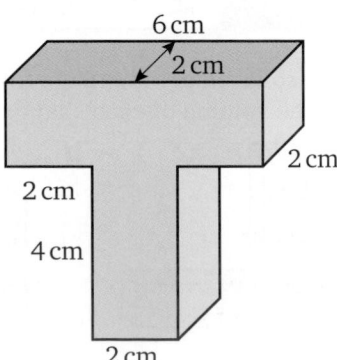

6 cm
2 cm
2 cm
2 cm
4 cm
2 cm

Hint
Divide each solid into cuboids.

7   This cuboid has a volume of 432 m³.

Work out the height, h, of the cuboid.

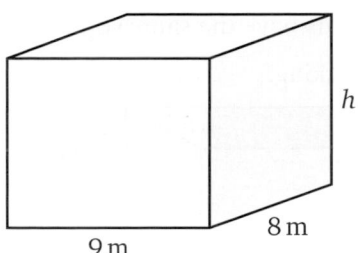

Not drawn
accurately

h

8 m

9 m

8   The table gives the measurements of some cuboids.

Copy and complete the table.

Cuboid	Length (cm)	Width (cm)	Height (cm)	Volume (cm³)
a	7	11		385
b	14		19	7182
c		4.1	10	282.9
d	15.5		3.8	565.44

9   Convert the following volumes to cubic centimetres.

a   8 m³   **b**   3.2 m³   **c**   0.765 m³   **d**   0.0568 m³

10   A 25 mm square hole is cut right through the centre of a cuboid as shown.

Find the volume of the remaining cuboid.

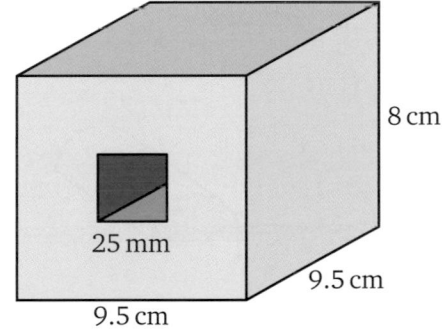

8 cm

25 mm

9.5 cm

9.5 cm

11   A concrete beam is 20 metres long, 0.3 metres wide and 0.4 metres thick.

How many cubic metres of concrete are needed to make the beam?

12   A garden is a rectangle of length 9 m and width 8.4 m.

The garden is to be covered with topsoil to a depth of 5 cm.

Topsoil costs £82.55 for a bag containing 1 m³ of topsoil or £38
for a bag containing 0.4 m³.

Work out the cheapest cost of the topsoil.

13   Twelve small boxes of matches are to be packed tightly into a carton.

Each box of matches has length 5 cm, width 3.5 cm and height 1.5 cm.

Work out the volume of the carton.

Work out the possible dimensions of the carton.
(The boxes of matches can be packed in layers.)

14 Do these cuboids have the same volume?

Show your working.

a

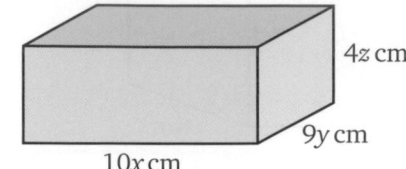

$4z$ cm

$9y$ cm

$10x$ cm

b

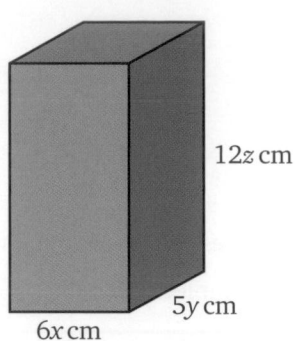

$12z$ cm

$5y$ cm

$6x$ cm

Learn... 2.2 Volume of a prism

A cuboid is a prism with a rectangular cross-section.

Remember that a prism is any solid with the same cross-section all the way through.

Here are some prisms with their cross-sections shaded.

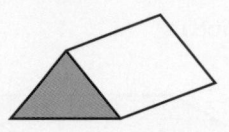
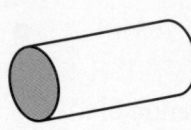
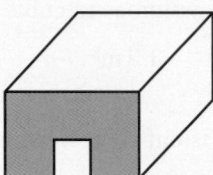
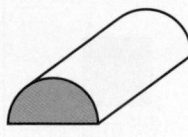
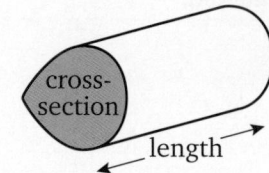

cross-section

length

Study tip

The formula for the volume of a prism will be given to you on the second page of the examination paper.

volume of prism = area of cross-section × length (or height)

This formula applies to any prism.

Example: Work out the volume of each of these prisms.

a

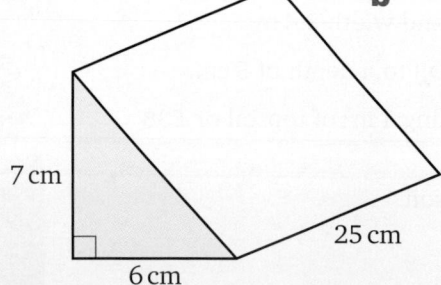

7 cm

6 cm

25 cm

b

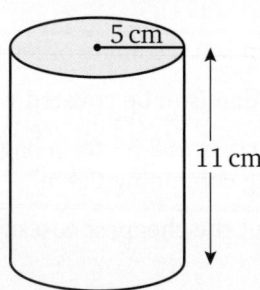

5 cm

11 cm

Solution: **a** The cross-section of this prism is a right-angled triangle with base 6 cm and perpendicular height 7 cm.

Using the formula, area of triangular cross-section = $\frac{1}{2}$ × base × height

$= \frac{1}{2} \times 6 \times 7$

Area of triangular cross-section = 21 cm²

Study tip

Remember:
- area is measured in square units
- volume is measured in cubic units.

Using the formula, volume = area of cross-section × length

$= 21 \times 25$

Volume = 525 cm³

b   The cross-section of this prism is a circle of radius 5 cm.

Using the formula, area of a circle $= \pi r^2$

$$= \pi \times 5^2$$

Area of cross-section $= 25\pi$

Using the formula, volume = area of cross-section × height

$$= 25 \times \pi \times 11$$

Volume $= 863.9\,\text{cm}^3$ (to 1 d.p.)

Study tip

Shade in the cross-section to make it clear what area you are working out.

Practise... 2.2 Volume of a prism   G F E D C

1   The area of the cross-section of each prism is given in these diagrams.

Work out the volume of each prism.

Remember to state the units of each answer.

a

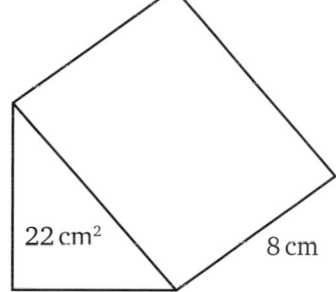

22 cm²   8 cm

c

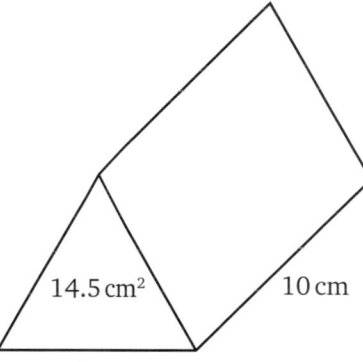

14.5 cm²   10 cm

b

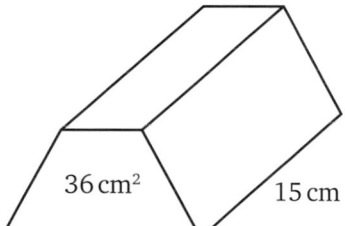

36 cm²   15 cm

d

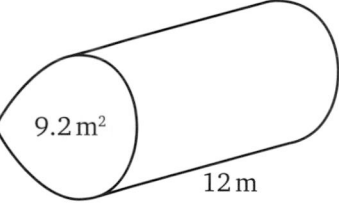

9.2 m²   12 m

2   Work out the volume of each of these **triangular prisms**.

a

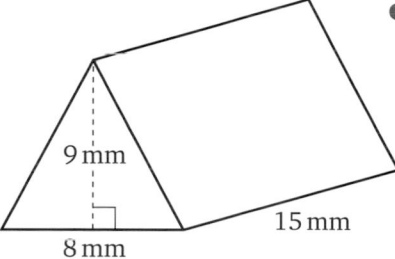

9 mm

8 mm   15 mm

c

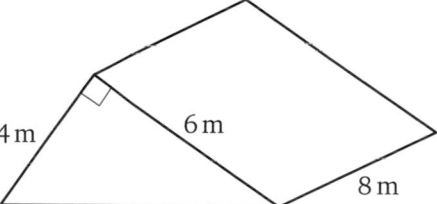

4 m   6 m

8 m

b

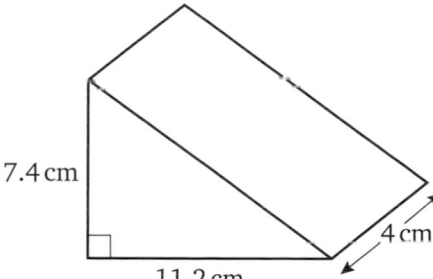

7.4 cm

11.2 cm   4 cm

C

3   Work out the volume of each **cylinder**.

a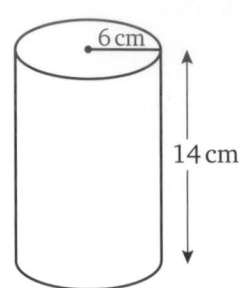

b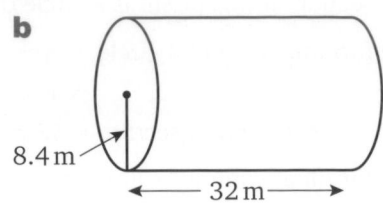

c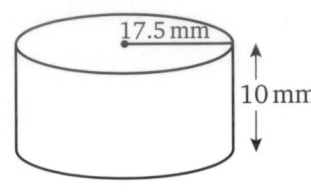

4   A prism has a volume of 132 cm³. The area of the cross-section of the prism is 33 cm².

Work out the height of the prism.

5   For each prism shown below, work out:

i   the area of the cross-section   **ii**   the volume.

> **Hint**
> Draw a sketch of the cross-section to help you.

a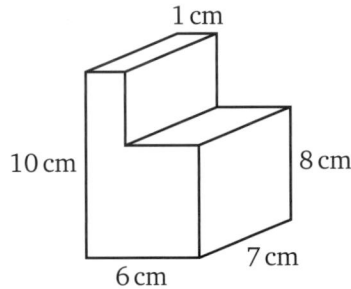

c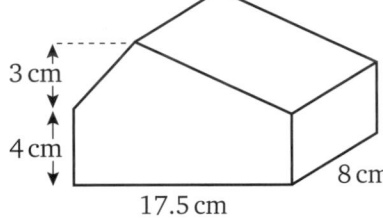

b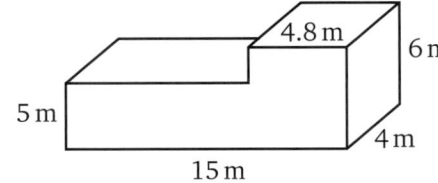

6   A cylinder of height 3.2 m has a volume of 15.68 m³.

Work out the area of the base of the cylinder.

⚠ 7   The diagram shows a plastic pipe of internal radius 4 cm and length 60 cm.

The plastic has a thickness of one centimetre.

Calculate the volume of plastic in the pipe.

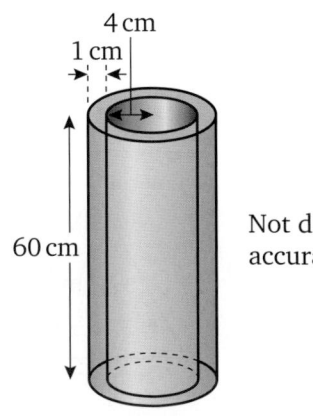

Not drawn accurately

⚙ 8   At a pre-school playgroup, each of the 36 children is given a beaker of milk.
The beakers are cylinders of radius 3 cm and height 8 cm and are three-quarters full.

Each milk carton contains 2.2 litres of milk.

Susie says that three cartons will be enough for all the children.

Is she correct?

Show your working.

> **Hint**
> 1000 cm³ = 1 litre

9 The volume of a prism is 90 cm³.
Find three different shapes of prism with this volume.
Give the dimensions of each one.

10 These two prisms have the same volume. Work out h.

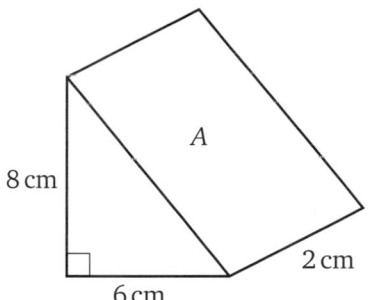 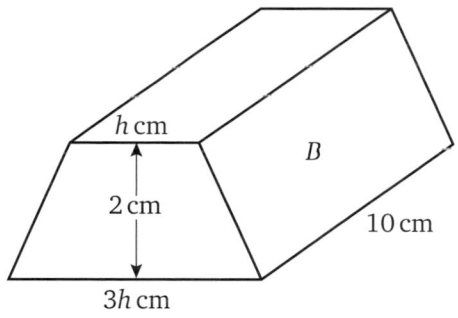

Not drawn accurately

A — 8 cm, 6 cm, 2 cm

B — h cm, 2 cm, $3h$ cm, 10 cm

Learn... 2.3 Surface area of a prism ⓚ

The total **surface area** of a three-dimensional shape is the sum of the area of all the **faces** of the shape.

For example, a cube where the length of each side is 3 cm is made up of six square faces, each measuring 3 cm by 3 cm.

The area of each face is 3 cm × 3 cm = 9 cm²

The total surface area of all six faces is 6 × 9 cm² = 54 cm²

It is often useful to draw the **net** of a solid to help you to see the individual areas.

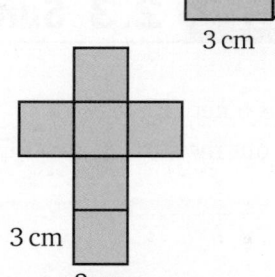

3 cm

3 cm

3 cm

Study tip

Remember to give the correct units for your answer. Area is always measured in square units.

Example: Work out the surface area of this triangular prism.

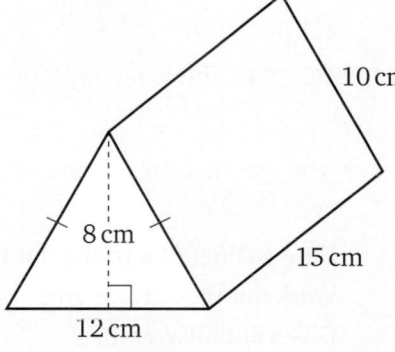

10 cm

8 cm

15 cm

12 cm

Solution: Sketch the net.

The middle rectangle (*A*) has area
12 × 15 = 180 cm²

The two outer rectangles (*B* and *C*) each have area 10 × 15 = 150 cm²

The triangles (*D* and *E*) each have area $\frac{1}{2}$ × 12 × 8 = 48 cm²

Total surface area
= 180 + (2 × 150) + (2 × 48)
= 576 cm²

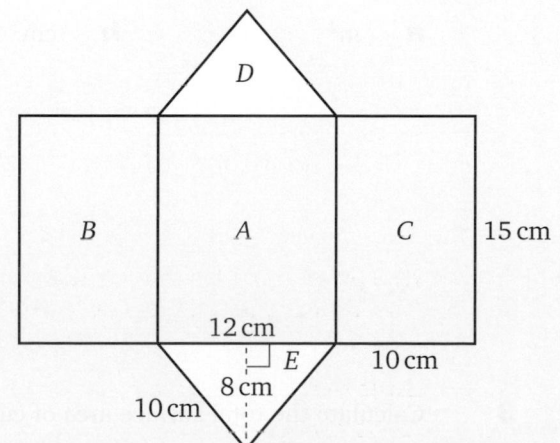

D

B   *A*   *C*   15 cm

12 cm

10 cm

8 cm *E* 10 cm

10 cm

Example: Work out the area of the curved surface of this cylinder.

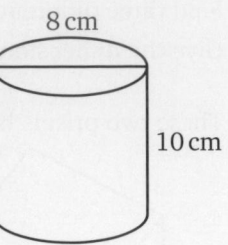

8 cm

10 cm

Solution: You are asked to work out the **curved** surface.
This means you don't have to include the flat ends.

The curved surface of the cylinder forms a rectangle when the net is drawn.

The length of the rectangle is equal to the circumference of the circular end of the cylinder.

Circumference = $2\pi r$ so the area of the curved surface = $2\pi r \times h$

In the cylinder shown, the radius is 4 cm (half the diameter).

area of the curved surface = $2 \times \pi \times 4 \times 10 = 80\pi$
or 251.3 cm² (to 1 d.p.)

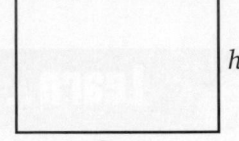

h

$2\pi r$

If you are asked to find the area of the **whole** cylinder, you must
add the area of the circular top and base to the area of the curved surface.

Practise... 2.3 Surface area of a prism (k) G F E D C

D

1 Here is a net of a cuboid.
Work out the surface area of the cuboid.

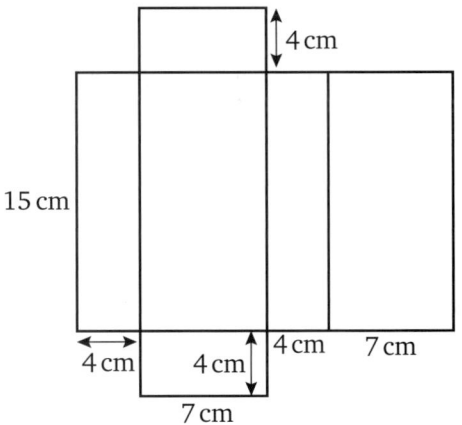

4 cm

15 cm

4 cm 4 cm 4 cm 7 cm

7 cm

2 Here is a net of a triangular prism.
Work out the surface area.

Give your answer in:

a m²   **b** cm²

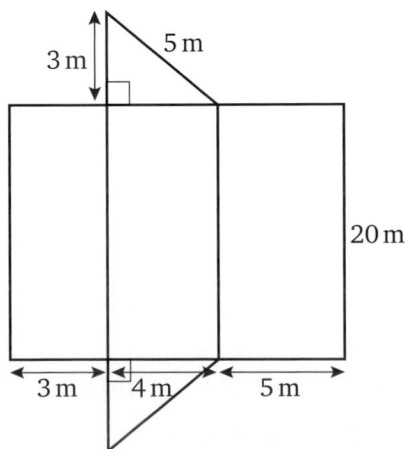

3 m 5 m

20 m

3 m 4 m 5 m

C

3 Calculate the total surface area of cubes with these side lengths.

a 7 cm   **b** 10 cm   **c** 5.4 cm

4   **a**   Calculate the total surface area of these cuboids.

i

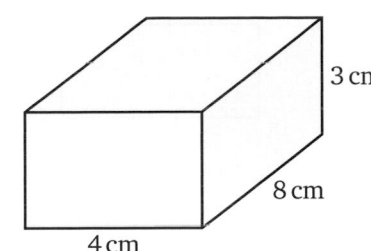

3 cm

8 cm

4 cm

ii

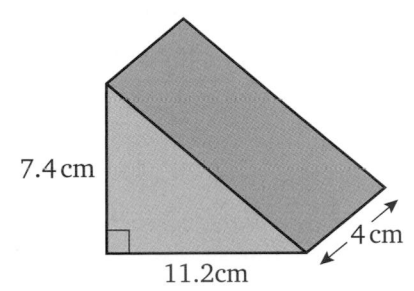

22 mm

18 mm

5.5 mm

b   Calculate the total surface area of these triangular prisms.

i

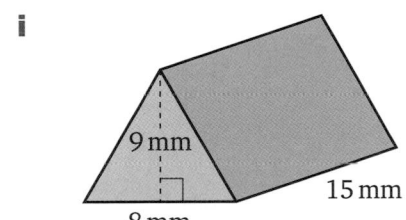

9 mm

8 mm

15 mm

ii

7.4 cm

11.2 cm

4 cm

5   Which of these units are correct for the surface area of a solid?

mm²   cm³   m²   mm   km²   cm²

6   Calculate the area of the curved surface of each of these cylinders.

a

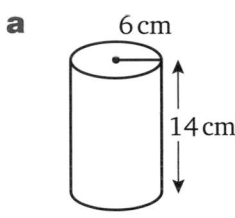

6 cm

14 cm

b

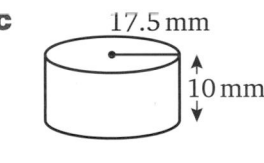

8.4 m

←32 m→

c

17.5 mm

10 mm

7   Jack says that the formula for the surface area of a cuboid is length × width × height.

Is he correct?

Give a reason for your answer.

8   Here are two closed cylinders. (They have a top and a base.)

Calculate the total surface area of each cylinder.

a

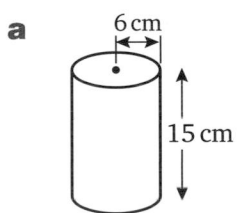

6 cm

15 cm

b

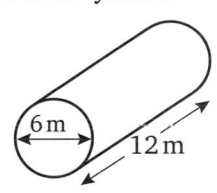

6 m

12 m

9   Andrew makes wooden jewellery boxes in the shape of cuboids of length 20 cm, width 15 cm and depth 10 cm. Each box has a lid.

The wood costs £18.75 for 1 square metre and on average he wastes 10% of each square metre.

He varnishes the outside of each box when he has made them.

A tin of varnish will cover an area of 1.5 m² and costs £7.99.

What is the cost of making each jewellery box?

Hint

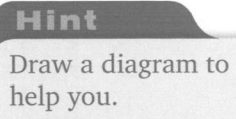

Draw a diagram to help you.

10 In this cuboid the surface areas of the three faces shown are 15 cm², 12 cm² and 20 cm².

Work out the volume of the cuboid.

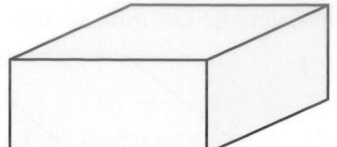

Not drawn accurately

11 Natalie has three wooden cubes that she is using in DT. The smallest cube has sides of length 3 cm. The medium-sized cube has sides of length 6 cm. The largest cube has sides of length 10 cm. She sticks them together to make the solid shown.

Natalie wants to paint the solid red. The tin of red paint she uses will cover an area of 0.5 m².

Will she have enough paint? Show your working.

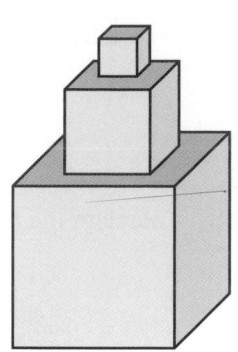

Not drawn accurately

12 The area of the curved surface of this cylinder is equal to three times the area of both ends added together. Express h in terms of r.

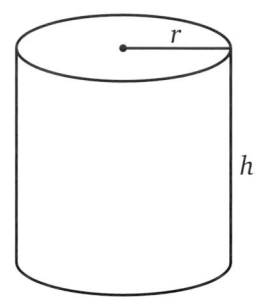

Not drawn accurately

2 Assess ⓚ

G

1 These solids are made from cubes of side 1 cm.

Find the volume of each solid.

a

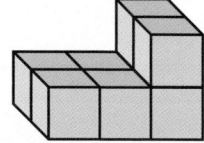

Not drawn accurately

b

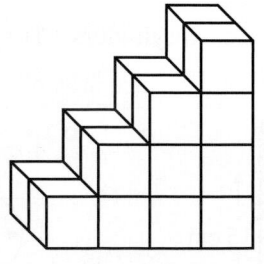

Not drawn accurately

2 These solids are made from cubes of side 1 m. Find the volume of each solid.

a

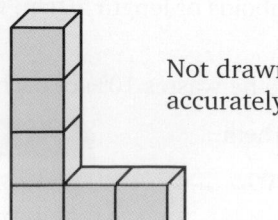

Not drawn accurately

b

Not drawn accurately

3   A prism has a total surface area of 0.75 m².

What is the surface area of the prism in cm²?

4   The table shows the measurements of some cuboids.

Cuboid	Length	Width	Height
a	14 cm	6 cm	3 cm
b	45 mm	22 mm	10 mm
c	3.2 m	6 m	4 m
d	12.4 cm	15.5 cm	11 cm

i   Work out the volume of each cuboid.

ii Calculate the total surface area of each cuboid.

Remember to state the units of each answer.

5   Calculate the volume of this cuboid.

Give your answer **a** in cm³ **b** in mm³.

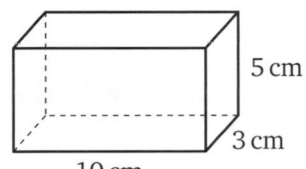

6   Calculate the volume of each of these prisms.

a

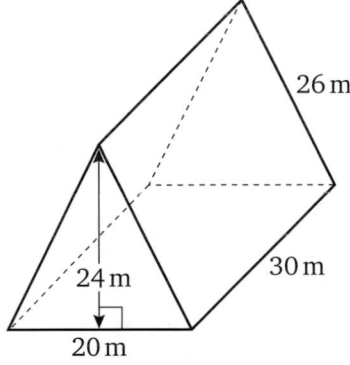

b

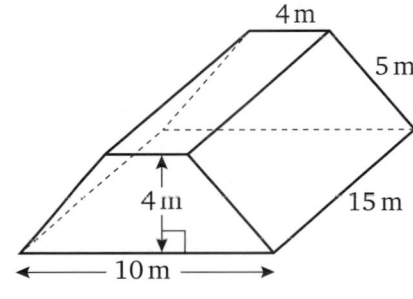

7   Here is a list of six formulae.

πr^2	length × width × height	2 × length + 2 × width
area of cross-section × length	$2\pi r$	$\frac{1}{2}$ × base × height

Write down which of these formulae represent:

a   a length   **b**   an area   **c**   a volume.

8   Work out the total surface area of this triangular prism.

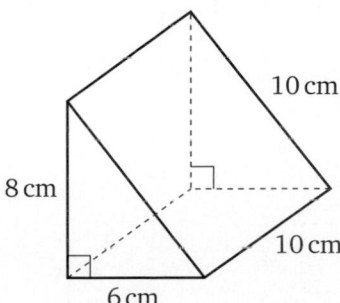

9   A metal pole is in the shape of a solid cylinder. It has a radius of 1.5 m and a length of 17 m.

Work out the volume of metal used for the pole.

Practice questions k

1   Centimetre cubes are fitted together to make a solid as shown on the left.

The solid is packed into a box as shown on the right.

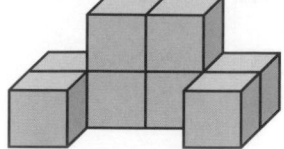 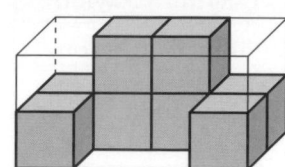

The box is a cuboid.
Work out the volume of the box.

(3 marks)
AQA 2009

2   A cuboid has a volume of 75 cm³.

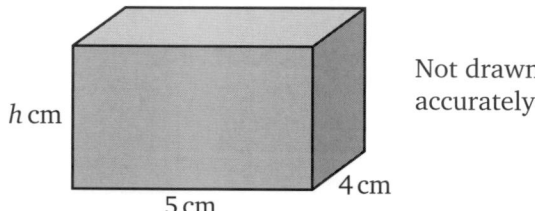

Not drawn accurately

h cm

5 cm   4 cm

The length is 5 cm.
The width is 4 cm.
Find the height, h cm.

(2 marks)
AQA 2008

3   The diagram shows a block of wood with uniform cross-section.
The cross-section is made of rectangles.
The block is 65 cm long.

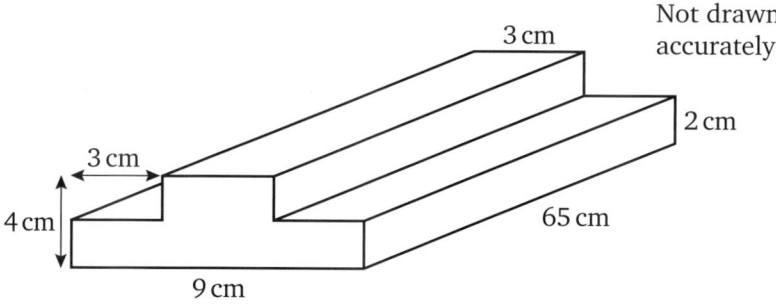

Not drawn accurately

3 cm
2 cm
3 cm
4 cm
65 cm
9 cm

Calculate the volume of the block.
State the units of your answer.

(5 marks)
AQA 2009

4   The diameter of a cylindrical water-butt is 55 cm.
The height is 82 cm.

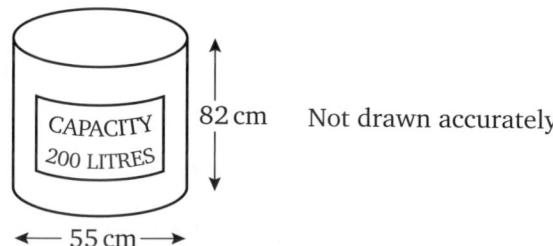

CAPACITY
200 LITRES

82 cm   Not drawn accurately

← 55 cm →

One litre = 1000 cm³
The label states that the capacity of the water-butt is 200 litres.
Is this accurate?
You **must** show your working.

(4 marks)
AQA 2008

3 Fractions and decimals

Objectives

Examiners would normally expect students who get these grades to be able to:

G

understand positive and negative integers

find the fraction of a shape shaded

put integers and simple fractions in order

find equivalent fractions

express simple decimals and percentages as fractions

F

add and subtract negative numbers

simplify fractions

calculate fractions of quantities

arrange fractions and decimals in order

E

multiply and divide negative numbers

express fractions as decimals and percentages

add and subtract fractions

D

find one quantity as a fraction or percentage of another

solve problems involving fractions

solve problems involving decimals

C

add and subtract mixed numbers

find the reciprocal of a number

round numbers to a given power of 10, up to three decimal places and one significant figure

multiply and divide fractions.

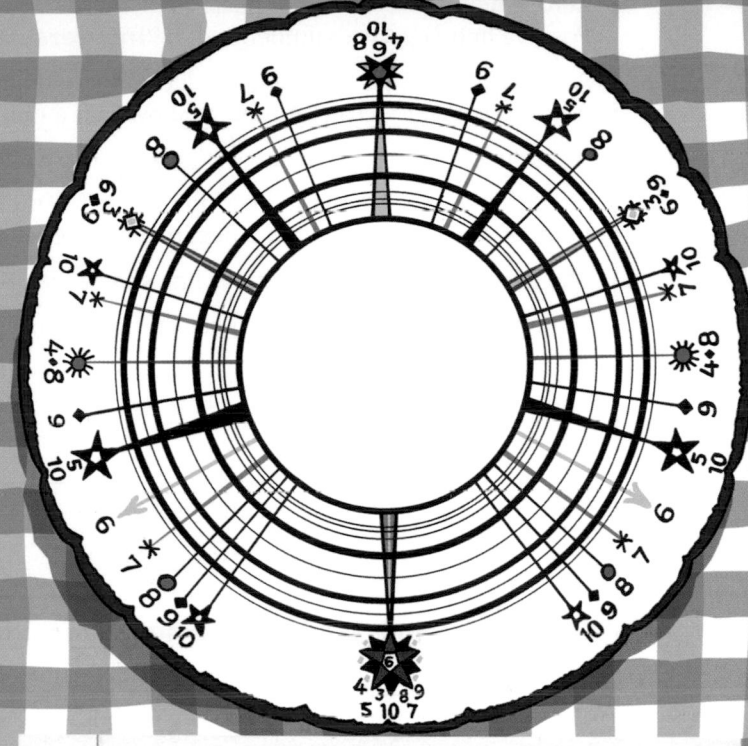

Did you know?

Plat diviseur

It is not easy to cut a pizza or a cake into pieces the same size, particularly if you need five or seven or nine pieces.

The French have a solution, the *plat diviseur*, or dividing plate, which has numbers marked round the edge to show where to cut for that number of pieces. Useful and beautiful!

Key terms

positive number	mixed number
negative number	rounding
integer	decimal place
equivalent fractions	significant figures
numerator	recurring decimal
denominator	reciprocal
improper fraction	

You should already know:

✔ how to add, subtract, multiply and divide simple numbers

✔ about simple fractions such as halves and quarters.

Learn... 3.1 Positive and negative numbers

Positive numbers are greater than zero and **negative numbers** are less than zero.
Zero is neither negative nor positive.
Positive and negative numbers can be **integers** (whole numbers) or non-integers such as $\frac{3}{4}$ or -1.53

A negative $(-)$ sign is always needed to show that a number is negative.
A positive sign $(+)$ can be used to show that a number is positive.

A number line helps to arrange numbers in order and to add and subtract them.

To **add** numbers, show the first number on the number line. Go to the right along the line to add a positive number or to the left to add a negative number (3 steps to the left to add -3).

The green arrows on the number line shows that $-4 + -3 = -7$

To **subtract**, show the first number on the number line. Go *left* to subtract a positive number or *right* to subtract a negative number.

The red arrow shows that $4 - -6 = 10$

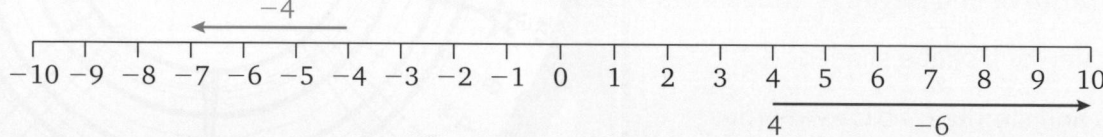

Calculating with positive and negative numbers

You need to know how to use your calculator to calculate with positive and negative numbers.

Your calculator may have a $\boxed{(-)}$ key. Use this to enter negative numbers into your calculator by pressing this key first, then the number.

Alternatively, you may have a $\boxed{+/-}$ key. To enter a negative number on your calculator, first press the number then $\boxed{+/-}$ to change it from positive to negative.

Example: Calculate:

    a $4 + -5$

    b -8×-6

    c $-5 + 6 + -8$

    d $60 \div -12$

Solution: **a**   Enter the calculation as $4 + \boxed{(-)} 5$ and press =
                    So $4 + -5 = -1$
                    (Alternatively, enter the calculation as $4 + 5 \boxed{+/-}$ and press =)

    b $-8 \times -6 = \boxed{(-)} 8 \times \boxed{(-)} 6 = 48$

    c $-5 + 6 + -8 = \boxed{(-)} 5 + 6 + \boxed{(-)} 8 = -7$

    d $60 \div -12 = 60 \div \boxed{(-)} 12 = -5$

Example: Harry has £34.65 in his bank account and has to pay a bill for £50. How much will he have in his account when he has paid the bill?

Solution: Amount in account is £34.65 − £50 = −£15.35
            So when Harry has paid the bill, he is overdrawn: he owes the bank £15.35.

Practise... 3.1 Positive and negative numbers

1 This is a table of average December temperatures in some parts of the world.

Place	Average temperature in degrees Celsius
Omsk, Russia	−13
Punte Arenas, Chile	+10
Scott Base, Antarctica	−5
Tromsø, Norway	−3
Victoria, Seychelles	+27

  a List the places in order of temperature, starting with the coldest.

  b How much higher is the temperature in Victoria than in Tromsø?

2 Work out: **a** $+12 - 15$ **c** $-17 \div -2$

  b 18×-25 **d** $25 - 30 - -18$

3 The temperature is 4°C at midday and -3°C at midnight. By how many degrees has the temperature fallen?

4 **a** A diver is at 12 m below sea level. How many metres will he have to rise to get to 2 m below sea level?

  b A diver at 3 m below sea level goes down 10 m. How far below sea level is he now?

  c A diver starts at 2 m below sea level and goes down half a metre per second. What depth is he at after 10 seconds?

5 In a quiz game, players score two points for a correct answer and lose a point for a wrong answer. If they do not answer, they score no points.

  a After 5 questions, Amy has 3 points. How many different ways could she have gained this score?

  b What possible scores could Ben have after 10 questions?

6 Becki has £45.56 in her account and then takes £100 out in cash. How much is in her account now?

7 Samir has nothing in his bank account. He uses the account to pay a bill of £35. How much does he have in his account now?

8 Pete's bank account is overdrawn by £36.70. He uses the account to pay a bill of £10.53. What will his account balance be now?

9 This is some information from Pip's bank statement.

Date	Details	Withdrawn	Paid in	Balance in account
17 Jul	Starting balance			− £103.25
17 Jul	Cheque number 001733	£25.00		
18 Jul	Monthly salary cheque		£1316.66	
22 Jul	Cash withdrawal	£100.00		
23 Jul	Gas bill standing order	£73.25		

Copy and complete the 'Balance in account' column to show how much Pip has in the account after each transaction.

10 Tom uses these numbers to write down five calculations with the answer −12.

-15 -6 -6 -6 -4 -3 -2 2 2 3 24

Write down the five calculations.

Study tip
Make sure you know how to use your calculator to do calculations with negative numbers.

Learn... 3.2 Fractions

Equivalent fractions are fractions that have the same value, such as $\frac{4}{5}$ and $\frac{8}{10}$

To find a fraction equivalent to another fraction, multiply or divide the **numerator** and the **denominator** of the fraction by the same number.

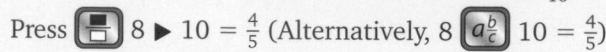

$$\overset{\times 2}{\frac{1}{2}\underset{\times 2}{=}\frac{2}{4}} \qquad \overset{\times 6}{\frac{1}{2}\underset{\times 6}{=}\frac{6}{12}} \qquad \overset{\div 6}{\frac{6}{12}\underset{\div 6}{=}\frac{1}{2}}$$

Fractions should be given in their simplest form when possible.
The simplest fraction in the list $\frac{1}{2}$, $\frac{2}{4}$, $\frac{3}{6}$ and $\frac{6}{12}$ is $\frac{1}{2}$

Your calculator can simplify a fraction such as $\frac{8}{10}$ using the fraction key 🔲 or $\boxed{a\frac{b}{c}}$

Press 🔲 8 ▶ 10 = $\frac{4}{5}$ (Alternatively, 8 $\boxed{a\frac{b}{c}}$ 10 = $\frac{4}{5}$)

If you enter a top-heavy fraction (also known as an **improper fraction**), the calculator will simplify it and may give it as a **mixed number**. Find out what your calculator will do. Some calculators will change an improper fraction to a mixed number (and vice versa) if you press (SHIFT) (S⇔D).

If your calculator will not change between improper fractions and mixed numbers, you will have to do it yourself.

To change an improper fraction such as $\frac{15}{4}$ to a mixed number, find how many times 4 goes into 15. It goes 3 times with 3 left over, so $\frac{15}{4}$ is $3\frac{3}{4}$ ($\frac{15}{4}$ is 15 quarters, 12 quarters make 3 whole ones and there are 3 quarters left over.)

To change a mixed number such as $3\frac{3}{4}$ to an improper fraction, multiply 3 by 4 to give 12 and add on 3, to give $\frac{15}{4}$. (3 whole ones are 12 quarters and there are 3 more quarters to be added on, giving 15 quarters.)

Study tip

Find out how to use your calculator to simplify fractions and to change between mixed numbers and top-heavy fractions.

Example: Write each fraction in its simplest form.

a $\frac{10}{15}$

b $\frac{45}{100}$

c $\frac{175}{50}$

Solution: **a** 🔲 10 ▶ 15 = $\frac{2}{3}$ (or 10 $\boxed{a\frac{b}{c}}$ 15 = $\frac{2}{3}$)

b 🔲 45 ▶ 100 = $\frac{9}{20}$ (or 45 $\boxed{a\frac{b}{c}}$ 100 = $\frac{9}{20}$)

c 🔲 175 ▶ 50 = $\frac{7}{2}$ = $3\frac{1}{2}$ (or 175 $\boxed{a\frac{b}{c}}$ 50 = $3\frac{1}{2}$)

Your calculator can also do fraction calculations. Use the fraction key to enter the fractions and use the normal ×, ÷, − and + keys to do the calculations.

Example: Calculate:

a $\frac{2}{3} + \frac{4}{5}$

b $1\frac{3}{4} \times 2\frac{1}{2}$

c $\frac{3}{8} \div \frac{7}{12}$

Solution: **a** 🔲 2 ▶ 3 ▶ + 🔲 4 ▶ 5 = $\frac{22}{15}$ (or 2 $\boxed{a\frac{b}{c}}$ 3 + 4 $\boxed{a\frac{b}{c}}$ 5 = $\frac{22}{15}$)

b Shift 🔲 1 ▶ 3 ▶ 4 ▶ × Shift 🔲 2 ▶ 1 ▶ 2 = $\frac{35}{8}$ (SHIFT) (S⇔D) = $4\frac{3}{8}$

(or 1 $\boxed{a\frac{b}{c}}$ 3 $\boxed{a\frac{b}{c}}$ 4 × 2 $\boxed{a\frac{b}{c}}$ 1 $\boxed{a\frac{b}{c}}$ 2 = $4\frac{3}{8}$)

c 🔲 3 ▶ 8 ▶ ÷ 🔲 7 ▶ 12 = $\frac{9}{14}$ (or 3 $\boxed{a\frac{b}{c}}$ 8 ÷ 7 $\boxed{a\frac{b}{c}}$ 12 = $\frac{9}{14}$)

To work out one quantity as a fraction of another, make the first quantity the numerator of the fraction and the second the denominator. You need to make sure the units of the two quantities are the same before you do this. Use your calculator to simplify the fraction.

So 20 minutes as a fraction of one hour = 20 minutes as a fraction of 60 minutes = $\frac{20}{60} = \frac{1}{3}$

Example: Write 30p as a fraction of £6.

Solution: 30p as a fraction of £6 is 30p as a fraction of 600p, which is $\frac{30}{600}$

Use your calculator to simplify the fraction. 30 ▶ 600 ▶ = $\frac{1}{20}$ (or 30 $\boxed{a\frac{b}{c}}$ 600 = $\frac{1}{20}$)

Example: In a mathematics exam, there are 35 marks for Section A and 45 marks for Section B. What fraction of the total exam marks are given for Section A?

Solution: Total number of marks for the exam is 35 + 45 = 80

Fraction of marks for Section A is $\frac{35}{80} = \frac{7}{16}$
(Simplify the fraction on your calculator.)

Study tip

Remember to give your answers in their simplest fraction form.

Practise...   3.2 Fractions    G F E D C

1 **a** Use your calculator to simplify these fractions.

i $\frac{12}{60}$ ii $\frac{22}{33}$ iii $\frac{75}{100}$ iv $\frac{125}{200}$ v $\frac{45}{180}$

b Simplify these fractions to find the odd one out.

i $\frac{7}{21}$ ii $\frac{15}{45}$ iii $\frac{1}{3}$ iv $\frac{9}{36}$ v $\frac{12}{36}$

2 $\frac{14}{16}$ is equivalent to $\frac{7}{8}$. Write down two more fractions equivalent to $\frac{7}{8}$

3 Use your calculator for this question.

a Express these improper fractions as mixed numbers.

i $\frac{10}{7}$ ii $\frac{15}{2}$ iii $\frac{17}{4}$ iv $\frac{105}{10}$ v $\frac{27}{5}$

b Express these mixed numbers as improper fractions.

i $2\frac{3}{4}$ ii $3\frac{2}{3}$ iii $1\frac{7}{8}$ iv $10\frac{1}{2}$ v $5\frac{5}{6}$

4 Use your calculator to write the first quantity as a fraction of the second.

a 25 minutes, $2\frac{1}{2}$ hours   **d** 20 cm, 1.8 m

b Half an hour, three hours   **e** 400 g, 1.2 kg

c 40p, £2.40

5 Here are nine shapes.

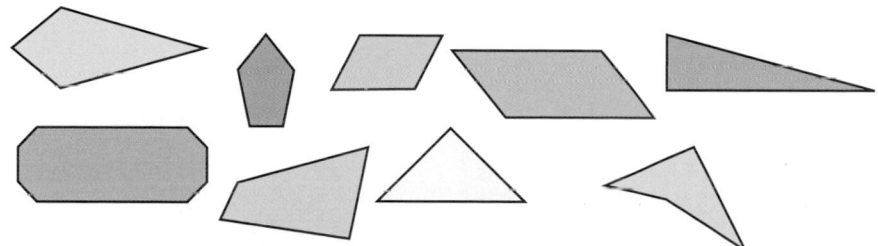

a How many quadrilaterals are there?

b What fraction of the total number of shapes are quadrilaterals?

c What fraction of the total number of shapes are parallelograms?

Hint

A quadrilateral is a shape with 4 sides.

D

6 Pigs have an average weight of 150 pounds and a stomach weighing 6 pounds.

a What fraction of a pig's total weight is the weight of its stomach?

Sheep have a different digestive system. They have an average weight of 120 pounds and a stomach weighing 30 pounds.

b What fraction of a sheep's total weight is the weight of its stomach?

! 7 Which of these expressions can be used to find x minutes as a fraction of y hours?

$\dfrac{60x}{y}$ $x \div 60y$ $60xy$ $\dfrac{x}{60y}$ $\dfrac{60y}{x}$

! 8 Find the missing fractions.

a $\dfrac{2}{3} \times \square = 1$ **c** $\dfrac{2}{3} - \square = 1$ **e** $\dfrac{p}{q} \times \square = 1$ **g** $\dfrac{p}{q} - \square = 1$

b $\dfrac{2}{3} + \square = 1$ **d** $\dfrac{2}{3} \div \square = 1$ **f** $\dfrac{p}{q} + \square = 1$ **h** $\dfrac{p}{q} \div \square = 1$

9 Sue's recipe for custard needs $1\frac{1}{2}$ pints of milk and $\frac{3}{8}$ pint of cream. How many pints is this altogether?

10 A pair of shoes costing £35 is reduced by £3.50 in a sale.

a What fraction of the original price is the reduction?

b What fraction is the sale price of the original price?

11 In New York on 6 September 2009, the sunrise time was 06:27 and the sunset time was 19:21. What fraction of the time from midnight on 5 September to midnight on 6 September was daylight?

Learn... 3.3 Working with fractions and decimals

Rounding

Numbers can be **rounded** to make them easy to work with and to understand. For example, if parents want to know how many students there are in a school, they probably want to know the approximate number, 900 for example, rather than the exact number 936.

Rounded to the nearest 100, 936 is 900. It is between 900 and 1000 and nearer to 900.

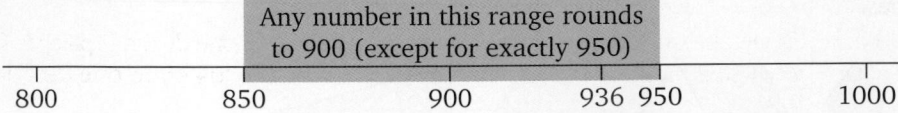

Rounded to the nearest 10, 936 is 940. It is between 930 and 940 and nearer to 940.

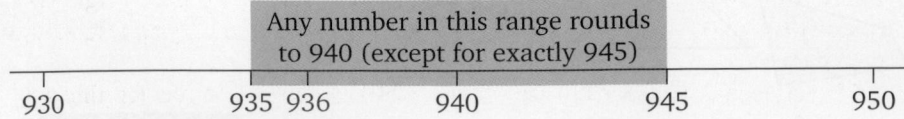

You also need to be able to round decimal numbers to the nearest integer, to one **decimal place**, two decimal places and so on.

Example: Round the number 7.846 to:

     a   the nearest integer   **b**   one decimal place   **c**   two decimal places.

Solution: **a**   7.846 is between 7 and 8 and nearer to 8.

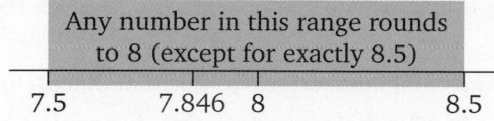

So, to the nearest integer, 7.846 is 8.

     b   7.846 is between 7.8 and 7.9 and nearer to 7.8. So 7.846 to one decimal place is 7.8

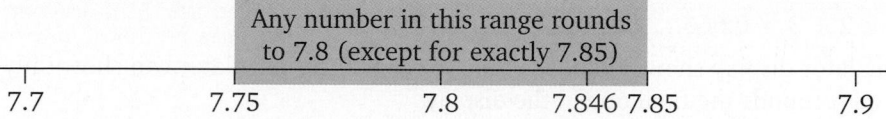

     c   To two decimal places, 7.846 is 7.85; it is between 7.84 and 7.85 and nearer to 7.85

Significant figures

You can also round numbers to different numbers of **significant figures**.

936 rounds to 900 and 0.0936 rounds to 0.09. The first is rounded to the nearest 100 and the second to two decimal places, but they are both rounded to one significant figure. There is one figure, 9, in each that is most important when considering the size of the number. This number is the first (or most) significant figure. Both numbers also need zeros to show you the place value of the 9 but these zeros are not significant figures.

(Zeros **can** be significant; for example, 1023 rounded to the nearest 10 is 1020. The zero in the hundreds position is significant but the zero in the units position is not.)

To two significant figures, 936 is 940 and
0.0936 is 0.094

> **Study tip**
>
> Make sure you understand the difference between rounding to a number of significant figures and rounding to a number of decimal places.

Example: Round these numbers to:

     a   the nearest integer   **i** 44.79   **ii** 0.5678   **iii** 204.45   **iv** 0.0235

     b   one decimal place   **i** 44.79   **ii** 0.5678   **iii** 204.45   **iv** 0.0235

     c   one significant figure.   **i** 44.79   **ii** 0.5678   **iii** 204.45   **iv** 0.0235

Solution: **a**   **i**   44.79 is between 44 and 45 and nearer to 45. So 44.79 to the nearest integer is 45

            ii   0.5678 is between 0 and 1 and nearer to 1. So 0.5678 to the nearest integer is 1

            iii   204.45 is between 204 and 205 and nearer to 204. So 204.45 to the nearest integer is 204

            iv   0.0235 is between 0 and 1 and nearer to 0. So 0.0235 to the nearest integer is 0

     b   **i**   44.79 is between 44.7 and 44.8 and nearer to 44.8. So 44.79 to one decimal place is 44.8

            ii   0.5678 is between 0.5 and 0.6 and nearer to 0.6. So 0.5678 to one decimal place is 0.6

            iii   204.45 is between 204.4 and 204.5 and nearer to 204.5. So 204.45 to one decimal place is 204.5

            iv   0.0235 is between 0.0 and 0.1 and nearer to 0.0. So 0.0235 to one decimal place is 0.0

     c   **i**   44.79 is between 40 and 50 and nearer to 40. So 44.79 to one significant figure is 40.

            ii   0.5678 is between 0.5 and 0.6 and nearer to 0.6. So 0.5678 to one significant figure is 0.6

            iii   204.45 is between 200 and 300 and nearer to 200. So 204.45 to one significant figure is 200

            iv   0.0235 is between 0.02 and 0.03 and nearer to 0.02. So 0.0235 to one significant figure is 0.02

Expressing fractions as decimals

Any fraction can be expressed as a decimal.

Some simple examples that you may already know are $\frac{1}{2} = 0.5$, $\frac{3}{4} = 0.75$, $\frac{3}{10} = 0.3$

To express a fraction as a decimal, use your calculator to divide the numerator by the denominator.

$\frac{3}{4} = 3 \div 4 = 0.75$ (Make sure your calculator is set to give a decimal answer not a fraction answer.)

0.75 is a **terminating decimal**.
$3 \div 4$ works out exactly, the calculation comes to an end after two decimal places.

Some fractions become **recurring decimals**. The division calculation does not stop.
Instead one digit, or a group of digits, repeats forever.

$\frac{1}{3} = 1 \div 3 = 0.333...$ This can also be written as $0.\dot{3}$

$\frac{2}{3} = 2 \div 3 = 0.666...$ This can also be written as $0.\dot{6}$

The calculator display shows that $\frac{2}{3}$ is 0.6666666667. The calculator can show only a limited number of digits and it rounds the final one in the display.

When decimals are used in calculations you have to round them appropriately.

$\frac{2}{3}$ to one decimal place is 0.7

$\frac{2}{3}$ to two decimal places is 0.67

$\frac{2}{3}$ to three decimal places is 0.667

$\frac{2}{3}$ to four decimal places is 0.6667 and so on.

Expressing fractions as percentages

To express a fraction as a percentage, change the fraction to a decimal and then multiply the decimal by 100%

$\frac{3}{4} = 0.75$

$0.75 \times 100\% = 75\%$

> **Study tip**
>
> In calculations, use all the figures already in your calculator whenever possible. Do not re-enter the number unless you really have to.

Example: **a**   What is $\frac{5}{12}$ as a decimal? Write your answer correct to three decimal places.

b   Use your answer to write $\frac{5}{12}$ as a percentage.

Solution: **a** $\frac{5}{12} = 5 \div 12 = 0.41666...$
$= 0.417$ to three decimal places.

> **Study tip**
>
> Make sure you always divide the numerator by the denominator when changing a fraction to a decimal.

b   So $\frac{5}{12}$ as a percentage is 41.7% (3 sf) or 42%, correct to the nearest whole percent.

Arranging fractions in order

To arrange fractions in order of size, first change them to decimals or percentages.

It is not easy to see which fraction, $\frac{3}{4}$ or $\frac{7}{9}$, is bigger, so change them both to decimals.

$\frac{3}{4} = 0.75$ and $\frac{7}{9} = 0.\dot{7}$

You can see that $\frac{7}{9}$ is a bit bigger than $\frac{3}{4}$

Example: Arrange these fractions in order of size, starting with the smallest.

$\frac{2}{3}, \frac{3}{5}, \frac{11}{18}, \frac{7}{11}$

Solution: $\frac{2}{3} = 0.\dot{6}$ $\frac{3}{5} = 0.6$, $\frac{11}{18} = 0.61\dot{1}$, $\frac{7}{11} = 0.\dot{6}\dot{3}$ $0.\dot{6}\dot{3}$ means 0.636363...

So the fractions in order of size are $\frac{3}{5}, \frac{11}{18}, \frac{7}{11}, \frac{2}{3}$

Alternatively, change them to percentages.

$\frac{2}{3} = 0.\dot{6} = 67\%$, $\frac{3}{5} = 0.6 = 60\%$, $\frac{11}{18} = 0.61\dot{1} = 61\%$, $\frac{7}{11} = 0.\dot{6}\dot{3} = 64\%$

The percentages here have been rounded to two significant figures.

Once again, the fractions in order of size are $\frac{3}{5}, \frac{11}{18}, \frac{7}{11}, \frac{2}{3}$

Reciprocals

When two numbers multiply together to make 1, the numbers are called the **reciprocals** of each other. So 2 and $\frac{1}{2}$ are the reciprocals of each other because $2 \times \frac{1}{2} = 1$

Your calculator can work out reciprocals both as fractions and as decimals. Look for the button labelled $\frac{1}{x}$ or x^{-1} and find out how to use it.

Example: Find the reciprocals of 0.2, $\frac{9}{20}$, 0.89

Solution: Reciprocal of 0.2 is 0.2 $\boxed{x^{-1}}$ $\boxed{=}$ 5

Reciprocal of $\frac{9}{20}$ is $\frac{20}{9} = 2\frac{2}{9}$

Reciprocal of 0.89 is 0.89 $\boxed{x^{-1}}$ $\boxed{=}$ 1.12 to three significant figures.

> **Study tip**
>
> To find the reciprocal of a **fraction**, swap the numerator and denominator.
>
> To find the reciprocal of a **mixed number**, convert it to an improper (top-heavy) fraction first. Then swap the numerator and denominator.

Fractions of quantities

You can work out a fraction of a given quantity on your calculator.

Example: Find four fifths of £3.50.

Solution: Four fifths of £3.50 is $\frac{4}{5} \times £3.50 = £2.80$

Example: A jacket costing £22 is reduced by $\frac{1}{3}$ in a sale. What is the sale price?

Solution: $\frac{1}{3}$ of £22 = $\frac{1}{3} \times £22 = £7.33$ (rounded to the nearest penny).

So the sale price is £22 − £7.33 = £14.67

(You could do this in one step by working out $\frac{2}{3}$ of £22 rather than working out $\frac{1}{3}$ and subtracting it.)

Practise...

3.3 Working with fractions and decimals

 G F E D C

F

1 There are approximately one million dairy cows in the US. $\frac{4}{5}$ of these are Holsteins. Approximately how many Holsteins are there in the US?

2 A pizza is cut into five equal pieces as shown. Work out the size of the angle marked x.

3 **a** Calculate $\frac{3}{4}$ of:

     i 56   **ii** £105   **iii** £15.65   **iv** 3.5 metres   **v** 500 grams

    b Calculate $\frac{3}{8}$ of:

     i 254   **ii** £25   **iii** $15   **iv** 3 hours   **v** 1 km

> **Hint**
>
> Round your answers if they do not work out exactly.

E

4 Express these fractions as:
- **a** decimals
- **b** percentages.

  i $\frac{4}{5}$ **ii** $\frac{9}{10}$ **iii** $\frac{11}{20}$ **iv** $\frac{23}{50}$ **v** $\frac{67}{100}$

5 Which of these fractions are equivalent to recurring decimals?

  a $\frac{3}{5}$ **b** $\frac{9}{11}$ **c** $\frac{5}{6}$ **d** $\frac{7}{20}$ **e** $\frac{4}{15}$

C

6 Round these numbers to:
- **a** the nearest 10
- **b** the nearest integer
- **c** one decimal place
- **d** two decimal places
- **e** three decimal places
- **f** one significant figure.

  i 12.89   **ii** 54.5   **iii** 109.87   **iv** 4.756   **v** 0.836

7 Round these numbers and quantities to one significant figure.
- **a** The height of Mount Everest, 8848 m
- **b** The length of the River Nile, 4135 miles
- **c** The number of words in the Bible, 181 253
- **d** The estimated population of the UK in 2013, which is 63 498 000 people
- **e** The diameter of a pound coin, 2.250 cm
- **f** The weight of a wren, 0.026 kg

8   **a** Match each number with its reciprocal.

$\frac{5}{9}$	1
1	$\frac{1}{7}$
0.4	2.5
15	$1\frac{4}{5}$
7	0.0667

- **b** Which number is the reciprocal of itself?
- **c** What happens when you multiply a number by its reciprocal?
- **d** Use your calculator to try to find the reciprocal of zero. What happens?

9   **a** Multiply 150 by $\frac{1}{4}$. What do you have to multiply the answer by to get back to 150?
  b Choose another number. Multiply it by 2.5.
  What do you have to multiply the answer by to get back to the original number?
  c What do your answers to part **a** and part **b** tell you about reciprocals?

⚠ 10 Match each number with its reciprocal.

$\frac{1}{x}$	$\frac{d}{c}$
$\frac{c}{d}$	$0.1x$
$\frac{10}{x}$	x
$15x$	$\frac{5}{2}x$
$0.4x$	$\frac{1}{15x}$

11 The perimeter of a square is 20 cm.
The sides of the square are enlarged by 10%

    a   By what percentage is the perimeter of the enlarged square bigger than that of the original?

    b   By what percentage is the area of the enlarged square bigger than that of the original?

12 Here are the ingredients for crème brulée pudding for eight people.

> 8 egg yolks
>
> 1 litre (1000 ml) cream
>
> 225 g sugar

Jane is making crème brulée for two people.
Work out how much of each ingredient she will need.

13 Jake scored 12 marks out of 25 in his first mathematics test and 14 out of 30 in his second.
In which test did he do better? Show how you found your answer.

14 Paul uses the standard formula for converting Fahrenheit temperatures (°F) to Celsius temperatures (°C),

$$C = \frac{5}{9}(F - 32)$$

Tim uses another version, $C = 0.56(F - 32)$

Find the difference between Paul's answers and Tim's answers when converting:

    a   an oven temperature of 400°F to Celsius

    b   a room temperature of 20°F to Celsius.

15 $\frac{5}{8}$ of a number is 40. What is the number?

16 $\frac{3}{4}$ of $\frac{2}{5}$ of a number is 18. What is the number?

3   Assess   (k)

1 Which of these fractions is not equivalent to the other three?

$$\frac{5}{6}, \frac{10}{12}, \frac{14}{18}, \frac{20}{24}$$

Show how you worked out your answer.

2 Paul has £153.29 in his bank account. His account has an overdraft.
He writes a cheque for £209.25. How much will he have in his account after the cheque goes through?

3 Find the missing numbers.

    a $2.5 \times \square = -5$ **c** $-4.5 + \square = -2$

    b $\frac{1}{2} \times \square = 1$ **d** $\square \times -3 = 1.5$

4 Which is the biggest fraction in this list?

    a $\frac{8}{9}$ **b** $\frac{6}{7}$ **c** $\frac{5}{6}$ **d** $\frac{9}{11}$ **e** $\frac{4}{5}$

G

F

E

5 Match each fraction with its percentage.

$\frac{2}{3}$		56%	
$\frac{17}{20}$		38%	
$\frac{3}{8}$		67%	
$\frac{5}{9}$		85%	
$\frac{4}{5}$		80%	

D

6 Jyoti has a dozen eggs. She uses three eggs for breakfast and two in a cake. What fraction of her eggs does she have left?

7 One day John gets 36 e-mails. 28 of them are work related and the rest are personal e-mails. What fraction of his e-mails are work related?

8 A video game runs at 30 frames a second. What is the total time taken by three scenes of 33 frames, 44 frames and 32 frames?

9 A skirt needs $1\frac{3}{4}$ yards of fabric and a jacket needs $2\frac{1}{8}$ yards. How much fabric is needed altogether for four skirts and three jackets?

10 In a clinical trial of two new drugs, 2135 out of 3000 patients taking Drug A got better and 1855 out of 2500 patients taking Drug B got better. Which drug appears to be the more effective?

11 A number when rounded to three decimal places is 0.015. Write down three possible values of the number. What is its smallest possible value?

12 Drew's annual salary is increased by $\frac{1}{4}$ and becomes £36 400. What was his original salary?

13 There are three girls and seven boys in the chess club. One more boy and one more girl join the club. Is the percentage of girls in the club now more, less or the same? Show how you worked out your answer.

C

14 Which of these numbers are the reciprocal of $\frac{5}{8}$?

  a   0.625   **c** $1\frac{3}{8}$ **e** $\frac{5}{8}$

  b $\frac{8}{5}$ **d** $1\frac{3}{5}$ **f**   1.6

15 The price of a shirt is reduced by one-fifth in a sale.
The next week, the sale price is increased by one-fifth.

Is the final price less than, greater than or the same as the original price? Explain how you worked out your answer.

Practice questions 🄚

1 A supermarket sells 600 kg of potatoes.
$\frac{1}{2}$ of the potatoes are sold in 10 kg bags.
$\frac{3}{10}$ of the potatoes are sold in 5 kg bags.
The rest of the potatoes are sold in 3 kg bags.
How many 3 kg bags does the supermarket sell?

(5 marks)

AQA 2006

4 Scatter graphs

Objectives

Examiners would normally expect students who get these grades to be able to:

D

draw a scatter graph by plotting points on a graph

interpret the scatter graph

C

draw a line of best fit on the scatter graph

interpret the line of best fit

identify the type and strength of the correlation.

Did you know?

Scatter graphs

Scatter graphs are frequently used in medical research to test for relationships. For example, a study of office workers found that those with a stressful job had higher blood pressure. Scatter graphs can also be used to test the effects of drugs on lowering blood pressure.

Key terms

scatter graph
coordinate
types of correlation
correlation
positive correlation
negative correlation
zero or no correlation
strength of correlation
line of best fit
outlier

You should already know:

✔ how to use coordinates to plot points on a graph

✔ how to draw graphs including labelling axes and adding a title.

Learn... 4.1 Plotting points on a scatter graph

Scatter graphs (or scatter diagrams) are used to show the relationship between two sets of data.

Before drawing a scatter graph you need to identify the scale on the axes.

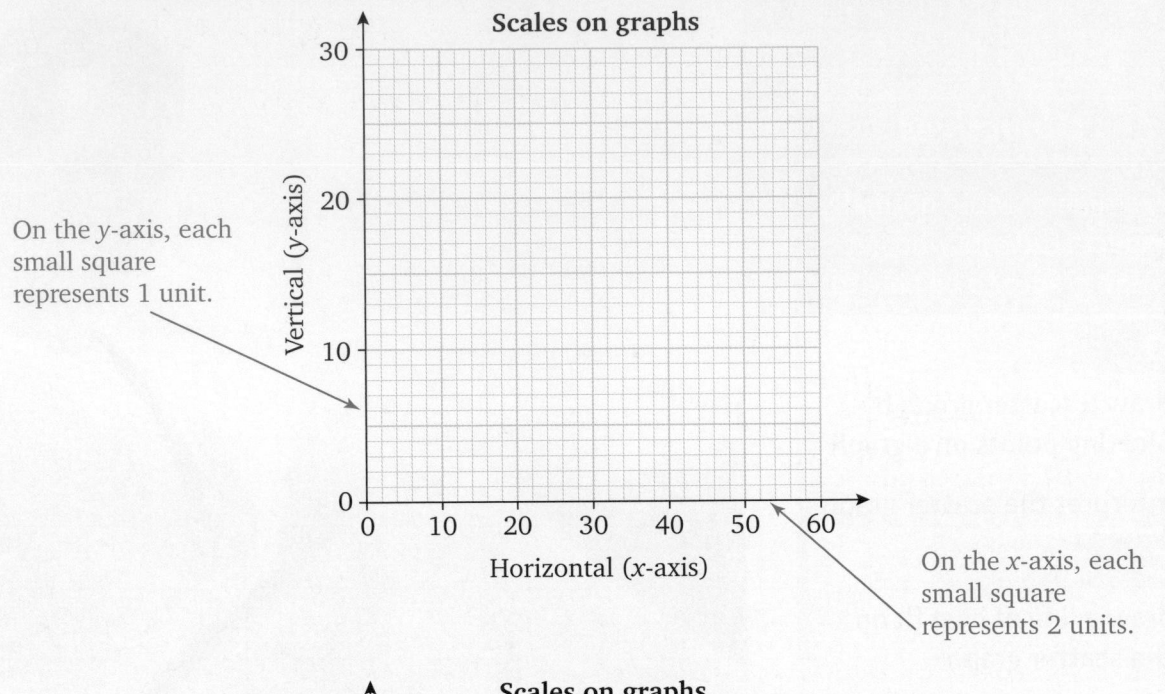

On the *y*-axis, each small square represents 1 unit.

On the *x*-axis, each small square represents 2 units.

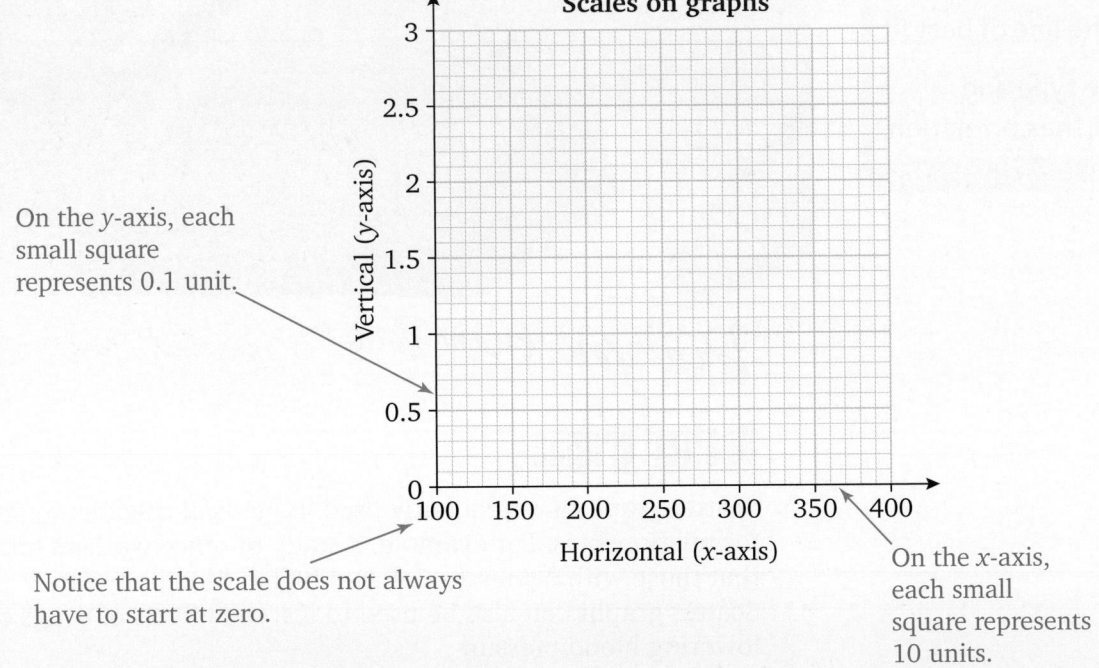

On the *y*-axis, each small square represents 0.1 unit.

Notice that the scale does not always have to start at zero.

On the *x*-axis, each small square represents 10 units.

Example: The table shows the temperature and numbers of ice creams sold on different days.

	Sun	Mon	Tue	Wed	Thu	Fri	Sat
Temperature (°C)	20	26	17	24	30	15	18
Ice cream sales	35	39	27	36	45	25	32

Show this information on a scatter graph.

Solution: The information can be plotted on a scatter graph using the **coordinate** points shown.

	Sun	Mon	Tue	Wed	Thu	Fri	Sat
Temperature (°C)	20	26	17	24	30	15	18
Ice cream sales	35	39	27	36	45	25	32
	(20, 35)	(26, 39)	(17, 27)	(24, 36)	(30, 45)	(15, 25)	(18, 32)

Temperature against ice cream sales

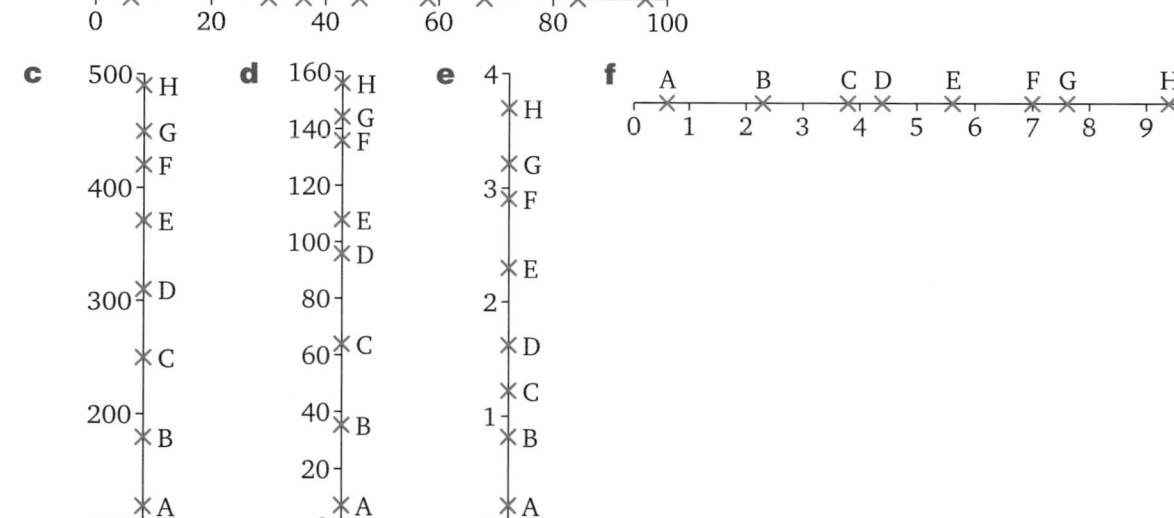

A jagged line is used to indicate a non-linear gap between O and the next value on the scale.

Study tip

Usually you should put the first set of data on the horizontal axis.

Study tip

Don't forget to label the axes and provide a title.

Practise... 4.1 Plotting points on a scatter graph k G F E D C

G

1 Write down the values of the following points.

a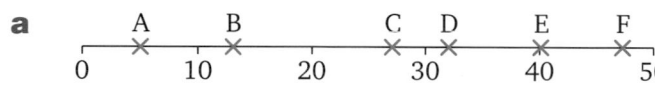

b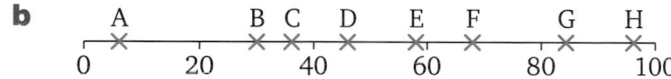

c **d** **e** **f**

F

2 The table shows the age and arm span of students in a school.

Age (years)	15	19	16	18	17	18	16	17
Arm span (cm)	78	84	76	80	71	78	80	83

Copy the axes and plot the points on the graph.

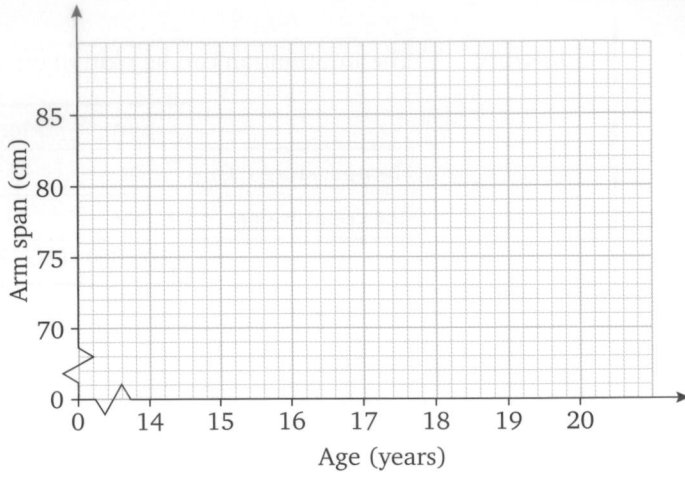

F
E

3 The table shows the age and value of second-hand cars.

Age of car (years)	Value of car (£)
5	3000
3	3400
4	2400
1	5200
6	2600
9	500
8	1600
10	600

Copy the axes and plot the points given in the table.

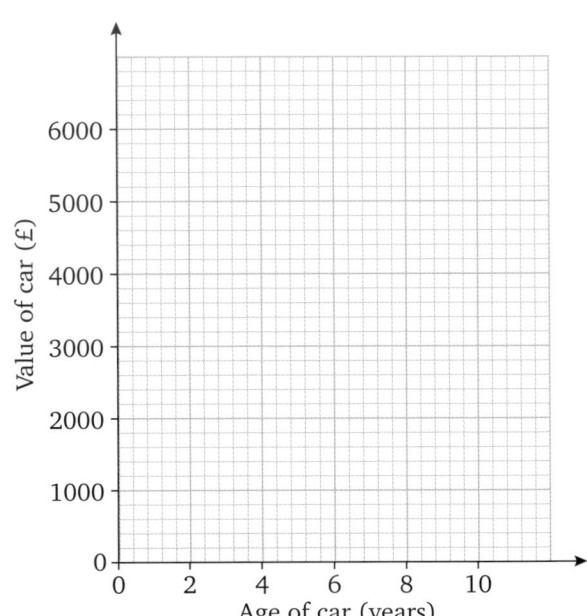

E

4 Copy and complete the table below, using the graph to find your values.

Point	A	B	C	D	E	F	G	H	I	J
Number of hours trained										
Fitness rating %										

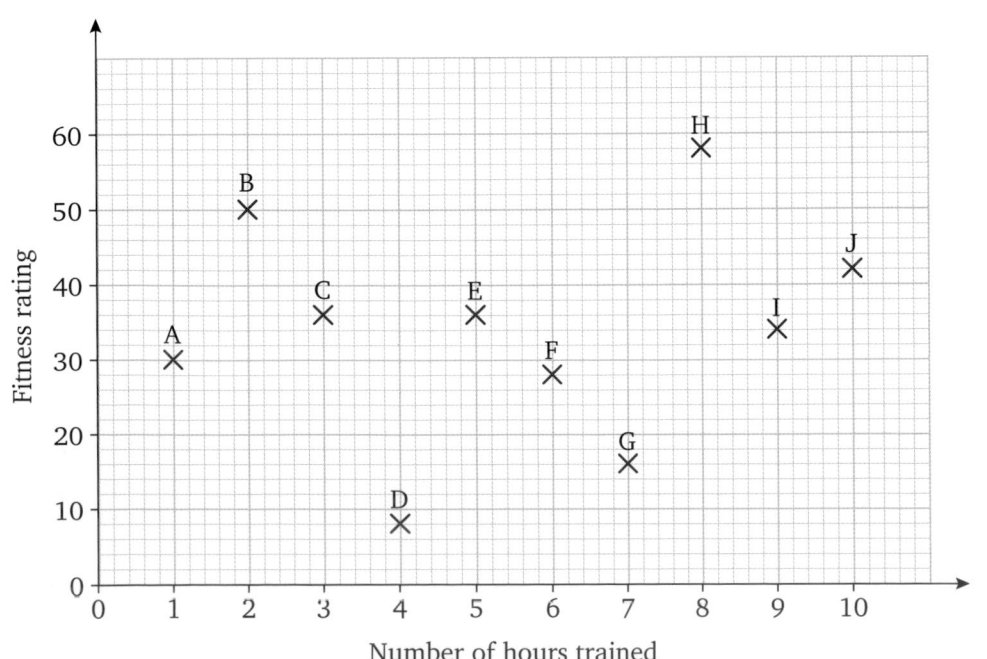

5 The following information shows the marks awarded to students on two exam papers.

French	31	14	65	28	55	59	44	77	40	49
Spanish	31	10	46	16	38	62	31	52	24	38

a Plot these points on a scatter graph.

b Tanya says that people who did well in Spanish also did well in French.
Is Tanya correct?
Give reasons for your answer.

  6 The table shows the infant mortality rate and the life expectancy for 10 countries.

Country	Egypt	France	Germany	India	Japan	Kenya	Nigeria	Pakistan	UK	Zimbabwe
Infant mortality	28.4	3.4	4	32.3	2.8	56	95.7	66.9	4.9	33.9
Life expectancy	71.8	80.9	79.1	69.2	82.1	56.6	46.5	64.1	78.8	44.3

Infant mortality is the number of deaths per 1000 births.
Life expectancy is given in years.

a Draw a scatter graph to show this information.

b What do you notice?

Learn... 4.2 Interpreting scatter graphs

Correlation measures the relationship between two sets of data.

It is measured in terms of **type** and **strength** of correlation.

Type of correlation

Positive correlation	Negative correlation	Zero or no correlation
Positive correlation is where an increase in one set of data results in an increase in the other set of data.	**Negative correlation** is where an increase in one set of data results in a decrease in the other set of data.	**Zero or no correlation** is where there is no obvious relationship between the two sets of data.

Example:
Temperature against ice cream sales. As the temperature increases, the number of ice cream sales increases.

Example:
Temperature against sales of coats. As the temperature increases, the sales of coats decreases.

Example:
Temperature against toothpaste sales. There is no obvious relationship between temperature and toothpaste sales.

Strength of correlation

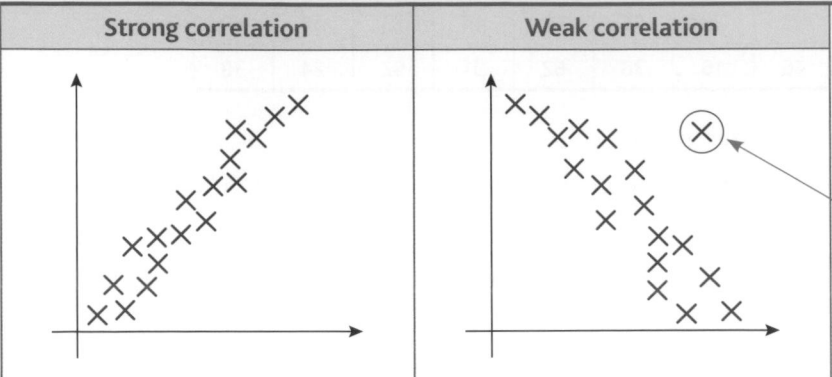

Strong correlation	Weak correlation	The strength of correlation is a measure of how close the points lie to a straight line (perfect correlation). Watch out for outliers which are values that do not fit in with the rest of the data. Correlation is usually measured in terms of strong correlation, weak correlation or no correlation.

Example: The graph shows the heights and shoe sizes of eight students.

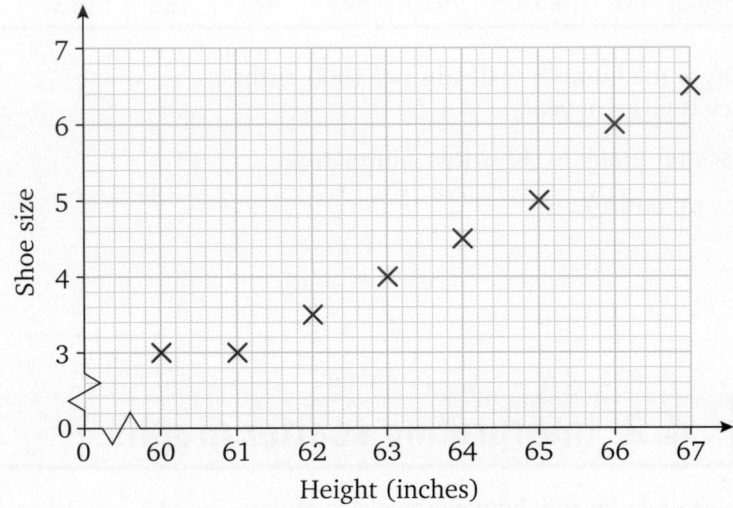

Describe the relationship between height and shoe size.

Solution: You can see that there is a relationship between height and shoe size.

As the height increases, the shoe size increases.

There is a **strong positive** correlation between height and shoe size.

Practise... 4.2 Interpreting scatter graphs ⓚ G F E D C

1 For each of the following:

a describe the type and strength of correlation

b write a sentence explaining the relationship between the two sets of data (for example, as the hours of sunshine increase so do the sales of iced drinks).

i The hours of sunshine and the sales of iced drinks.

ii The number of cars on a road and the average speed.

iii The distance travelled and the amount of petrol used.

iv The cost of a house and the number of bedrooms.

v The amount of sunshine and the sale of umbrellas.

2 For each of these scatter graphs:

a describe the type and strength of correlation

b write a sentence explaining the relationship between the two sets of data.

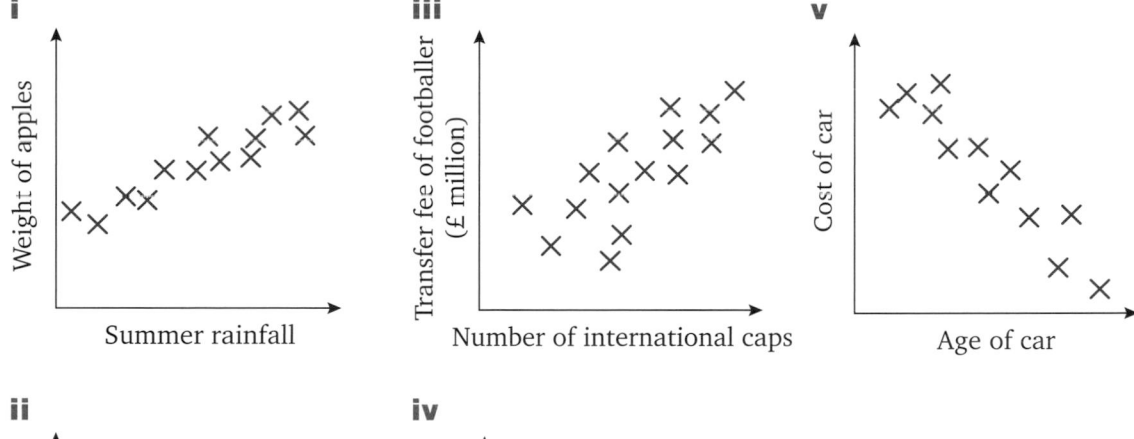

i Weight of apples / Summer rainfall

iii Transfer fee of footballer (£ million) / Number of international caps

v Cost of car / Age of car

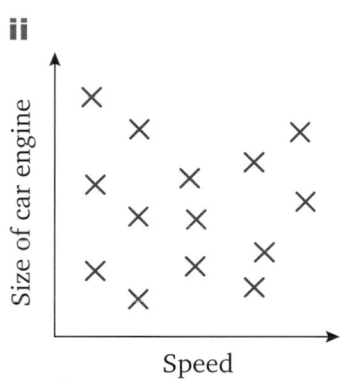

ii Size of car engine / Speed

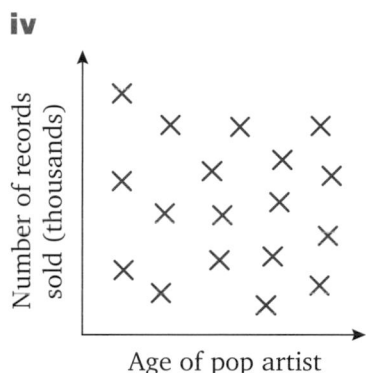

iv Number of records sold (thousands) / Age of pop artist

3 The table shows the ages and arm spans of seven students in a school.

Age (years)	16	13	13	10	18	10	15
Arm span (inches)	62	57	59	57	64	55	61

a Represent the data on a scatter graph.

b Describe the type and strength of correlation.

c Write a sentence explaining the relationship between the two sets of data.

4 The table shows the hours of sunshine and rainfall in 10 seaside towns.

Sunshine (hours)	Rainfall (mm)
650	11
400	30
530	28
640	11
520	24
550	20
480	26
600	15
550	16
525	23

a Represent the data on a scatter graph.

b Describe the type and strength of correlation.

c Write a sentence explaining the relationship between the two sets of data.

D

5 For each graph, write down two variables that might fit the relationship.

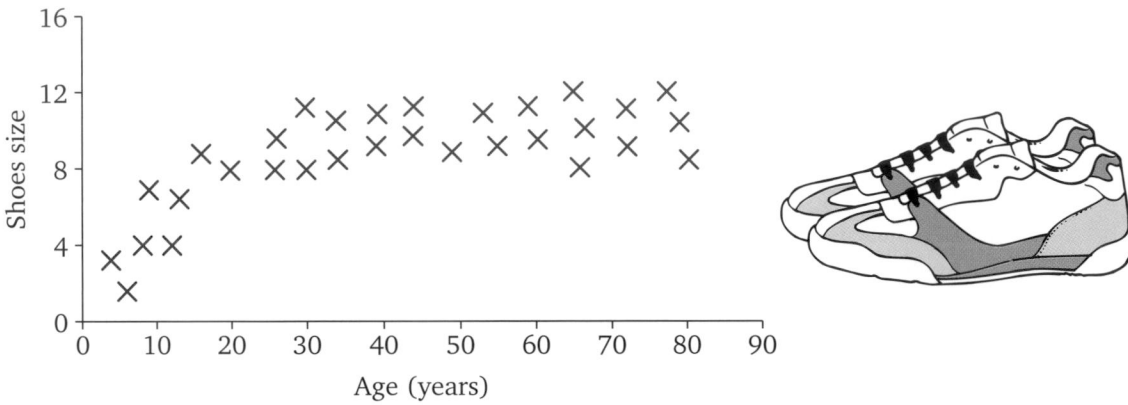

a   b   c

6 The scatter graph shows the ages and shoe sizes of a group of people.

a Describe the type and strength of correlation.

b Give a reason for your answer.

7 Ron is investigating the fat content and the calorie values of food at his local fast-food restaurant.

He collects the following information.

	Fat (g)	Calories
Hamburger	9	260
Cheeseburger	12	310
Chicken nuggets	24	420
Fish sandwich	18	400
Medium fries	16	350
Medium cola	0	210
Milkshake	26	1100
Breakfast	46	730

a Describe the correlation between fat and calories.

b Does the relationship hold for all the different foods? Give a reason for your answer.

Hint

If you are asked to describe correlation you should draw a scatter graph first and then describe the type and strength of correlation.

 **Learn...** **4.3 Lines of best fit**

A **line of best fit** is drawn to represent the relationship between two sets of data on a scatter graph.

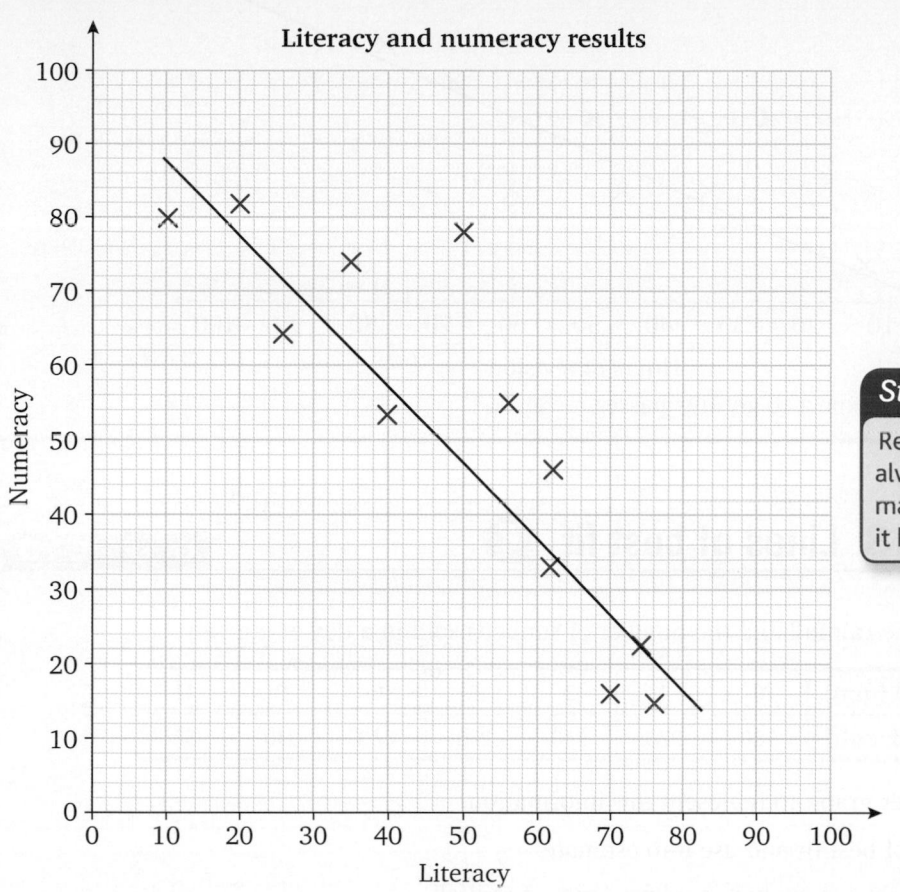

Study tip

Remember: your line does not always need to pass through as many points as possible, nor does it have to pass through the origin.

In this example, one of the values does not seem to fit the rest of the data.

This is called an **outlier** or rogue value.

Ignore these values when drawing a line of best fit.

You should draw the line of best fit so that:

- it gives a general trend for all of the data on the scatter graph
- it gives an idea of the strength and type of correlation
- there are roughly equal numbers of points above and below the line.

You can use the line of best fit to estimate missing data.

A line of best fit should only be drawn where the correlation is strong.

Study tip

When you are drawing your line of best fit, you will usually have a 'corridor of success'. This means that if your line of best fit falls within this 'corridor', you are correct.

Example:

The graph shows the number of hours' revision and the number of GCSE passes for 10 students.

Draw a line of best fit.

Dinah studies for 60 hours. How many GCSE passes is she likely to get?

Solution:

By drawing the line of best fit you can use the graph to estimate the number of GCSE passes.

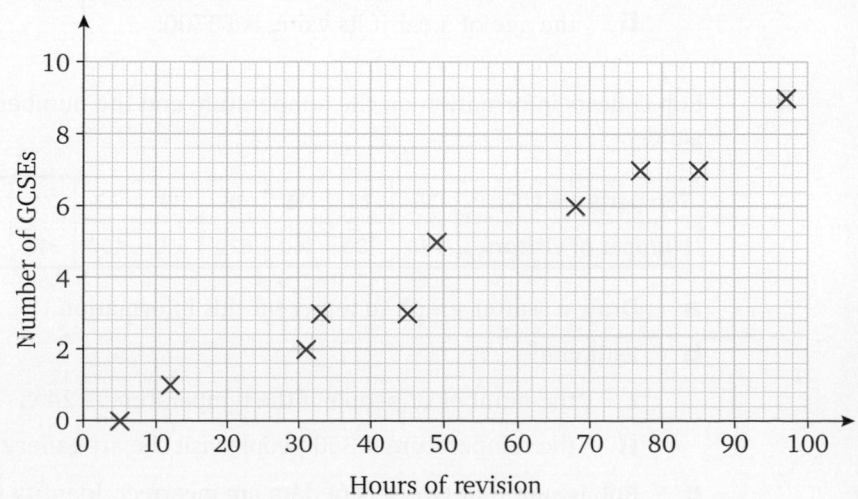

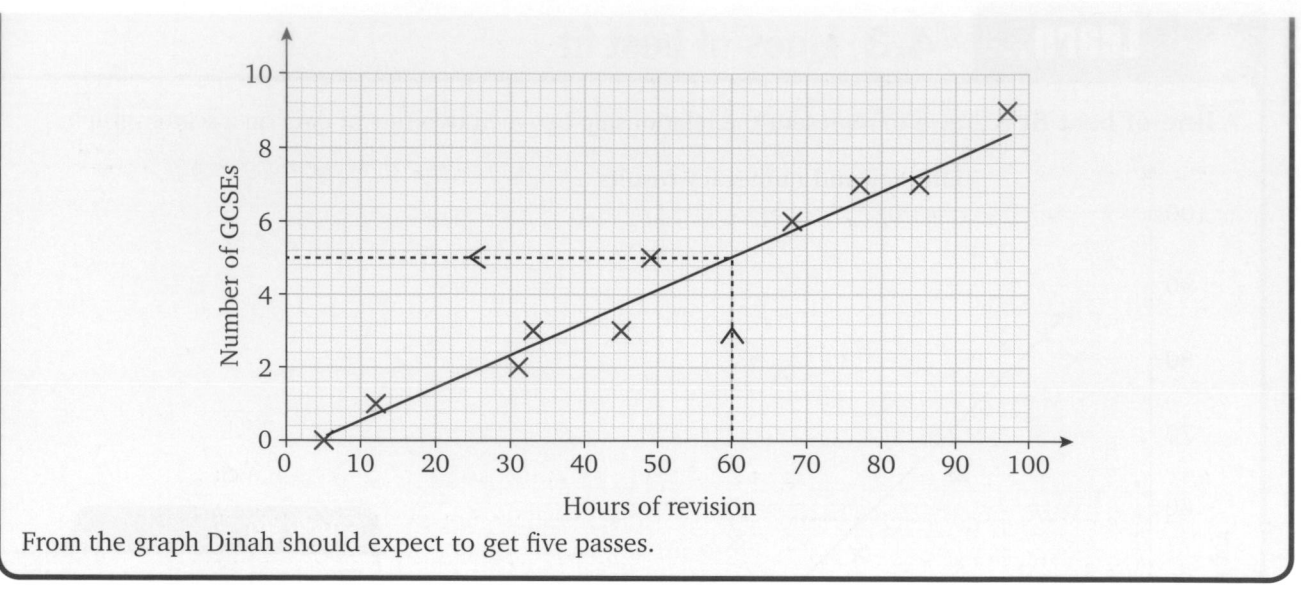

From the graph Dinah should expect to get five passes.

Practise... 4.3 Lines of best fit (k)

G F E D C

D

1 The table shows the rainfall and the number of sunbeds sold in a day at a resort.

Amount of rainfall (mm)	0	1	2	5	6	9	11
Number of sunbeds sold	380	320	340	210	220	110	60

  a Draw a scatter graph to represent this information.

  b Draw a line of best fit and use it to estimate:

    i the number of sunbeds sold for 4 mm of rainfall

    ii the amount of rainfall if 100 sunbeds are sold.

2 The table shows the age and value of seven second-hand cars of the same model.

Age of car (years)	2	1	4	7	10	9	8
Value of car (£)	4200	4700	2800	1900	400	1100	2100

  a Draw a scatter graph to represent this information.

  b Draw a line of best fit and use it to estimate:

    i the value of a car if it is 7.5 years old

    ii the age of a car if its value is £3700.

3 Rob collects information on the temperature and the number of visitors to an art gallery.

Temperature (°C)	15	25	16	18	19	22	24	23	17	20	26	20
Number of visitors	720	180	160	620	510	400	310	670	720	530	180	420

  a Draw a scatter graph to represent this information.

  b Estimate:

    i the number of people if the temperature is 24°C

    ii the temperature if 350 people visit the art gallery.

  c Rob is sure that two sets of data are incorrect. Identify these two sets of data on your graph.

4 Readings of two variables, A and B, are shown in the table.

A	1	2	3	4	5	6	7	0.8	2.1	3.2	3.9	5.1	6.2	7.1
B	1.8	8.8	20	33	48	73	95	2	9	18	31	49	72	98

a Draw a scatter graph to represent the data.

b Describe the correlation between the two sets of data.

c Draw a curve of best fit and use this to estimate:

i the value of B if A = 2.5

ii the value of A if B = 64

5 The table shows the actual age and reading age of six girls and six boys in a class.

Girls	Ann	Bano	Carrie	Dianne	Elseph	Florence
Actual age (months)	60	65	71	61	68	66
Reading age (months)	59	63	68	61	64	64

Boys	Jack	Kevin	Leon	Manjeet	Nabeel	Oscar
Actual age (months)	63	66	70	64	67	69
Reading age (months)	58	60	64	59	63	65

a What do you notice about the data?

b If Paul is 68 months old, what is his likely reading age?

c If Gail is 6 years old, what is her likely reading age?

d Which student has a reading age which is the same as their actual age?

6 The table shows the distances from the equator and average temperatures for 12 cities.

The distance is measured in degrees from the equator.

The temperature is measured in degrees Celsius.

City	Distance from equator (°)	Average temp. (°C)
Bangkok	13	28
Beijing	39	12
Boston	42	9
Cairo	30	22
Cape Town	33	17
Copenhagen	55	8
Gibraltar	36	19
Istanbul	40	14
London	51	10
Moscow	55	4.2
Mumbai	18	27
Perth	32	18

a What do you notice?

b Dubai is 25° north of the equator.
Use these data to find the average temperature in Dubai.

c What other factors might affect temperatures?

4 Assess

D

1 The information below shows the marks of eight students in history and geography.

Student	A	B	C	D	E	F	G	H
History	25	35	28	30	36	44	15	21
Geography	27	40	29	32	41	48	17	20

Draw a scatter graph to represent this information and comment on the relationship between the history and geography marks.

2 The following table shows the hours of TV watched and test marks for 10 students.

Student	1	2	3	4	5	6	7	8	9	10
TV hours	4	7	9	10	13	14	15	20	21	25
Test mark	9	90	74	30	74	66	95	38	35	30

a Draw a scatter graph to represent this information and comment on the relationship between the figures.

b Two students do not seem to 'fit the trend'.
Which ones are they? Explain why.

C

3 The tables show the relationship between the area (in thousands of km²) of some European countries and their populations (in millions) given to 2 s.f.

	Monaco	Malta	Jersey	Netherl.	UK	Germ.	Italy	Switz.	Andorra	Denm.
Area	0.0020	0.32	0.12	42	250	360	300	41	0.47	43
Population	0.030	0.40	0.090	16	60	83	58	7.3	0.068	5.4

	France	Austria	Turkey	Greece	Spain	Eire	Latvia	Sweden	Norway	Iceland
Area	550	84	780	130	500	70	65	450	320	100
Population	60	8.2	67	11	40	3.9	2.4	8.9	4.5	0.28

Draw a scatter graph of these data and comment on the graph.

4 The table shows the distance jumped in long jump trials and the leg length of the jumpers.

Leg length (cm)	71	73	74	75	76	79	82
Distance jumped (m)	3.2	3.1	3.3	4.1	3.9	4	4.8

a Draw a scatter graph to represent this information.

b Use a line of best fit to estimate:

i the leg length of an athlete who jumped a distance of 3.5 m

ii the distance jumped by an athlete with a leg length of 85 cm.

c Explain why one of those estimates is more reliable than the other.

5   Adnan is comparing A Level textbooks in order to test the hypothesis
'Books with more pages weigh more'.

He records the number of pages and then weighs each textbook.

His results are shown in the table below.

Number of pages	82	90	140	101	160	140	111	152	202
Weight (g)	165	155	210	192	245	96	190	231	280

a   One of the readings is a rogue value.
Which reading is an outlier?
Give a reason why this might occur.

b   Is Adnan's hypothesis true or false.
Show your working to justify your answer.

Practice questions (k)

1   The length and wingspan, in centimetres, of seven common garden birds is shown in the table.

Bird	Length (cm)	Wingspan (cm)
Starling	21	40
Blackbird	25	34
Blue tit	11	19
Greenfinch	15	26
Dove	32	51
Sparrow	15	23
Great tit	14	24

a   Copy and complete the scatter graph
opposite. *(2 marks)*

b   Describe the strength and type of
correlation. *(1 mark)*

c   Draw a line of best fit on your
scatter graph. *(1 mark)*

d   Use your line of best fit to estimate
the wingspan of a thrush whose
length is 20 cm. *(1 mark)*

e   It is **not** sensible to use your line of
best fit to estimate the wingspan of
a pigeon whose length is 41 cm.
Explain why. *(1 mark)*

AQA 2008

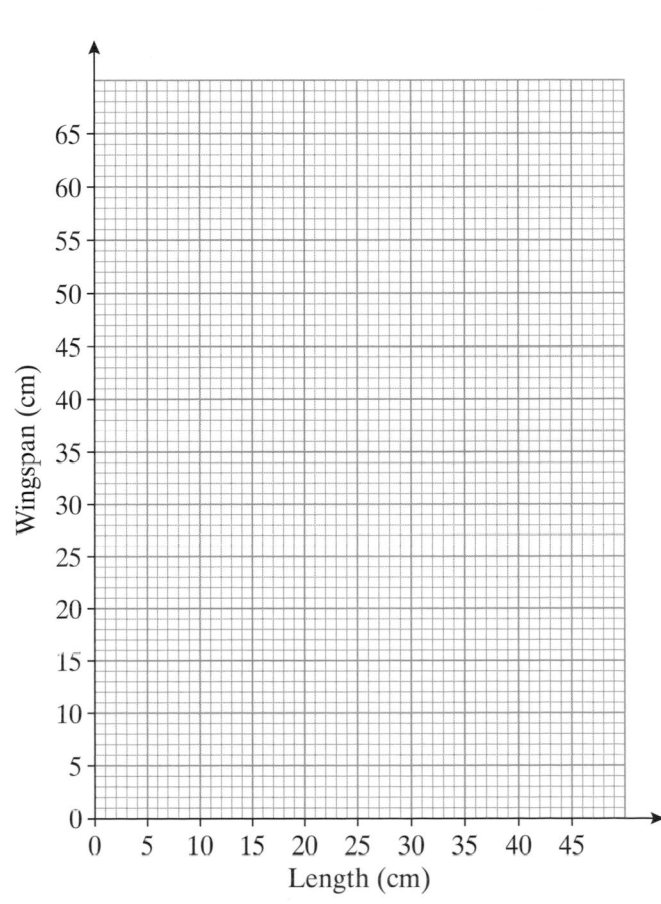

5 Equations and inequalities

Objectives

Examiners would normally expect students who get these grades to be able to:

F

solve a simple equation such as $5x = 10$ or $x + 4 = 7$

E

solve an equation involving fractions such as $\frac{x}{3} = 4$ or $2x - 3 = 8$

D

solve more complicated equations such as $3x + 2 = 6 - x$ or $4(2x - 1) = 20$

represent and interpret inequalities on a number line

C

solve an equation such as $4x + 5 = 3(x + 4)$ or $\frac{x}{2} - \frac{x}{8} = 9$ or $\frac{2x - 7}{4} = 1$

solve an inequality such as $2x - 7 < 9$

find the integer solutions of an inequality such as $-8 < 2n \leqslant 5$

Did you know?

'Ink blots to space rockets'

$\bigcirc + 3 = 21$

What is the number under the blob?

You can guess the answer without knowing any algebra.

You can't design a space rocket by guesswork, but this chapter will show you how to take the first steps in solving complicated equations.

Then you might end up designing the next space rocket.

Key terms

unknown
solve/solution
operation
inverse operation
brackets
denominator

inequality
$<$ (less than)
$\leqslant$ (less than or equal to)
$>$ (greater than)
$\geqslant$ (greater than or equal to)
integer

You should already know:

✔ how to collect like terms

✔ how to use substitution

✔ how to multiply out brackets by a positive or negative number.

 **Learn...**   **5.1 Simple equations**

Equations are used when you are trying to find an **unknown** value. Follow these steps to find the value of the unknown. This is called the **solution**.

- Think about the **operations** $(+, -, \times, \div)$ that have been applied to x.

- Reverse these operations, doing the same to both sides of the equation.

- Where there are two operations, reverse the second operation first,
  e.g. $2x + 3$ means 'multiply x by 2, then add 3', so the **inverse operations** will be 'subtract 3, then divide by 2'.

Example: Solve the equation:

$3x = 21$ Remember that $3x$ means $3 \times x$

Solution: $\dfrac{3x}{3} = \dfrac{21}{3}$ Divide both sides by 3.

$x = 7$

> **Study tip**
>
> Check your answer by substituting it back into the equation to see whether it fits, e.g. 3×7 does equal 21.

Example: Solve the equation:

$x + 9 = 4$

Solution: $x + 9 - 9 = 4 - 9$ Subtract 9 from both sides.

$x = -5$

Example: Solve the equation:

$\dfrac{x}{8} = 1$

Solution: $\dfrac{x}{8} \times 8 = 1 \times 8$ Multiply both sides by 8.

$x = 8$

Example: Solve the equation

$5x - 2 = 13$

Solution: This is an equation with two operations, $\times$ and $-$.

Reverse the 'subtract 2' operation first:

$5x - 2 + 2 = 13 + 2$ Add 2 to both sides.

$5x = 15$

$\dfrac{5x}{5} = \dfrac{15}{5}$ Divide both sides by 5.

$x = 3$

Practise...   **5.1 Simple equations**

F

1   Solve these equations.

a $2x = 12$	**d** $4a = 6$	**g** $x - 3 = 8$	**j** $a + 9 = 2$
b $3y = 18$	**e** $6b = 15$	**h** $y + 4 = 12$	**k** $b - 1 = -3$
c $5z = 35$	**f** $2c = -4$	**i** $z + 1.5 = 4.8$	**l** $c + 7.9 = 2.2$

E

2   Solve these equations.

a $\dfrac{x}{2} = 6$ i $23 = 4z + 7$

b $\dfrac{y}{4} = 5$ j $3 = 2a + 9$

c $\dfrac{z}{5} = 1$ k $6 = 5b + 11$

d $\dfrac{a}{10} = 0.4$ l $8c - 15 = 9$

e $\dfrac{b}{7} = 0$ m $15 - 2x = 9$

f $\dfrac{c}{3} = -2$ n $7 - 3y = 10$

g $3x - 5 = 13$ o $4 = 13 - 6z$

h $2y + 1 = 9$ p $0 = 28 - 4t$

> **Hint**
>
> If the unknown is on the right side of the equation, swap it around before you start to solve it.

3   a   Make up five different equations that have the answer $z = 3$

     Use a different style for each equation:

- one which requires division
- one which requires multiplication
- one which requires addition
- one which requires subtraction
- one which requires a combination of operations.

   b   Make up three different equations that have the answer $t = -5$

4   Tony thinks of a number, doubles it and adds 11.
The answer is 19.
Write this as an equation.
Solve the equation to find Tony's number.

5   Jackie thinks of a number, multiplies it by 7 and adds 5.
The answer is 47.
Write this as an equation.
Solve the equation to find Jackie's number.

6   Sol goes out with a £5 note in his pocket.
He buys x snack bars at 40p each.
He has 20p left.
Find the value of x.

7   The angles in a triangle add up to 180°.
Write down an equation in x.

Solve your equation to find the value of x.

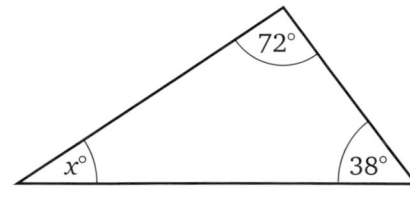

8   The angles in a quadrilateral add up to 360°.
Write down an equation in y.

Solve your equation to find the value of y.

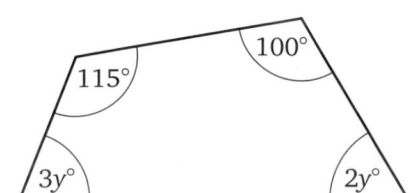

 **Learn...** 5.2 **Harder equations**

These include equations where x appears on both sides.

Follow these steps to **solve** the equation:

- Collect together on one side all the terms that contain the **unknown** letter (x).
- Collect together on the other side all the other terms.
- Remember signs belong with the term **after** them.
- Take one step at a time – do not try to do two steps at once.

Example: Solve the equations:

a $2x + 3 = 18 - x$

b $3y + 9 = 5y - 8$

Solution:

a $2x + 3 + x = 18 - x + x$ Add x to both sides (this collects all the x terms

$3x + 3 = 18$ together on the left-hand side).

$3x + 3 - 3 = 18 - 3$ Take 3 from both sides (this collects all the numbers

$3x = 15$ on the right-hand side).

$\dfrac{3x}{3} = \dfrac{15}{3}$ Divide both sides by 3.

$x = 5$

b $3y + 9 - 3y = 5y - 8 - 3y$ Take $3y$ from both sides (this collects all the y

$9 = 2y - 8$ terms on the right-hand side).

$9 + 8 = 2y - 8 + 8$ Add 8 to both sides.

$17 = 2y$

$\dfrac{17}{2} = \dfrac{2y}{2}$ Divide both sides by 2.

$8.5 = y$

$y = 8.5$ Write the equation with y on the left.

Study tip

Collect the terms in y on the side that has the largest number of them already.

Practise... 5.2 **Harder equations**   G F E D C

1 Solve these equations.

a $4x + 1 = 2x + 13$ **e** $6p + 2 = 9 + 4p$ **i** $7c - 1 = 3 - c$

b $2y - 3 = y + 4$ **f** $3 + q = 17 - 6q$ **j** $25 + 2d = 5d + 4$

c $5z - 2 = 8 + 3z$ **g** $7 + 2a = 2 - 3a$ **k** $6 - 7e = 3 - 6e$

d $t + 3 = 9 - 3t$ **h** $8b - 3 = 2b - 15$ **l** $5f + 10 = 2 + f$

2 Jared solves the equation $9x - 2 = 5 - 4x$

His first step is $5x - 2 = 5$

What mistake has Jared made?

D

D

3　Ella solves the equation $5y + 6 = 2 - y$

She writes down $6y = 4$

What mistake has Ella made?

4　Dean solves the equation $3x - 11 = 4 + 2x$

He gets the answer $x = 7$

Can you find Dean's mistake?

5　Rick solves the equation $2y + 5 = 3 - 3y$

He gets the answer $y = -2$

Can you find Rick's mistake?

⚠ 6　$4z - 3 = \bullet - 2z$

The answer to this equation is $z = 5$

What is the number under the blob?

⚠ 7　$2a + \bullet = 5 - 7a$

The answer to this equation is $a = -1$

What is the number under the blob?

⚠ 8　**a**　If $b = 11$, find the value of $3b - 8$

　　b　Using your answer to part **a**, explain why $b = 11$ is **not** the solution of the equation $3b - 8 = 19 - 2b$

⚠ 9　**a**　If $c = -4$, find the value of $9 - 5c$

　　b　Using your answer to part **a**, explain why $c = -4$ is **not** the solution of the equation $6c + 13 = 9 - 5c$

Learn... 5.3 Equations with brackets

For equations such as $3(2x - 1) = 12$ your first step is to deal with the **bracket**.

This usually means multiplying out the bracket.

In the first example below, you could start with division instead.

Example:　Solve the equations:

　　a　$4(3x - 1) = 32$

　　b　$7 - 3(y + 2) = 5 - 4y$

Solution:　**a**　$4(3x - 1) = 32$

Multiply out the bracket first, then follow the rules for solving equations.

$$12x - 4 = 32$$ 　　Remember to multiply **both** terms in the bracket by 4.

$$12x - 4 + 4 = 32 + 4$$ 　　Add 4 to both sides.

$$12x = 36$$

$$\frac{12x}{12} = \frac{36}{12}$$ 　　Divide both sides by 12.

$$x = 3$$

Alternative method:

$$4(3x - 1) = 32$$

$3x - 1 = 8$	Divide both sides by 4.
$3x - 1 + 1 = 8 + 1$	Add 1 to both sides.
$3x = 9$	
$\dfrac{3x}{3} = \dfrac{9}{3}$	Divide both sides by 3.
$x - 3$	

This alternative method works because 4 is a factor of 32.
It cannot be used for all equations with brackets, as the next example shows.

b $7 - 3(y + 2) = 5 - 4y$

Multiply out the bracket first, then follow the rules for solving equations.

$7 - 3y - 6 = 5 - 4y$	Note: $-3 \times +2 = -6$
$1 - 3y = 5 - 4y$	The numbers on the left-hand side have been collected.
$1 - 3y - 1 = 5 - 4y - 1$	Subtract 1 from both sides.
$-3y = 4 - 4y$	
$-3y + 4y = 4 - 4y + 4y$	Add $4y$ to both sides.
$y = 4$	

> **Study tip**
>
> Don't try to do two steps at once – most students make mistakes if they rush their working.

Practise... 5.3 Equations with brackets   G F E D C

1   Solve these equations.

a $5(x + 3) = 55$ **d** $4(a + 1) = 24$

b $2(y - 4) = 16$ **e** $7(b - 2) = 7$

c $9 = 3(z - 7)$ **f** $13 = 2(c + 5)$

2   Solve these equations.

a $4(p + 2) = 2p + 9$ **f** $6 + c = 5(c - 2)$ **k** $3(y - 4) + 2(4y - 2) = 6$

b $6(q - 3) = 17 - q$ **g** $11d - 1 = 3(d + 1)$ **l** $10 - 3(k + 2) = 7 - k$

c $2(5t - 1) = 13$ **h** $2(1 - 2e) = 5 - 3e$ **m** $23 = 6 - 4(t - 5)$

d $5a + 3 = 4(a - 2)$ **i** $2 - 5f = 3(2 - f)$ **n** $4(p - 3) - 3(p - 4) = 14$

e $3(2b - 3) = 1 + 7b$ **j** $6(2 + 3x) = 11x + 5$ **o** $2(q - 9) - (7q - 3) + 25 = 0$

3   Natalie thinks of a number, adds 7 and then doubles the result.
Her answer is 38.
Write this as an equation.
Solve the equation to find Natalie's number.

4   Rob thinks of a number, subtracts 5 and then multiplies the result by 4.
His answer is 32.
Write this as an equation.
Solve the equation to find Rob's number.

D

C

Learn... 5.4 Equations with fractions

At some stage in solving an equation with a fraction, you have to clear the fraction by multiplying both sides by the **denominator**.

For example, if the equation contains $\frac{x}{3}$, you will multiply by 3.

If there is more than one fraction, say $\frac{3x}{5}$ and $\frac{x}{2}$, you will multiply by both denominators.

In this case, this is $5 \times 2 = 10$

Harder equations have more than one term on the top of the fraction. There is an 'invisible bracket' around the terms on top of an algebraic fraction.

Example: Solve the equation

$$\frac{x}{3} - 2 = 5$$

Solution: This is an example of the simplest type of equation with a fraction.

$\frac{x}{3} - 2 + 2 = 5 + 2$ Start by adding 2 to both sides.

$\frac{x}{3} = 7$ Now the fraction term is on its own.

$\frac{x}{3} \times 3 = 7 \times 3$ Multiply both sides by 3 (the **denominator**).

$x = 21$

Example: Solve the equation

$$\frac{3x}{5} - \frac{x}{2} = 1$$

Solution: This is an example where there is more than one fraction.

You need to multiply by both denominators, in this case, $5 \times 2 = 10$

Multiply each term by 10.

$10 \times \frac{3x}{5} = \frac{30x}{5} = 6x$

$10 \times \frac{x}{2} = \frac{10x}{2} = 5x$

$10 \times 1 = 10$

$6x - 5x = 10$

$x = 10$

> **Study tip**
>
> Don't forget to multiply the right-hand side as well as the left-hand side.

Example: Solve the equation

$$\frac{5x + 2}{4} = 3$$

Solution: This is an example of a harder equation with more than one term on the top of the fraction.

$\frac{(5x + 2)}{4}$ is the same as one-quarter of $(5x + 2)$

Multiply by 4 to get $5x + 2$

$5x + 2 = 12 \longleftarrow 4 \times 3$

$5x + 2 - 2 = 12 - 2$ Subtract 2 from both sides.

$5x = 10$

$\frac{5x}{5} = \frac{10}{5}$ Divide both sides by 5.

$x = 2$

> **Hint**
>
> You should put in the invisible bracket before you start your working.

Practise... 5.4 Equations with fractions  G F E D C

1 Solve these equations.

a $\frac{x}{2} - 5 = 4$

b $\frac{y}{5} + 3 = 7$

c $5 = 1 + \frac{z}{3}$

d $7 + \frac{a}{3} = 8$

e $9 - \frac{b}{2} = 2$

f $\frac{c}{6} + 5 = 2$

g $\frac{4x + 1}{3} = 11$

h $\frac{2y - 7}{5} = 3$

i $1 = \frac{9 - z}{3}$

j $\frac{p + 3}{4} = 5$

k $\frac{3q + 8}{2} = 13$

l $\frac{4t - 3}{3} = 7$

m $\frac{x}{5} + \frac{x}{3} = 8$

n $\frac{y}{2} - \frac{y}{8} = 3$

o $\frac{5z}{6} - \frac{7z}{12} = 4$

2

a $\frac{5a - 1}{2} = a - 5$

b $\frac{2b - 5}{8} = 5 - b$

c $c - 7 = \frac{11 - c}{3}$

d $\frac{3p}{2} = 5 - \frac{p}{6}$

e $\frac{q}{3} - \frac{1}{4} = \frac{q}{6}$

f $\frac{3t}{8} + \frac{1}{4} = \frac{2t}{5}$

3 Faria says the answer to the equation $\frac{x + 2}{5} = 4 - x$ is $x = 9$

Use substitution to check whether Faria is correct.

4 Ed and Gary solve the equation $\frac{4y - 3}{5} = 2y + 3$

Ed gets the answer $y = -2$ and Gary gets $y = -3$

Check their answers to see which of them is correct.

5 The equation $\frac{6p - 5}{2} = 4 + 3p$ cannot be solved. Why?

Learn... 5.5 Inequalities and the number line

The four **inequality** symbols are:

<	≤	>	≥
less than	less than or equal to	greater than	greater than or equal to

A number line shows the range of values for x.

An open circle shows that the range does not include that end of the line.

For example $x > 1$ or $y < 5$

A closed circle shows that the range does include that end of the line.

For example $x \leqslant 3$ or $y \geqslant 5$

This is the number line for $x > 1$

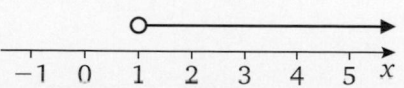

x could be any number greater than 1... *but not 1.*

The open circle shows that x can be close to 1 but not equal to 1.

This is the number line for $x \leqslant 3$

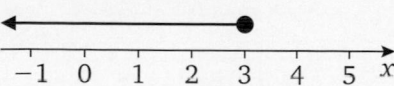

x could be any number less than or equal to 3.

The closed circle shows that x can be equal to 3.

This is the number line for $x < -1$ or $x \geqslant 2$

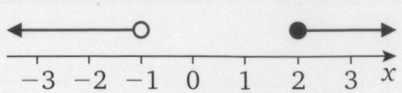

x could be any number less than -1 or it could be any number greater than or equal to 2. x cannot be a number between -1 and 2.

Example: Show the inequality $-2 \leqslant x < 3$ on a number line.

Solution: If x is an integer, it could be $-2, -1, 0, 1, 2$ *but not 3.*

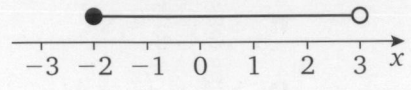

The open circle shows that x can be close to 3 but not equal to 3. The closed circle shows that x can be equal to 2.

Practise... 5.5 Inequalities and the number line

D

1 Write down the inequalities shown by these number lines.

a

b

c

d

2 Show each of these inequalities on a number line.

a $x > 1$ **d** $x < 2$ **g** $-4 \leqslant x < 3$

b $x > -5$ **e** $x \leqslant -1$ **h** $x < 4$ or $x \geqslant 6$

c $x \geqslant 0$ **f** $-2 < x < 1$ **i** $x \leqslant -2$ or $x > 0$

3 Explain why it is incorrect to write $2 < x < -6$

4 Nic gets £10 a week in pocket money.
Nic asks Joe how much he gets each week.
Joe says 'I get more than £6 but less than you.'
Joe's pocket money is made up of pound coins and 50 pence pieces.
List the possible amounts Joe might get.

5 Natalie is five feet and six inches tall.
Olwen is five feet and two inches tall.
Pippa is taller than Olwen but not as tall as Natalie.
Show Pippa's height on a number line.
Explain why you cannot make a list of possible heights for Pippa.

Learn... 5.6 Solving inequalities

Some inequalities are very similar to equations.

The inequality $3x - 2 > 4$ is similar to the equation $3x - 2 = 4$

To solve this inequality, use inverse operations as you would with the equation.

$3x - 2 + 2 > 4 + 2$ 　　　Add 2 to both sides.

$3x > 6$ 　　　Divide both sides by 3.

$x > 2$

You may be asked to list **integer** values (whole numbers) that satisfy an inequality.

For example, the integers that satisfy $-3 \leqslant x < 5$ are $-3, -2, -1, 0, 1, 2, 3, 4$.

Sometimes you have to combine these two skills, as in the example below.

Example:　　List all the integer values of n such that $-5 < 2n \leqslant 6$

Solution:　　Divide every term in the inequality by 2
$-2.5 < n \leqslant 3$

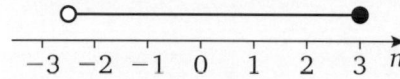

Integer values for n are: $-2, -1, 0, 1, 2, 3$

Practise... 5.6 Solving inequalities

1　Solve these inequalities.

　　a　$3x - 2 \geqslant 4$ 　　　　　　**d**　$5 + 2p > 1$

　　b　$2y + 7 \leqslant 16$ 　　　　　　**e**　$8 < 2 + 3q$

　　c　$4z + 12 < 0$ 　　　　　　**f**　$5 > 13 - x$

2　List all the integer values of n such that:

　　a　$-3 < n < 4$ 　　　　　　**e**　$0 < 3n < 15$

　　b　$1 \leqslant n < 6$ 　　　　　　**f**　$-4 < 2n \leqslant 6$

　　c　$-5 < n \leqslant -1$ 　　　　　　**g**　$-10 \leqslant 4n < 12$

　　d　$-2 \leqslant n \leqslant 1$ 　　　　　　**h**　$-5 \leqslant 5n \leqslant 8$

3　Find the largest integer that satisfies the inequality $5 - 2x \geqslant 1$

4　Find the smallest integer that satisfies the inequality $7 < 3(2x + 9)$

5　List all the pairs of positive integers, x and y, such that $3x + 4y \leqslant 15$

6　Jiffa is 14 years old.

She says to her Uncle Asif, 'How old are you?'

He says, 'In 9 years' time I shall be more than twice as old as I was when you were born.'

Write down an inequality and solve it to find the greatest age Asif could be.

5 Assess (k)

F

1 Solve these equations.

   a $9x = 81$ **b** $y - 4 = 12$ **c** $10z = 50$

E

2 Solve these equations.

   a $\frac{a}{3} = 9$ **c** $2d - 5 = 6$ **e** $8 + 3f = 5$

   b $4c + 11 = 3$ **d** $5e + 4 = 12$ **f** $p + 5 = 14 - 2p$

D

3 Solve these equations.

   a $2q - 1 = 5 - q$ **c** $4 + 3n = n - 10$ **e** $49 = 7(3t - 2)$

   b $6m - 7 = 2m + 3$ **d** $5(u + 1) = 35$ **f** $3(v - 4) = 9 + 2v$

4 Write down the inequalities shown by these number lines.

   a

       $-5 \;\; -4 \;\; -3 \;\; -2 \;\; -1 \;\; 0 \;\; 1 \;\; 2 \;\; 3 \quad x$

   b

       $-5 \;\; -4 \;\; -3 \;\; -2 \;\; -1 \;\; 0 \;\; 1 \;\; 2 \;\; 3 \quad y$

C

5 Solve these equations.

   a $4(w - 2) + 2(3w + 1) = 44$ **c** $\frac{y}{4} + 3 = 7$ **e** $\frac{x}{5} + \frac{x}{10} = 6$

   b $5(2x - 3) = 7 + 4(x - 1)$ **d** $4 - \frac{k}{3} = 6$

6 Solve these inequalities.

   a $6a - 7 \geqslant 5$ **b** $3b + 10 < 4$

7 Find the largest integer that satisfies the inequality $2x + 3 < 17$

8 List all the integer solutions of the inequality $-8 < 3n \leqslant 9$

Practice questions (k)

1 An equilateral triangle is one where all the sides are the same length.

This triangle has lengths $(4x - 2)$ cm, $(2x + 5)$ cm and $(6x - 9)$ cm.

Find the value of x that makes this triangle equilateral.

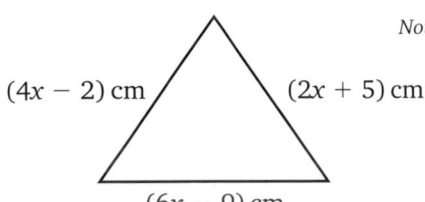

Not drawn to scale

$(4x - 2)$ cm $(2x + 5)$ cm

$(6x - 9)$ cm

(4 marks)

AQA 2009

Enlargements

Examiners would normally expect students who get these grades to be able to:

F

state the scale factor of an enlargement

E

enlarge a shape by a positive scale factor

find the measurements of the dimensions of an enlarged shape

D

enlarge a shape by a positive scale factor from a given centre

C

find the ratio of corresponding lengths in similar shapes and identify this as the scale factor of enlargement

use ratios in similar shapes to find missing lengths.

Did you know?

Screen sizes

The screens for monitors or televisions come in many different sizes. The two larger screens in the photograph above look as though they are enlargements of the smaller screen. Enlargements have to satisfy certain conditions which you will learn about in this chapter.

Television screens come in two different shapes: $4:3$ and $16:9$

- If you measure an older style TV, the $4:3$, you will find that for every 4 units of width there are 3 units of height.
- If you measure a widescreen TV screen, which is $16:9$, for every 16 units of width there are 9 units of height.

An enlargement of $4:3$ with a scale factor of 4 would be $4 \times 4:4 \times 3$ which equals $16:12$. Therefore the ratio $16:9$ is not an enlargement of $4:3$. This is why people filmed in $4:3$ format look fatter when shown in widescreen.

Strangely, televisions are measured across the diagonal and still in inches!

Key terms

enlargement
transformation
similar
scale factor
centre of enlargement
vertex, vertices
ratio

You should already know:

✔ how to plot coordinates in all four quadrants

✔ about units of length and how to use them

✔ about ratio and how to simplify a ratio

✔ how to use the vocabulary of transformations: mapping, object and image

✔ how to recognise and use corresponding angles

✔ how find the area of simple shapes including a rectangle and a triangle.

6.1 Introduction to enlargement and scale factor

Enlargements are a type of **transformation**.

They are the only transformations at GCSE that change the size of a shape.

All the other transformations (reflections, rotations and translations) keep the image the same size as the original shape. The shapes are **congruent**.

An enlargement changes the size of an image but not the shape.

All the lengths will be changed but all the angles will stay the same. The shapes are **similar**.

For example, if you take a photograph to be enlarged, the new photograph will be bigger but the picture does not change in any other way.

Example: These two diagrams are the same shape.
The shapes are similar.
One is an enlargement of the other.

What is the **scale factor** of the enlargement?

Solution: The scale factor tells us how many times bigger the shape has been made. To find it you need to take two corresponding sides, one on the original (object) and one on the new one (image).

In this diagram the corresponding lengths are 3 units and 6 units. The length on the image is 2 times that on the object.

So, the scale factor = 2

Every length on the image is twice the size of the corresponding length on the object.

Example: Copy this diagram onto squared paper and then enlarge the shape by scale factor 3.

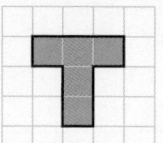

Solution: Before you start, look at the lengths of the lines already given on the original shape.

As they are to be enlarged by a scale factor of 3, each of these lengths will be three times longer in the image.

Starting at the top left-hand side of the shape, the top is 3 units in length.

The top of the enlarged shape will be $3 \times 3 = 9$ units long.

Move around the shape and enlarge each side in turn.

The side was 1 unit long originally so on the enlarged shape it will be $1 \times 3 = 3$ units long.

Continue in this way until you get back to the starting point.

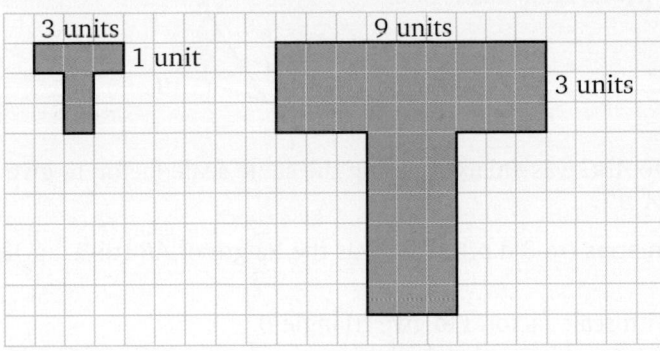

Practise...

6.1 Introduction to enlargement and scale factor

G F E D C

1 In these diagrams, *A* has been enlarged to give *B*.

What is the scale factor of each enlargement?

a
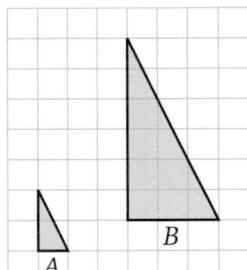

b
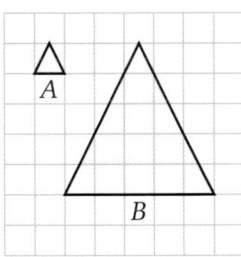

c
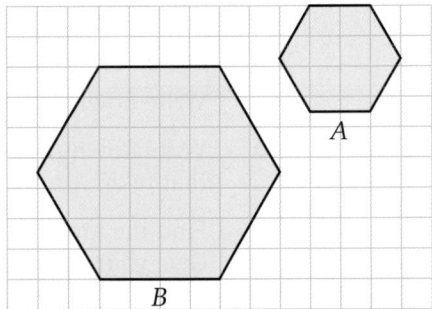

2 A trapezium *ABCD* is enlarged to form the trapezium *EFGH*.

The scale factor of the enlargement is 4.

$AB = 2.5$ cm $DC = 2$ cm $AD = 1.5$ cm $BC = 1.5$ cm

Work out the lengths of the sides:

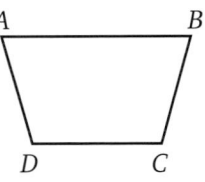

Not drawn accurately

a *EF*   **b** *HG*   **c** *EH*   **d** *FG*

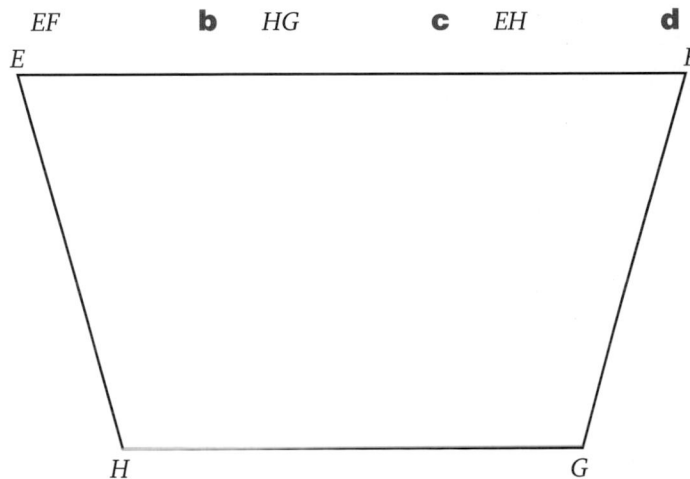

Not drawn accurately

Hint

EF means the line joining *E* and *F*.

E
D

C

3 Enlarge each of these shapes with a scale factor 2.

a 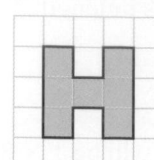   **b** 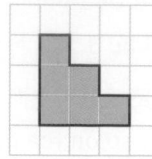   **c**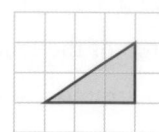

4 **a** Enlarge the shape with a scale factor of 3.

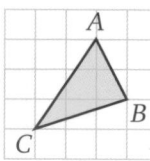

b A similar triangle to *ABC* was enlarged, using the same scale factor, to give an image triangle *A'B'C'*.

If *A'B'* was 6.708 metres (to 3 d.p.), what was the length of *AB* (to 3 d.p.)?

5 Triangle *A* is enlarged with scale factor 3 to give triangle *B*.

a One side of triangle *B* has length 7.5 cm.

What is the length of the corresponding side of triangle *A*?

b One angle of triangle *B* is 45°.

What is the size of the corresponding angle in triangle *A*?

6 The diagram shows the plan for a garden. It consists of a lawn with three square flower beds.

The smallest flowerbed, *X*, is 1.4 metres by 1.4 metres.

a *Y* is an enlargement of *X* with a scale factor of 2.
Write down the dimensions of *Y*.

b *Z* is an enlargement of *Y* also with a scale factor of 2.
Write down the dimensions of *Z*.

c Write down the scale factor of the enlargement that takes *X* to *Z*.

d Find the area of each flowerbed.
Give your answers to two decimal places.

e Find the area of the lawn.
Give your answer to two decimal places.

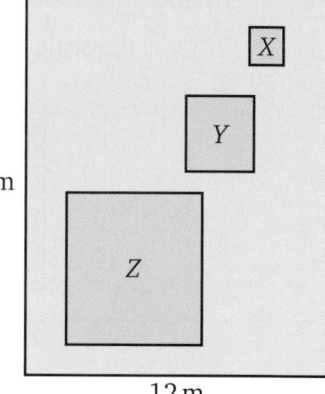

14 m

12 m

7 **a** Julie has a photograph of her cat. She wants to have the photograph enlarged to put on the cover of her portfolio.

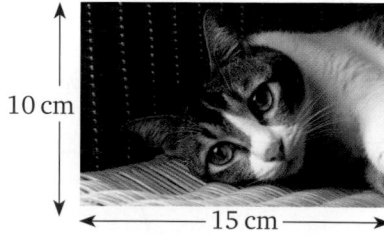

10 cm

15 cm

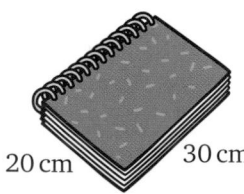

20 cm   30 cm

She wants the picture to fill the cover of the portfolio.
What is the scale factor of the enlargement she needs?

b Julie also wants to enlarge the photograph to fit a frame to go on her wall.
The frame is 90 cm wide.

i Find the scale factor to be used to enlarge the original photograph to fit the frame.

ii Find the height of the frame.

iii If the photograph on the folder was enlarged to fit the frame, find this scale factor.

Learn... 6.2 Centres of enlargement

When diagrams are drawn on sets of axes, extra information is needed to perform an enlargement.

The **centre of enlargement** is given as a pair of coordinates.

This tells you where to put the enlargement on the axes.

The centre of enlargement can be anywhere including inside, outside or on the edge of the object.

In all diagrams shown here, the same scale factor has been used but the centre of enlargement, marked with a cross, is different.

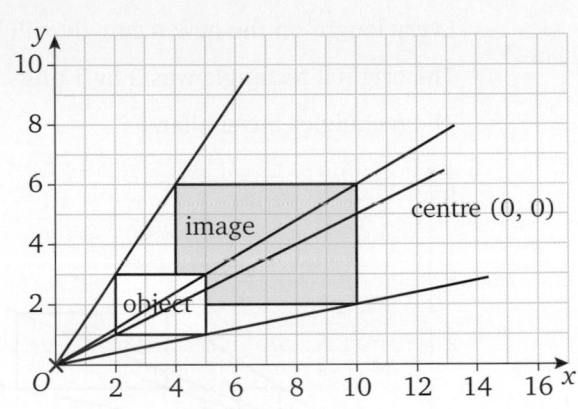

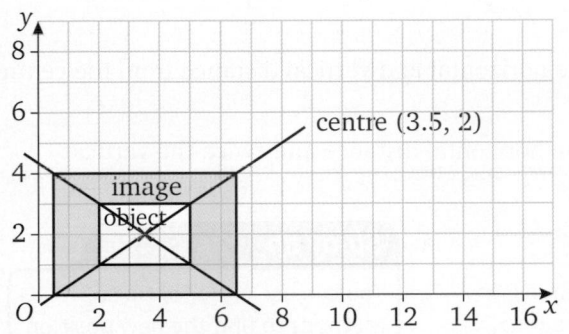

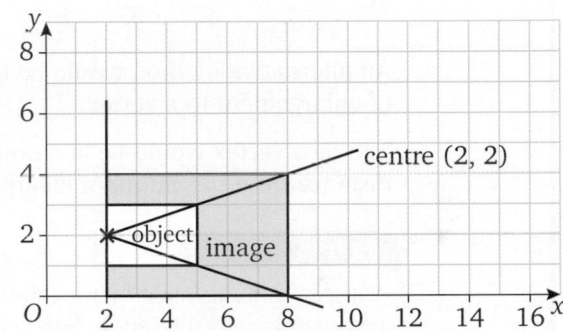

Example: Enlarge the rectangle *A* by scale factor 2, centre of enlargement (1, 1).

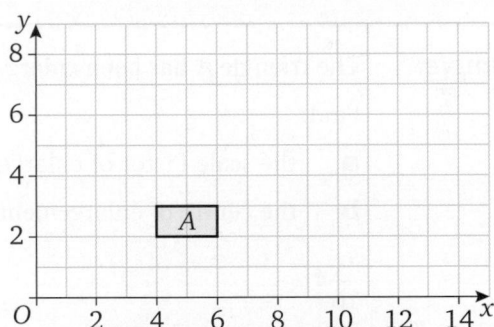

Solution: To enlarge a shape:

1. Plot the centre of enlargement on the grid with a cross.

2. Choose a **vertex** (corner) of the shape. Join the centre of enlargement to this vertex and extend the line past the vertex.

3. Measure the distance from the centre of enlargement to the vertex and multiply this by the scale factor. In this case, the scale factor is 2.

4. This is the new distance from the centre of enlargement to the corresponding vertex on the new rectangle. Measure this distance along the line you have drawn and mark the new point.

5. Repeat this for all other **vertices**.

> **Study tip**
>
> Always use a sharp pencil and a ruler. Make sure that the lines are drawn exactly through the intersection of the lines of the grid.

> **Study tip**
>
> There are usually two vertices that are easier to draw because the construction lines do not cross over the shape itself.
>
> Do these first!

When the enlargement is finished, the distances from the vertices to the point of enlargement will be twice as long.

Every length on the new rectangle will be twice as long as it was before.

The original rectangle was 2 by 1 units. The enlarged rectangle is now 4 by 2 units.

The rectangles are similar.

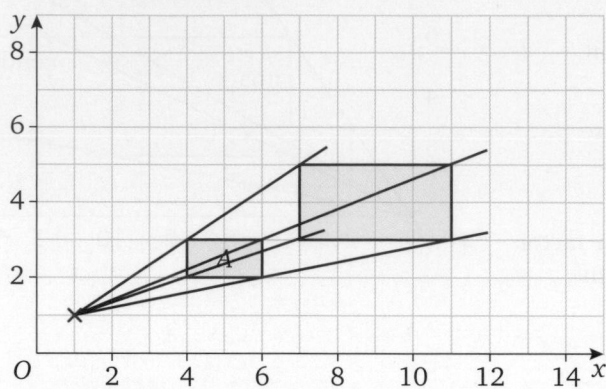

An alternative method would be to count the horizontal and vertical distance from the centre of enlargement to a vertex.

The new vertex would be at a point twice the horizontal distance and twice the vertical distance from the centre of enlargement.

Hint

You can use the scale factor to check the dimensions of the enlarged rectangle. You can use this fact to help you draw an accurate diagram and to check your enlargement.

Study tip

You can use either of these methods to find the new position of a vertex. You can even use a combination of both!

Example: The triangle *A* has been enlarged to triangle *B*.

Find:

a the scale factor of enlargement

b the centre of enlargement.

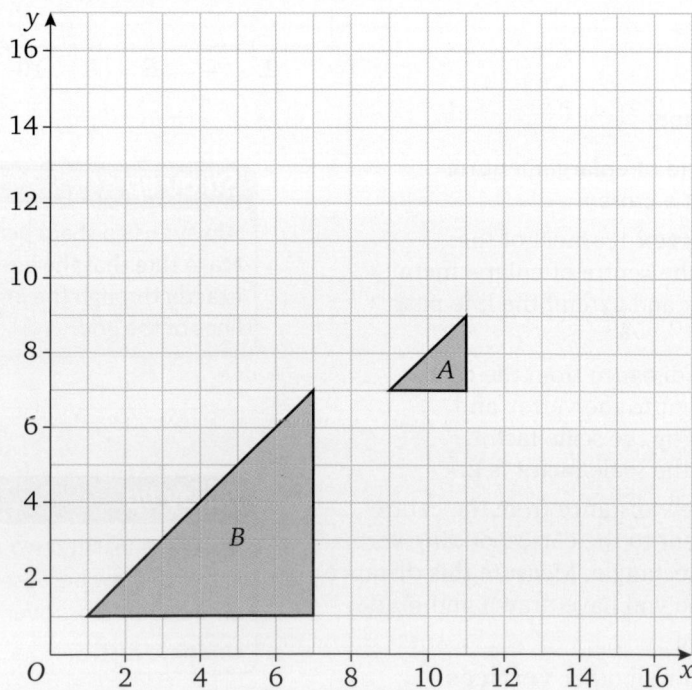

Solution: **a** Measure a side on the enlarged shape *B* and a corresponding side on the original shape *A*.

For example the 'bottom line' of *B* measures 6 units and the 'bottom line' of *A* measures 2 units.

The scale factor $= \dfrac{\text{enlarged length}}{\text{original length}} = \dfrac{6}{2} = 3$

The scale factor is 3. Every length on the enlarged triangle is 3 times the corresponding length on the original triangle.

The distance of each vertex in triangle *B* is 3 times further from the centre of enlargement than the corresponding vertex in triangle *A*.

b To find the centre of enlargement, start by joining a vertex in object *A* with the corresponding vertex in the enlarged triangle *B*. Extend the line back past *A*.

Now do the same for anther pair of vertices in *A* and *B*.

The two lines will meet at a point.

This point is the centre of enlargement.

For this enlargement, the centre of enlargement is (13, 10).

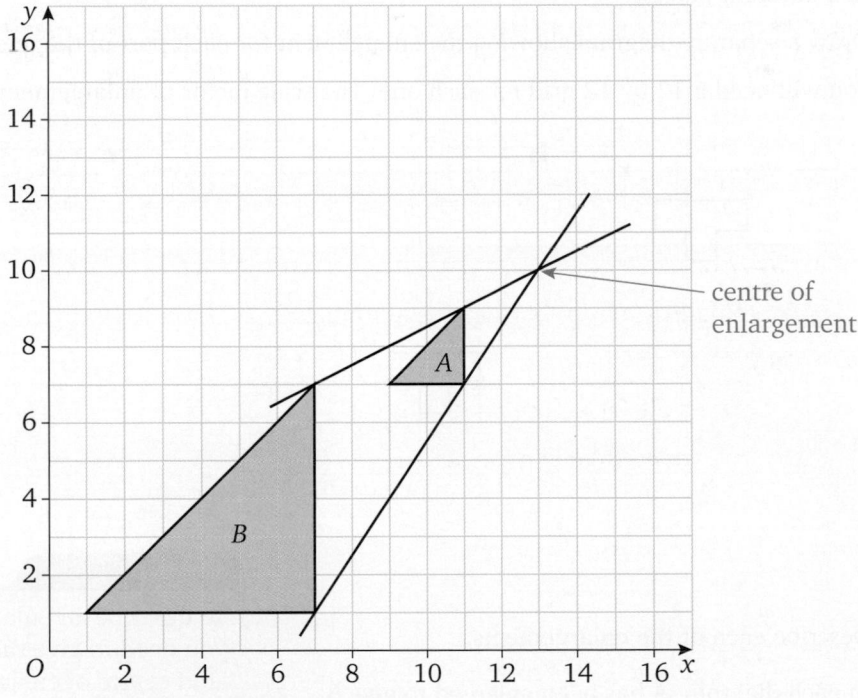

Study tip

Once you have identified the centre of enlargement, choose a vertex.

Then check that:

the distance of the vertex on the enlarged image from the centre of enlargement = (scale factor) × distance of the corresponding vertex in the original object from the centre of enlargement.

Practise... **6.2 Centres of enlargement**

D

1 Copy each shape onto squared paper. (You will need a 12 by 12 grid for each part of the question.)

Enlarge each shape with scale factor 2 and centre of enlargement X.

Use the grid position marked with a cross as the centre of enlargement.

a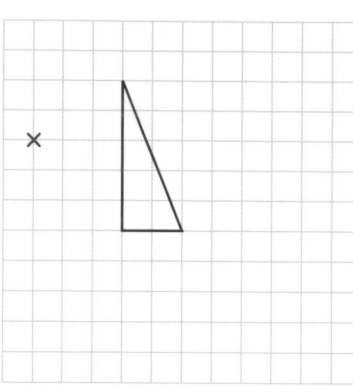

b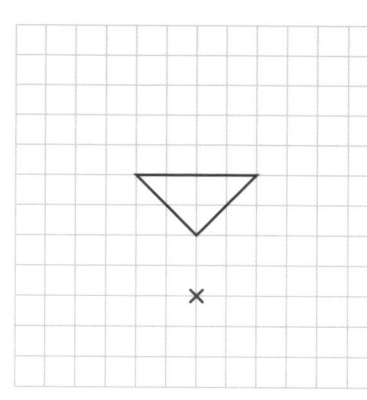

c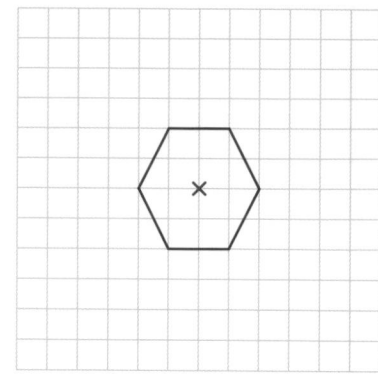

2 Each part of this question shows the same shape but the centre of enlargement is in a different place.

Draw a separate diagram showing the enlargement for each part of the question.

You will need a 12 by 12 grid for each one. The scale factor of enlargement is 3.

a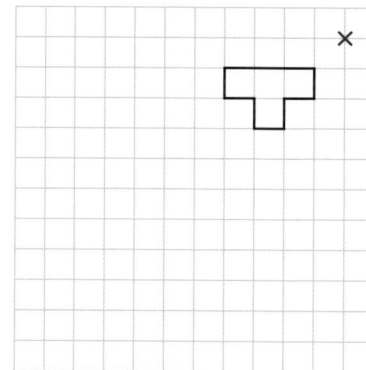

b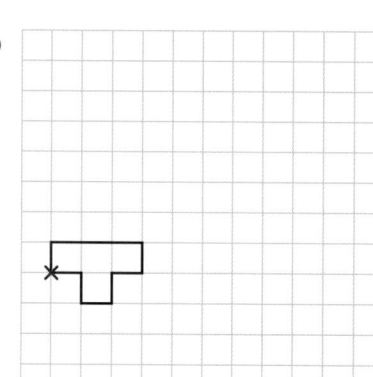

c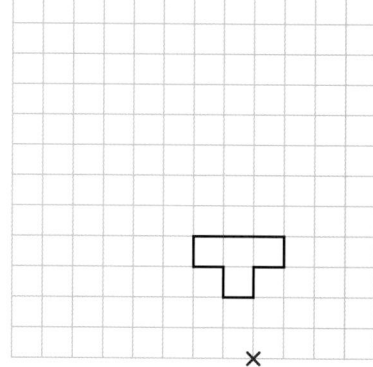

Hint

To describe an enlargement fully you need to give the scale factor and centre of enlargement.

3 Describe each of the enlargements.

In each diagram, *A* has been enlarged to give *B*.

a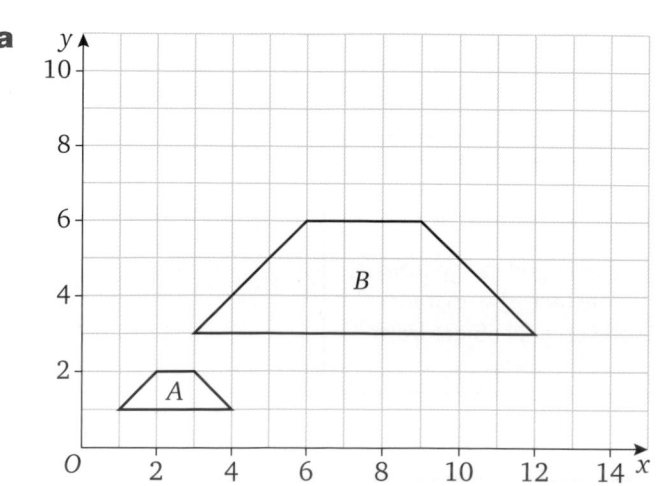

b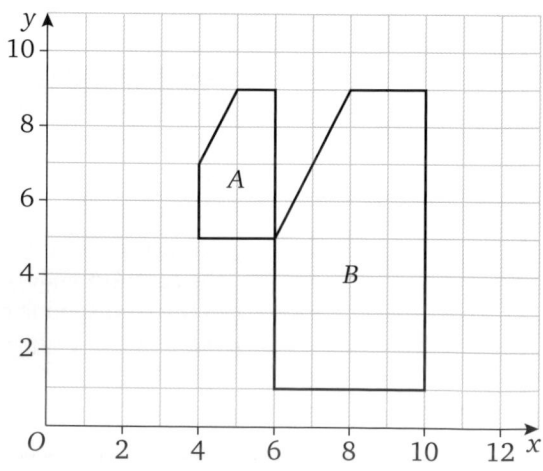

c

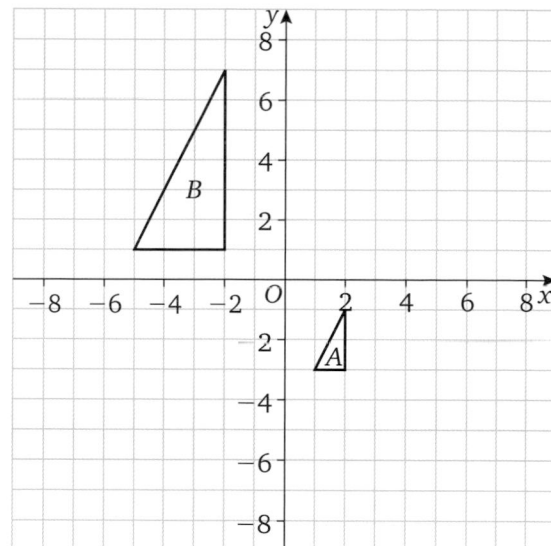

4   Describe fully the enlargement of triangle *ABC* to triangle *DEF*.

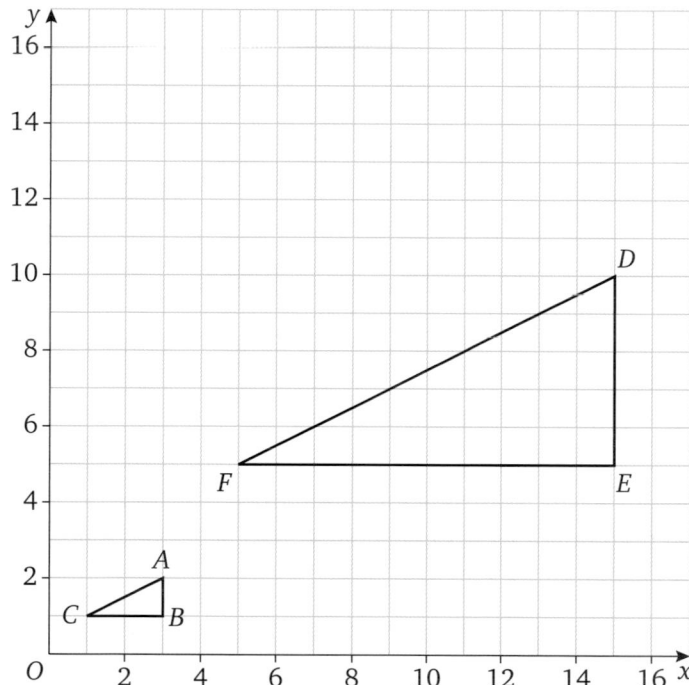

⚠ 5   **a**   **i**   Draw a pair of axes with values from −9 to 7.

   ii   Plot and label triangle *B* with vertices at (−4, 1), (−4, −4) and (−6, −1).

b   Draw the image of triangle *B* after an enlargement of scale factor 3, with centre of enlargement (−9, −2).
Label the image *C*.

c   What are the coordinates of the vertices of *C*?

⚠ 6   **a**   **i**   Draw a pair of axes with x-values from 0 to 16 and y-values from 0 to 8.

   ii   Plot and label rectangle *E* with vertices at (6, 2), (6, 4), (10, 4) and (10, 2).

b   Draw the image of rectangle *E* after an enlargement of scale factor 1.5, with centre of enlargement (0, 0).
Label the image *F*.

c   What are the coordinates of the vertices of *F*?

7 A jewellery designer was asked to make a pendant which perfectly matched a pair of earrings. In order for them to look similar, he decided that the pendant should be an enlargement of the earrings. He worked out that a scale factor of 3 would be most suitable.

Here is the plan of one of the earrings.
Each square represents a square 0.5 cm by 0.5 cm.

Copy this diagram onto squared paper and draw the plan for the pendant.

The centre of enlargement is marked by a cross on the diagram.

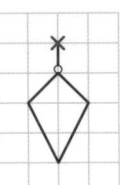

 **Learn...** **6.3 Enlargements, similar shapes and ratio**

Triangle *ABC* is an enlargement of triangle *DEF* with a scale factor of 2. This means that the triangles are similar.

Every side on triangle *ABC* is twice the length of the corresponding side on triangle *DEF*.
The corresponding angles are equal.

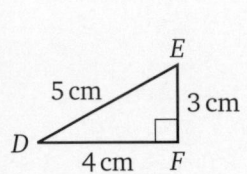 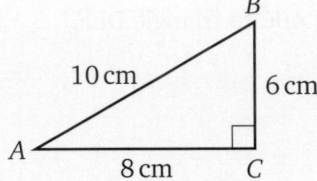

Not drawn accurately

The corresponding sides are all in the same **ratio** 2 : 1

$AC : DF = 8 : 4$ Divide both sides by 4.
$ = 2 : 1$

$BC : EF = 6 : 3$ Divide both sides by 3.
$ = 2 : 1$

and

$AB : DE = 10 : 5$ Divide both sides by 5.
$ = 2 : 1$

Ratios can be simplified or cancelled down in the same way as fractions.

This is done by dividing both sides by the same number until you cannot do it any more.
It is then in its simplest form.

Example: Rectangle *EFGH* is an enlargement of rectangle *ABCD*.

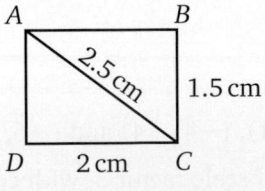 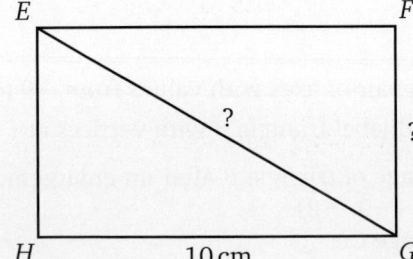

Not drawn accurately

a Write down the ratio of *DC* : *HG* in its simplest form.

b What is the scale factor of the enlargement?

c Find the length of *FG*.

d Find the length of the diagonal *EG*.

e Work out the perimeter of each rectangle.

f What is the ratio of the perimeter of *ABCD* to the perimeter of *EFGH*?

Solution:

a $DC = 2\,\text{cm}$ $HG = 10\,\text{cm}$

$DC : HG = 2 : 10$

$\qquad\qquad = 1 : 5$ Divide both sides by 2

The scale factor is the value of n when the ratio of the corresponding lengths is written in the form $n : 1$ or $1 : n$.

b The scale factor is taken from the ratio once it is in the form $1 : n$ or $n : 1$

Scale factor of the enlargement $= 5$

c $BC = 1.5\,\text{cm}$

$FG = 1.5 \times 5 = 7.5\,\text{cm}$

d $AC = 2.5\,\text{cm}$

$EG = 2.5 \times 5 = 12.5\,\text{cm}$

> **Study tip**
>
> Whenever you are asked to find missing lengths, always check afterwards that the ratio of the original length to the enlarged length is correct.

e Perimeter of $ABCD = 2 + 1.5 + 2 + 1.5 = 7\,\text{cm}$

Perimeter of $EFGH = 10 + 7.5 + 10 + 7.5 = 35\,\text{cm}$

f Comparing the perimeters of the two rectangles:

perimeter of $ABCD$: perimeter of $EFGH = 7 : 35$

$\qquad\qquad\qquad\qquad\qquad\qquad = 1 : 5$ Divide both sides by 7.

This is the same ratio as before.

Perimeter is also a length.

The ratios of all corresponding lengths in the diagram should be the same because the shapes are similar.

Example: Are these shapes similar? Is shape A an enlargement of shape B?

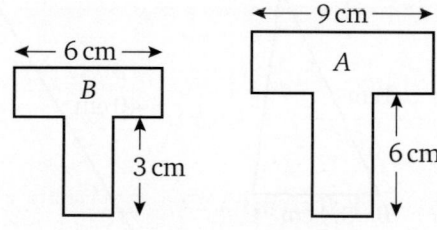

Not drawn accurately

Solution: Ratio of 'tops' of shapes $= 9 : 6$ Divide both sides by 3

$\qquad\qquad\qquad\qquad\qquad = 3 : 2$ Divide both sides by 2

$\qquad\qquad\qquad\qquad\qquad = 1.5 : 1$

Scale factor $= 1.5$

> **Hint**
>
> To read off a scale factor from a ratio, the ratio must be in the form $n : 1$ or $1 : n$

Ratio of corresponding 'sides' of shapes $= 6 : 3$ Divide both sides by 3

$\qquad\qquad\qquad\qquad\qquad\qquad\qquad = 2 : 1$

Scale factor $= 2$

The scale factors are different, so these shapes are not similar. A is **not** an enlargement of B.

Practise...

6.3 Enlargements, similar shapes and ratio

G F E D C

D

1 Triangles *A* and *B* are equilateral.

a What is the ratio of the lengths?
Give your answer in its simplest form).

b Find the perimeter of each equilateral triangle.

c What is the ratio of the perimeters?
Give your answer in its simplest form.

d What is the scale factor of the enlargement?

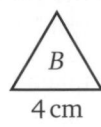
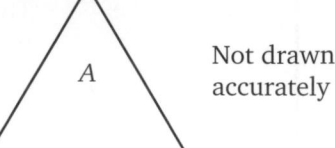

Not drawn accurately

4 cm

12 cm

2 The large triangle is an enlargement of the small triangle.

a What is the ratio of the bases of the triangles?
Give your answer in its simplest form.

b What is the scale factor of the enlargement?

c Find the missing height of the enlarged triangle.

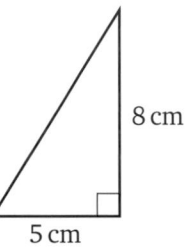
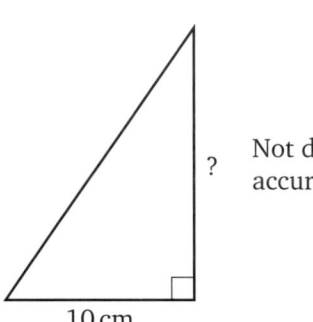

8 cm

5 cm

? Not drawn accurately

10 cm

3 Triangle *DEF* is an enlargement of triangle *ABC*.

a Work out the ratio of the length of *AB* to the length of *DE*. Give your answer in the form 1 : *n*.

b Find the length of the side *EF*.

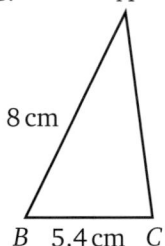
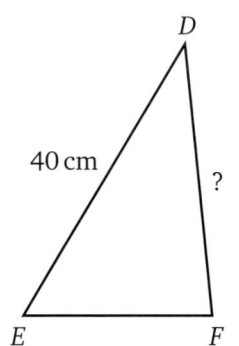

A

8 cm

B 5.4 cm *C*

D

40 cm

? Not drawn accurately

E *F*

C

4 In the following diagrams, decide if the larger shape is an enlargement of the smaller one.

In both parts, all corresponding angles are equal.

a
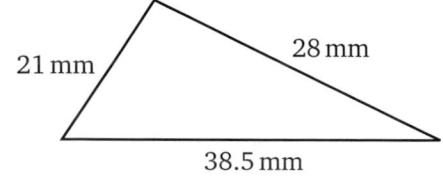

3 mm 4 mm

5.5 mm

21 mm 28 mm

38.5 mm

Not drawn accurately

b
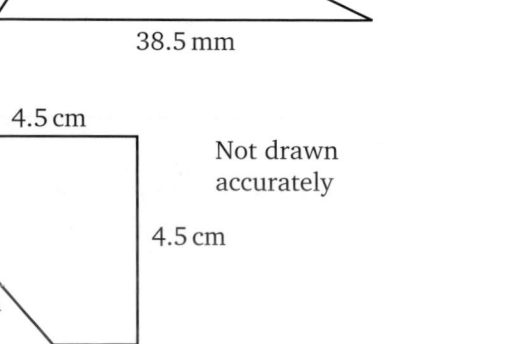

1.5 cm

1.5 cm

0.5 cm

4.5 cm

4.5 cm

Not drawn accurately

1 cm

5 These triangles are enlargements of each other. Work out the missing lengths.

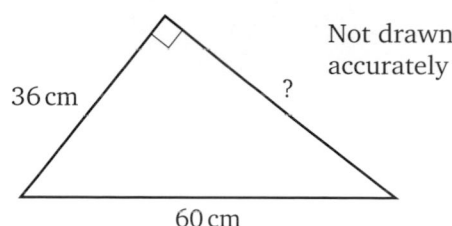

Not drawn accurately

6 These triangles are enlargements of each other.

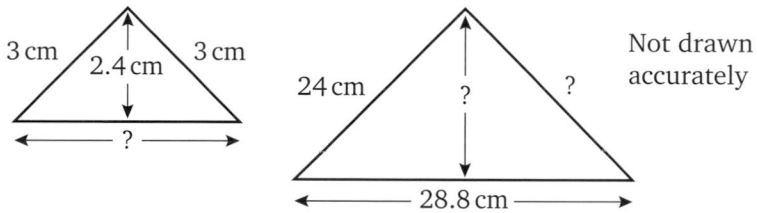

Not drawn accurately

a Find the ratio of the corresponding sides.

b Find any missing lengths.

! 7 Here is a diagram of some stepladders.

There are two similar triangles in this diagram.

a Draw them out as two separate diagrams.

b Transfer the measurements onto these diagrams.

c What is the length of the rope?

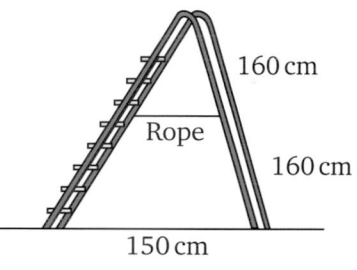

Not drawn accurately

8

Richard wants to know if an enlargement of the photograph will fit the frame. The photo has dimensions 15 cm by 10 cm.
The frame measures 42 cm by 28 cm.

a Are the shapes similar? If so, what is the scale factor?

b What would be the size of the frame needed if the photograph had been enlarged by scale factor 4?

9 Russian wooden dolls are made so that one doll will fit completely inside the next one.

They are similar.

By measuring the heights of the dolls in the picture, see if you can find an approximate scale factor relating the first doll to the second, the second to the third and so on.

Are all the scale factors the same?

6 Assess (k)

F

1 State the scale factor of the following enlargement.

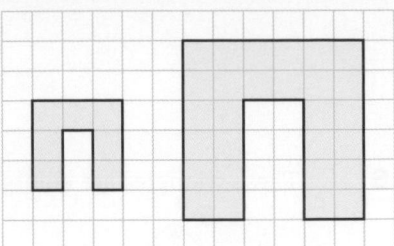

E

2 Copy this shape and draw an enlargement of the shape, scale factor 3.

On the enlarged shape, what are the lengths of the two parallel sides?

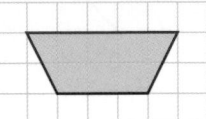

D

3 Copy this shape and enlarge it with scale factor 2 about the centre of enlargement shown.

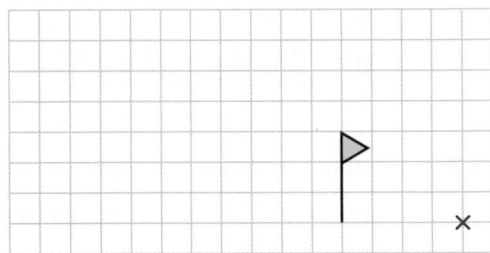

D
C

4   **a**   **i**   Draw a pair of axes with x- and y-values from 0 to 16.

  ii   Plot and label triangle A with vertices (6, 7), (6, 11) and (10, 11).

  b   Draw the image of triangle A after an enlargement of scale factor 3, with centre of enlargement (7, 10).
  Label this triangle B.

  c   What are the coordinates of the vertices of B?

C

5 A tennis court is an enlargement of a table tennis table.

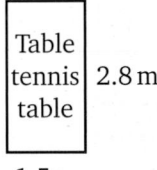

Table tennis table   2.8 m

1.5 m

Tennis court   ?   Not drawn accurately

10.5 m

The tennis court is similar to the table-tennis table.
One is an enlargement of the other.

  a   Work out the scale factor of the enlargement.

  b   Work out the length of the tennis court.

  c   Work out the area of the table-tennis table and the area of the tennis court.

  d   Work out the ratio of the area of the table tennis table to the area of the tennis court.
  Give your answer in the form $1:n$.

Practice questions (k)

1 Triangle *PQR* is an enlargement of triangle *ABC* with scale factor 5.

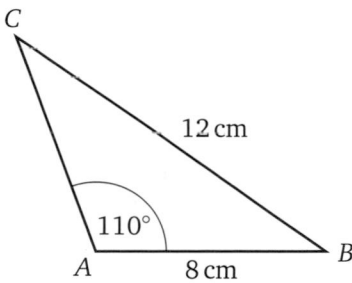
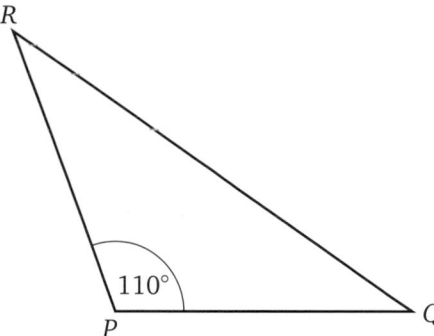

Calculate the length of *RQ*.   *(2 marks)*

AQA 2007

2 **a** **i** Copy shape *A* onto a grid.

  ii Enlarge the shape by a scale factor of 2.

  iii Label your new shape *B*.   *(2 marks)*

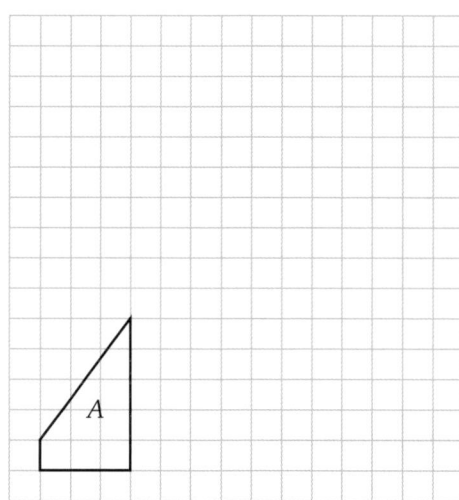

  b Which of these statements are true?

  i Shape *B* is congruent to shape *A*.

  ii The angles of shape *B* are the same as the angles of shape *A*.

  iii The perimeter of shape *B* is twice the perimeter of shape *A*.

  iv The area of shape *B* is twice the area of shape *A*.   *(4 marks)*

AQA 2006

Objectives

Examiners would normally expect students who get these grades to be able to:

C

solve equations such as $x^3 + x = 12$ using systematic trial and improvement methods.

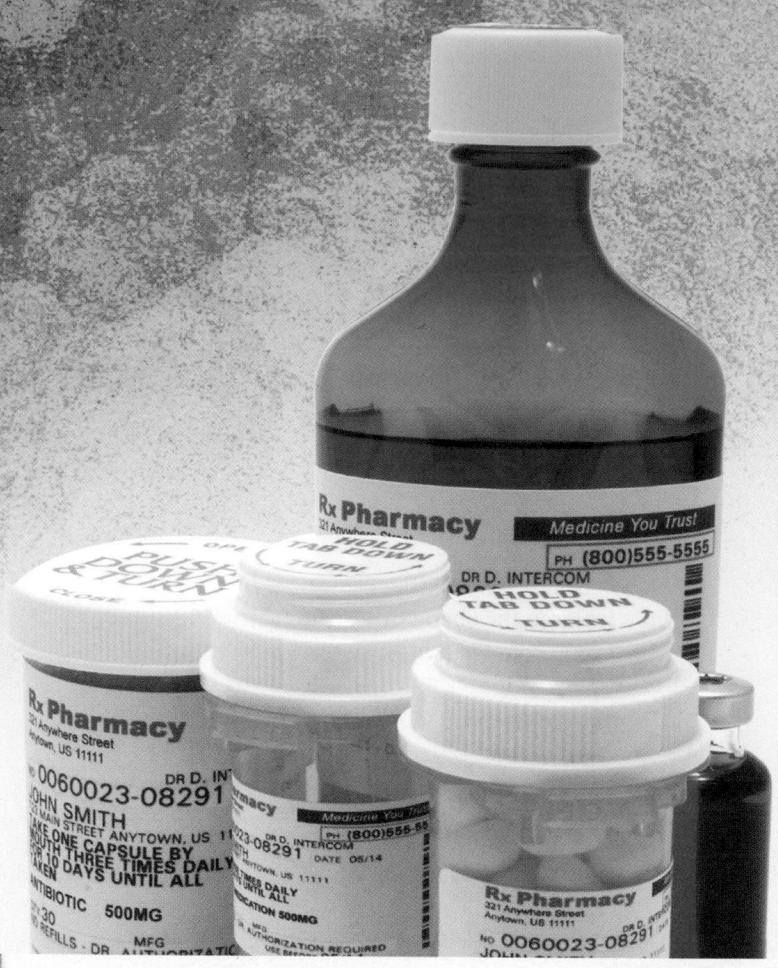

Did you know?

Trial and improvement

Trial and improvement (also know as trial and error) has many uses in the real world. It is often used by engineers when they develop complex equipment. For example, engineers will trial different fuel flow rates when determining the maximum thrust from a jet engine.

Also doctors may use trial and improvement to test different combinations of drugs for diabetes, epilepsy and high blood pressure. For the future, scientists are developing supercomputers which will act as 'virtual humans'. This will allow doctors to match different combinations of drugs to different patients.

Key terms

trial and improvement
decimal place

You should already know:

✔ how to substitute into algebraic expressions

✔ how to rearrange formulae

✔ how to use the bracket and power buttons on your calculator.

Learn... 7.1 Trial and improvement

Trial and improvement is a method for solving problems using estimations which get closer and closer to the actual answer. Trial and improvement is used where there is no exact answer so you will be asked to give a rounded answer. On the examination paper you will be told when to use a trial and improvement method.

If you are told that $x^3 + x = 50$ then you can work out that the answer lies between 3 and 4 because:

$3^3 + 3 = 30$ which is too small

and $4^3 + 4 = 68$ which is too large.

You know that the answer lies between 3 and 4 so you might try 3.5

$3.5^3 + 3.5 = 46.375$ This is too small.

As 3.5 is too small and 4 is too large, you know that the answer lies between 3.5 and 4 so you might try 3.7 or 3.8.

You can keep going with this method to get an answer which is more and more accurate.

The question will tell you how accurate your answer should be.

> **Study tip**
>
> It is a good idea to lay out your working carefully. A table can be helpful.

Example: Use trial and improvement to solve $x^3 - x = 40$

Give your answer to one **decimal place**.

Solution: You can try out some different values to get you started.

Trial value of x	$x^3 - x$	Comment
1	0	Too small
2	6	Too small
3	24	Too small
4	60	Too large

40

> **Study tip**
>
> On some examination questions you will be told where the answer lies. For example, you may be told that there is a solution between 2 and 3.

The answer 40 lies between 24 and 60.

This tells you that x lies between 3 and 4.

You might try 3.5

3.5	39.375	Too small
3.6	43.056	Too large

Again, you can see that 40 lies between 39.375 and 43.056

This tells you that x lies between 3.5 and 3.6

You should try 3.55

The answer to one decimal place is either 3.5 or 3.6

Work out the value for 3.55 to see if it is larger than 40.

If it is too large, then 3.55 is too large and the answer to one decimal place is 3.5

If it is too small, then 3.55 is too small and the answer to one decimal place is 3.6

3.55	41.188875	Too large

You know that x lies between 3.5 and 3.55

But any answer between 3.5 and 3.55 is the same as 3.5 to one decimal place.

The required answer is 3.5 to one decimal place.

Practise... 7.1 Trial and improvement G F E D C

C

1 Mavis the farmer knows the area of her square fields but not the length.
Use trial and improvement to find the length of the fields.
Give your answer to two decimal places.

a Area 120 m²   **b** Area 600 m²   **c** Area 320 m²

2 Find, using trial and improvement, a solution to the following equations.
Give your answers correct to one decimal place. Remember to show all your working.

a $x^3 + x = 10$ **c** $x^3 - 5x = 400$

b $x^3 + x = 520$ **d** $x - x^3 = 336$

3 Use trial and improvement to solve the equation $x^3 + x = 75$
Give your answer to one decimal place.
The table has been started for you.

Trial value of x	$x^3 + x$	Comment
2	10	Too low
3	30	Too low
4	68	Too low
5	130	Too high

So now we know that the value lies between 4 and 5.

4.5	95.625	Too high
?		
?		

4 Use trial and improvement to find solutions to the following equations.
Give your answer to two decimal places.

a $a^3 - 10a = 50$ if the solution lies between 4 and 5

b $x^3 - x = 100$ if the solution lies between 4 and 5

⚠ **c** $5x - x^3 = 10$ if the solution lies between −2 and −3

5 Use trial and improvement to find solutions to the following equations.
Give your answer to two decimal places.

a $t^3 - 5t = 10$ if t lies between 2 and 3

b $x^3 - 5x = 60$ if x lies between 4 and 5

c $x(x^2 + 1) = 60$ if x lies between 3 and 4

⚠ **d** $p^3 + 6p = -50$ if p lies between −3 and −4

6 Use trial and improvement to find a negative solution to the equation $y^3 + 60 = 0$

⚠ **7** The equation $x^3 - 4x^2 = -5$ has two solutions of x between 0 and 5.
Use trial and improvement to find these solutions.
Give your answer to three decimal places.

! 8 Use trial and improvement to find the value of $x^2 - \dfrac{1}{x} = 5$ where x lies between 2 and 3.

Give your answer to two decimal places.

? 9 The difference between the square of a number and the cube of a number is 100.

Find the number to one decimal place.

? 10 This solid consists of a central square and four equal arms.

The volume of the solid is $100\,\text{cm}^3$.

Find the value of x correct to two decimal places.

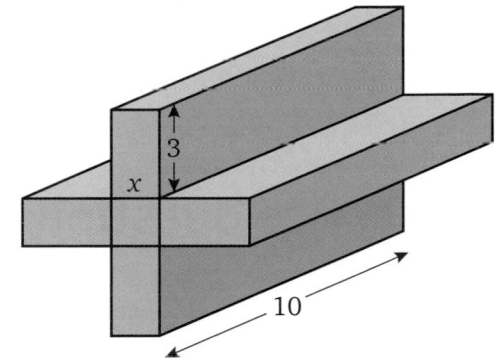

Assess ⓚ

1 Use trial and improvement to solve the equation $x^3 - 4x = 100$
Give your answer to one decimal place.
The table has been started for you.

Trial value of x	$x^3 - 4x$	Comment
3	15	Too small
4	48	Too small
5	105	Too large

2 The equation $x^3 + 8x^2 = 20$ has two negative solutions between 0 and -8.

Use trial and improvement to find these solutions.

Give your answer to two decimal places.

3 A cuboid measures $x \times x \times (x + 2)$.

The volume of the cuboid is $50\,\text{cm}^3$.

Use trial and improvement to find x.

Give your answer to three decimal places.

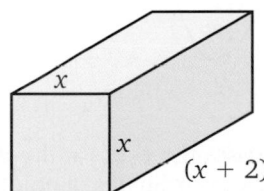

4 Use trial and improvement to find solutions to the following equations.

Give your answer to two decimal places.

a $x^3 + 5x = 50$ if the solution lies between 3 and 4

b $y^3 + 3y = 10$ if the solution lies between 1 and 2

c $x^3 - x = 100$ if the solution lies between 4 and 5

d $3x - x^3 = 25$ if the solution lies between -3 and -4

! 5 Use trial and improvement to find solutions to the following equations.

Give your answer to two decimal places.

a $x^3 + x = 60$ if x lies between 3 and 4

b $x^3 - 12x = 0$ if x lies between 2 and 6

C

6 Use trial and improvement to find the value of $8x - x^3 = 3$ where x is negative.

Give your answer to two decimal places.

7 Use trial and improvement to find the value of $t^3 + t^2 = 10$ where $1 \leqslant t \leqslant 2$

Give your answer to two decimal places.

Practice questions *k*

1 Kerry is using trial and improvement to find a solution to the equation $8x - x^3 = 5$
Her first two trials are shown in the table.

x	$8x - x^3$	Comment
2	8	too high
3	−3	too low

Copy and continue the table to find a solution to the equation.
Give your answer to one decimal place. *(3 marks)*

AQA 2007

2 The sketch shows the graph of $y = x^3 - 3x - 8$
The graph passes through the points $(2, -6)$ and $(3, 10)$.

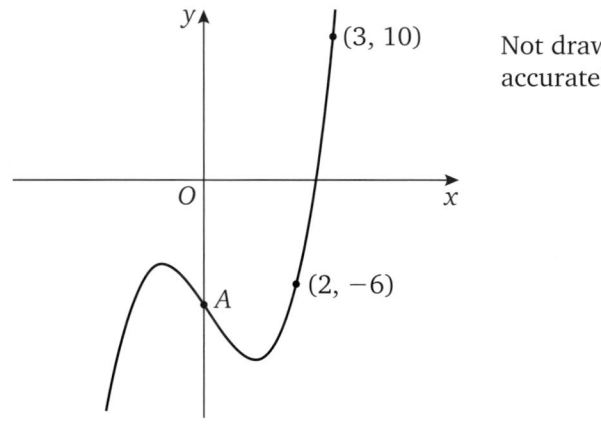

Not drawn accurately

a The graph crosses the y-axis at the point A.
Write down the coordinates of point A. *(1 mark)*

b Use trial and improvement to find the solution of:
$x^3 - 3x - 8 = 0$
Give your answer to one decimal place. *(4 marks)*

AQA 2008

8 Percentages and ratios

Objectives

Examiners would normally expect students who get these grades to be able to:

F

understand that percentage means 'number of parts per 100' and use this to compare proportions

E

work out a percentage of a given quantity

D

increase or decrease by a given percentage

express one quantity as a percentage of another

use ratio notation, including reduction to its simplest form and its links to fraction notation

solve simple ratio and proportion problems, such as finding and simplifying a ratio

C

work out a percentage increase or decrease

solve more complex ratio and proportion problems

solve ratio and proportion problems using the unitary method.

Key terms

percentage	ratio
unitary method	unitary ratio
VAT (Value Added Tax)	proportion
rate	

Did you know?

The origins of mathematical symbols

15th century	17th century	Now
P⸱ͻ	ͻ̶	%

Did you know that the symbol % for percent and : for ratio were not introduced until relatively recently? The % sign probably developed from the symbol shown above. This appeared in an Italian manuscript dating from 1425. In Italian 'each hundred' is 'per cento', in French it is 'pour cent' and in English 'per cent'.

An Englishman, William Oughtred, was the first to use a colon : for ratios in his book, *Canones Sinuum* in 1657.

Find out when other symbols such as $+$, $-$, $\times$, $\div$ and $=$ were introduced. What did they use before then?

You should already know:

✔ how to add, subtract, multiply and divide simple numbers with and without a calculator

✔ about place values in decimals (for example, $0.7 = \frac{7}{10}$, $0.07 = \frac{7}{100}$)

✔ how to put decimals in order of size

✔ how to simplify fractions by hand and using a calculator

✔ how to write a fraction as a decimal and vice versa

✔ how to change a percentage to a fraction or decimal, and vice versa.

 **Learn...** 8.1 Finding a percentage of a quantity

Sometimes writing a **percentage** as a fraction can help you find a percentage of a quantity.

For example, to shade 75% of this shape:

$75\% = \dfrac{75}{100} = \dfrac{3}{4}$, so shade three quarters of the shape

To write a percentage as a fraction or decimal, divide by 100:

$75\% = 75$ out of $100 = \dfrac{75}{100}$

Also $75\% = 75 \div 100 = 0.75$

You can use your calculator's fraction key to simplify fractions.

(As $\frac{3}{4} = \frac{6}{8}$, any 6 of the 8 triangles could be shaded.)

You can use your calculator to work out percentages of other quantities.

This is the decimal equivalent of the percentage you wish to find.

To find a percentage of a quantity on a calculator:
- **divide** the quantity **by 100** (to find 1%)
- then **multiply by the percentage** you need.

Finding 1% first is sometimes called the **unitary method**.

Or use a **multiplier:**
- write the percentage as a multiplier
- then **multiply** by the quantity.

To increase or decrease by a given percentage:
- find the percentage of the quantity (as above)
- for a percentage increase, add to the original quantity
  for a percentage decrease, subtract from the original quantity

Or use a **multiplier:**
- write the new quantity as a percentage of the original quantity
- convert this percentage to a multiplier
- **multiply by the original quantity.**

Multipliers

You can use a multiplier to find a percentage of a quantity or to increase or decrease a quantity by a percentage.

For example:
- **to find 35% of a quantity**, the multiplier is $35 \div 100 = \mathbf{0.35}$
- **to increase a quantity by 35%**, the multiplier is $135 \div 100 = \mathbf{1.35}$ ◄—— because $100\% + 35\% = 135\%$
- **to decrease a quantity by 35%**, the multiplier is $65 \div 100 = \mathbf{0.65}$ ◄—— because $100\% - 35\% = 65\%$

Example: Find $26\frac{1}{2}\%$ of £9.47.

To find $26\frac{1}{2}\%$
Use 26.5 if you prefer.

Solution: $26\frac{1}{2}\%$ of £9.47 $= £9.47 \div 100 \times 26\frac{1}{2}$
$= £2.50955$
$= £2.51$ To find 1%
(to the nearest penny)

Round to the nearest penny.

Alternative method using multiplier
$26\frac{1}{2}\% = 26.5\% = 0.265$ as a decimal
$26\frac{1}{2}\%$ of £9.47 $= 0.265 \times 9.47$
$= £2.51$
(to the nearest penny)

Example: Increase £72 by 30%

Solution: 30% of £72 $= 72 \div 100 \times 30$
$= 21.6$

To find 1%, then 30%

New amount $= 72 + 21.6$
$= £93.60$

Alternative method using multiplier
New amount $= 100\% + 30\% = 130\%$
Multiplier $= 1.30$ or 1.3

New amount $= 1.3 \times 72$
$= £93.60$

Study tip
Take care to write money correctly.
Here the answer is £93.60, not £93.6

Example: Decrease 3.25 litres by 42%

Solution: 42% of 3.25 $= 3.25 \div 100 \times 42$
$= 1.365$

New amount $= 3.25 - 1.365$
$= 1.885$ litres

Alternative method using multiplier
New amount $= 100\% - 42\% = 58\%$
Multiplier $= 0.58$

New amount $= 0.58 \times 3.25$
$= 1.885$ litres

Does your calculator have an 'Ans' key?
You can use it instead of entering 1.365 again here.

8.1 Finding a percentage of a quantity

G F E D C

1   Copy each shape onto squared paper. Shade the given percentage.

a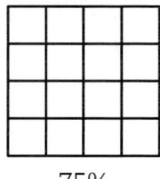
75%

b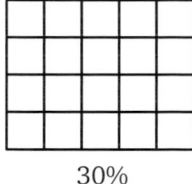
30%

c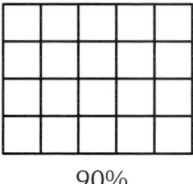
90%

2   **a**   Use one of the methods shown in Learn 4.1 to work out:

i 20% of £380	**iii** 62% of 3500 litres	**v** 37% of 600 g
ii 25% of £7000	**iv** 85% of 40 km	**vi** 18% of 750 ml.

    b   Use a different method to check your answers.

3   **a**   Write down the multiplier for working out 40% of a quantity.

> **Hint**
> This is how you find the multiplier for working out 40% of a quantity:
> Multiplier = 40 ÷ 100 = 0.4

    b   Copy and complete this table of multipliers.

To find	40%	1%	15%	24%	9%	6%	12.5%	3.5%	225%
Multiply by		0.01		0.24		0.06			

    c   Use the multipliers from your table to work out:

i 40% of 250	**iv** 24% of £900	**vii** 12.5% of £140
ii 1% of 420	**v** 9% of £50	**viii** 3.5% of £72.60
iii 15% of 640	**vi** 6% of £230	**ix** 225% of £42.70.

4   A school has 60 teachers.

85% of the teachers work full time; the rest work part time.

    a   How many teachers work full-time?

    b   How many teachers work part-time?

5   Louise says '60% of £19 is eleven pounds and four pence.'

Is she correct?

Show working to support your answer.

6   **a**   Write down the multiplier for increasing a quantity by 10%

> **Hint**
> After an increase of 10%, the new quantity is 100% + 10% = 110% of the original quantity.
> The multiplier = 110 ÷ 100 = 1.10

    b   Copy and complete these tables.

To increase by	10%	20%	5%	7.5%
Multiply by			1.05	

To decrease by	10%	20%	5%	7.5%
Multiply by		0.8		

    c   Use the multipliers from your table to work out:

i 90 increased by 10%	**v** £375 decreased by 10%
ii 150 g increased by 20%	**vi** £549 decreased by 20%
iii 240 m increased by 5%	**vii** 620 kg decreased by 5%
iv £364 increased by 7.5%	**viii** 480 litres decreased by 7.5%

G
F
E
E
D

D

7　**a**　Increase 250 m by 40%　　**d**　Decrease 37.5 litres by 12%

　　b　Increase 80 kg by 70%　　**e**　Increase £54.60 by 43%

　　c　Decrease 24 miles by 5%　　**f**　Decrease £180 by 62.5%

　　Check your answers using a different method.

8　The price of a magazine is £2.50.

　　What is the new price after a 6% increase?

　　Check your answer using a different method.

9　The table gives the original prices of some sports equipment.
　　The shop reduces these prices by 20% in a sale.

　　Find the new prices.

Item	Original price
Football	£15.90
Tennis racket	£65.75

10　The population of a city is 275 300.
　　It is expected to increase by 3% next year.

　　What is the expected population next year?

　　Give your answer to the nearest hundred.

11　The prices of each of these items are given excluding **VAT**.
　　Find the cost of each item including VAT at the **rate** given.

a

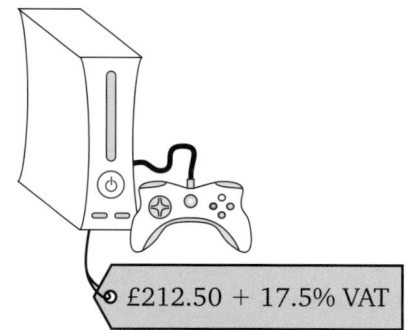

£212.50 + 17.5% VAT

c

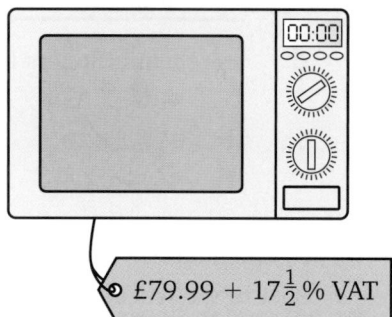

£79.99 + $17\frac{1}{2}$% VAT

b

Cost of electricity:
£134.92 + 5% VAT

12　Three quarters of a million people sat GCSE Mathematics in the UK last year.
　　Of these people, 51% were female.

　　How many more females than males sat GCSE Mathematics in the UK last year?

13　A sponsored swim raised £480 for charity.

　　The organisers give 35% to a children's charity and 25% to an animal sanctuary.
　　They give the rest to a local hospice.

　　How much money do they give to the local hospice?
　　You **must** show your working.

14　A supermarket has offered Paul a job.

　　He can choose to work on Saturday or Sunday.
　　The table gives the hours of work.
　　He earns £6.40 per hour on Saturday. He earns 25% more
　　per hour on a Sunday than he does on a Saturday.
　　On each day he has a 1 hour *unpaid* lunchbreak.

　　On which day does Paul earn more?

	Hours
Saturday	9am – 5pm
Sunday	10am – 4pm

15   A jar contains 80 sweets. The sweets are red, yellow, green, blue or orange.

25% of the sweets are red.
20% of the sweets are yellow.
There are 10% more orange sweets than red sweets.
50% of the remaining sweets are blue.

How many green sweets are there?

 **Learn...**

8.2 Writing one quantity as a percentage of another

To write one quantity as a percentage of another:
- divide the first quantity by the second; this writes them as a decimal (or write the first quantity as a fraction of the second)
- then multiply by 100% to change the decimal or fraction to a percentage

To write an increase or decrease as a percentage:
- find the difference between the old quantity and the new quantity; this gives the increase or decrease
- divide the increase (or decrease) by the **original** amount or write the increase (or decrease) as a fraction of the **original** amount
- then multiply by 100% to change the decimal or fraction to a percentage

Sometimes you may need to write one part as a percentage of the whole amount (as in the first example below).

The quantities must always be in the **same units**.

You can also use this method to find a percentage profit or loss.

Example: Last season a school's football team won 18 matches, drew 4 matches and lost 10 matches.

    a   What percentage of the matches were won?

    b   What percentage were drawn?

    c   What percentage were lost?

Solution: You must write each number as a percentage of the total number of matches.

The total number of matches = 18 + 4 + 10 = 32

    a   percentage of games that were won = $\frac{18}{32} \times 100\% = 18 \div 32 \times 100\% = 56.25\%$

        or using the fraction key: percentage won = $\frac{18}{32} \times 100\% = 56\frac{1}{4}\%$

    b   percentage of games that were drawn = $\frac{4}{32} \times 100\% = 4 \div 32 \times 100\% = 12.5\%$

        or using the fraction key: percentage drawn = $\frac{4}{32} \times 100\% = 12\frac{1}{2}\%$

    c   percentage of games that were lost = $\frac{10}{32} \times 100\% = 10 \div 32 \times 100\% = 31.25\%$

        or using the fraction key: percentage lost = $\frac{10}{32} \times 100\% = 31\frac{1}{4}\%$

Add the percentages to check the answer: 56.25% + 12.5% + 31.25% = 100% ✓

Example: Before Heidi joined a gym, she weighed 72 kg. She now weighs 69 kg.
What is the percentage decrease in her weight?

Solution: Decrease = 72 − 69 = 3 kg

Percentage decrease = $\frac{3}{72} \times 100\% = 3 \div 72 \times 100\% = 4.166...\%$

or using the fraction key $\frac{3}{72} \times 100 = 4\frac{1}{6}\%$

So the percentage decrease is 4.2% (to one decimal place).

Study tip

Remember to divide by the **original** amount.

Example: Jack's pay rate has gone up by 45 pence to £8.55 per hour.
Find the percentage increase.

Solution: The increase in Jack's hourly pay rate = 45 pence

To work in pence, use
£8.55 = 855 pence

His original hourly pay rate was 855 − 45 = 810 pence

Percentage increase = $\frac{45}{810}$ × 100% = 45 ÷ 810 × 100% = 5.555...%

The percentage increase in Jack's hourly pay rate = 5.6% (to 1 d.p.)

or $\frac{45}{810}$ × 100% = $5\frac{5}{9}$%

You get the same answer if you work in pounds:
percentage increase = 0.45 ÷ 8.10 × 100% = 5.6% (to 1 d.p.)

Study tip

You must use the **same units** in your division sum.

Practise...

8.2 Writing one quantity as a percentage of another

When answers are not exact, round them to one decimal place.

D

1   Write the first quantity as a percentage of the second quantity.

a   96p,   £3

b   £22 500,   £90 000

c   34 kg,   85 kg

d   60 cm,   5 m

e   270 g,   5 kg

f   350 cm,   2 m

Hint

1 m = 100 cm
1 kg = 1000 g

2   In a class, 21 out of the 28 students walk to school.
What percentage of the class walk to school?

3   A farmers' market will be held on 8 days in September.
What percentage of the month is this?

4   A local authority collected 88 000 tonnes of waste for recycling last year.
9000 tonnes of this was glass.
What percentage of the waste was glass?

5   A school's athletic team is made up of 16 girls and 19 boys.
What percentage of the team are:

a   girls   **b**   boys?

C

6   A garden centre buys plants for 56 pence each.
It sells them for 99 pence each.
Work out the percentage profit.

Hint

The percentage profit is the
percentage increase in price.

7 Sharon buys a motorbike for £3400.
She sells it a year later for £2900.
Work out her percentage loss.

8 This year a school has 1237 students. Last year there were 1329 students.
Find the percentage decrease in the number of students in the school.

9 The price of a packet of biscuits goes up from 98 pence to £1.09.
Find the percentage increase in the price.

10 A furniture shop reduces its prices in a sale.

   a Work out the percentage reduction in the price of:

     i the table

     ii one chair.

   b Dan buys a table and four chairs.
Work out the percentage reduction in the total price.

Table
Was £490
Now £395

Chair
Was £95 (each)
Now £70 (each)

11 The cost of Greg's car insurance has gone up from £420 to £480.

Greg works out 60 ÷ 480 × 100. He says the cost has increased by 12.5%

   a What mistake has he made?

   b What is the actual percentage increase in the cost of the insurance?

12 Write:

   a eighty thousand as a percentage of two million

   b £75 million as a percentage of £5 billion

   c 90 cm as a percentage of 1.75 m

   d 750 g as a percentage of 3.6 kg

   e 37.5 hours as a percentage of 1 week.

13 A manufacturer makes a rectangular rug that is 160 cm long and 120 cm wide.
The manufacturer decides to increase both dimensions of the rug by 25%

Find the percentage increase in:

   a the perimeter of the rug

   b the area of the rug.

14 The table gives the number of visits to some countries made by UK residents in 2004 and 2008.

Compare the percentage changes in the number of visits made to each of these countries.

Study tip

When you are asked to compare sets of data with a different amount of data in each set you should use percentages.

Visits abroad by UK residents (thousands)		
	2004	**2008**
Bulgaria	297	360
Greece	2709	2096
Italy	2974	3372
Slovakia	38	170
Turkey	1124	1936

Source: Travel Trends 2008 (Crown copyright)

15 A newspaper gives a table showing the changes in the quantities of milk and cream used between 2006 and 2010.

Work out the percentage changes and comment on your results.

Food	Average per person per week	
	2006	**2010**
Whole milk	497 ml	432 ml
Skimmed milk	1.13 litres	1.15 litres
Cream	22 ml	19 ml

16 Jacob takes a maths test and a science test in December. He takes another test in each subject the following June. The table shows his scores.
Paul says "I improved most in science".
His teacher says "Actually you improved most in maths".

How did Paul decide? How did his teacher decide?

You **must** shows your working to justify your answer.

	December	June
Maths	46%	62%
Science	53%	71%

Learn... 8.3 Using ratios and proportion

Ratios are a good way of comparing quantities. The quantities must be in the same units.

Two (or more) ratios that simplify to the same ratio are called equivalent ratios.

For example, $8:12$ and $100:150$ are equivalent because they both simplify to $2:3$.

To simplify a ratio, divide each part by the same number.

£3 = 300 pence
When the amounts are in the **same units**, you can omit the units.

For example, the ratio of £3 to 40 pence $= 300:40 = 30:4 = 15:2$

Each number is divided by 10, then 2

You can use the fraction key on your calculator to simplify ratios.

This is the **simplest form** of this ratio. It uses the smallest possible whole numbers.

Sometimes ratios are divided further until one side is 1. This gives the $1:n$ (or the $n:1$) form. These are called **unitary ratios**.

Dividing $15:2$ by 2 gives the ratio $7\frac{1}{2}:1$ or $7.5:1$

Dividing the original ratio $300:40$ by 40 also gives this.

The scales of maps and models are often given as unitary ratios.

The **unitary method** is based on working out what happens with **one** unit of something. It can be used to solve a variety of different problems involving ratio and **proportion**.

There are some links between ratios and fractions.

For example, suppose a brother and sister share an inheritance in the ratio $3:4$
- This means that for every £3 the brother gets, the sister gets £4.
- The brother's share is $\frac{3}{4}$ of the sister's share. The sister's share is $\frac{4}{3}$ or $1\frac{1}{3}$ times the brother's share.
- The brother gets $\frac{3}{7}$ of the whole inheritance and the sister gets the other $\frac{4}{7}$

The **multiplier method** multiplies the quantity by the fraction representing the ratio.

Example: A model of a car is made using a scale of $1:50$

    a The model car is 9 centimetres long.
How long is the real car in metres?

    b The real car is 2 metres wide. How wide is the model car in centimetres?

Solution: **a** The ratio $1:50$ means that 1 cm on the model car represents 50 cm on the real car.
To find the length of the real car, multiply the length of the model car by 50.
Length of the real car = 9 cm × 50 = 450 cm
Length of the real car in metres = 450 ÷ 100 = 4.5 m

> 1 metre = 100 centimetres
> You can change the units before or after using the scale.

    b The width of the real car = 2 m = 200 cm
To find the width of the model car, divide the width of the real car by 50.
Width of model = 200 ÷ 50 = 4 cm

Example: Liam earns £97.20 for working 15 hours in a supermarket.

How much does he earn for 24 hours at the same rate of pay?

> The amount Liam earns is **proportional** to the time he works. (If he works twice as long, he gets paid twice as much. If he works 3 times as long, he gets paid 3 times as much … and so on.)

Solution: For 15 hours Liam earns £97.20.

Unitary method

For 1 hour he earns £97.20 ÷ 15 = £6.48   Divide the pay for 15 hours by 15.

For 24 hours he earns £6.48 × 24 = £155.52   Multiply the pay for 1 hour by 24.

Always check that your answer looks reasonable.
Here the pay for 24 hours is more than that for 15 hours. ✓

Multiplier method

$£97.20 \times \dfrac{24}{15} = £155.52$

Multiplying by $\dfrac{24}{15}$ does the same as dividing by 15 and multiplying by 24.

Example: **a** Which jar of coffee gives the best value for money?

    b Give a reason why you might decide to buy one of the other jars.

Solution: You can use the **unitary method** to solve 'best buy' problems.

    a Find the cost of **1 gram** in each jar.
Working in pence gives easier numbers to compare.

Small jar: Cost of 50 g = 156 pence
               Cost of 1 g = 156p ÷ 50
                       = 3.12 pence

> There are sometimes other methods you could use.
> In this problem you could compare the cost of 100 g.

Medium jar: Cost of 100 g = 229 pence
               Cost of 1 g = 229p ÷ 100
                       = 2.29 pence

> Small jar: 100 g (2 jars) costs 156p × 2 = 312 pence
> Medium jar: 100 g costs 229 pence
> Large jar: 100 g ($\frac{1}{2}$ jar) costs 445p ÷ 2 = 222.5 pence
> This also shows the large jar gives the best value for money

Large jar: Cost of 200 g = 445 pence
               Cost of 1 g = 445p ÷ 200
                       = 2.225 pence

The cost of 1 gram of coffee is **least** in the large jar so the large jar gives the best value for money.

    b You might buy a smaller jar if you only want a small amount of coffee (or if you do not have £4.45 to spend).

Example: Here is a recipe for blackberry and apple jam.

Sharon has picked 500 g of blackberries.

What quantity of apples and sugar does she need to use?

> Recipe: Blackberry and Apple Jam
> * 800 g Blackberries
> * 600 g Apples
> * 1kg Sugar

Solution: Writing the quantity of sugar as 1000 g gives the ratio of blackberries : apples : sugar
= 800 g : 600 g : 1000 g

You can change the quantity of blackberries from 800 g to 500 g in two steps.
Dividing by 8 reduces the quantity to 100 g. Then multiplying by 5 increases it to 500 g.

	Blackberries	**Apples**	**Sugar**
÷8	800 g	600 g	1000 g	÷8
	100 g	75 g	125 g	
×5	500 g	375 g	625 g	×5

Alternatively
You could divide by 200 to give the simplest form 4 : 3 : 5
Then to change the 4 into 500, you need to multiply by 125.
Doing this to all parts gives 500 : 375 : 625

If you prefer, you can divide by 800 to reduce the quantity of blackberries to **1 g** (the unitary method), then multiply by 500. This also gives the correct answer but the numbers are a bit harder.

In ratio and proportion questions you can multiply or divide by anything you like. But you must do the same to all the parts or quantities.

> **Study tip**
> Write all parts in the same units before simplifying a ratio.

Practise... 8.3 Using ratios and proportion G F E D C

1 **a** Write down three different pairs of numbers that are in the ratio 1 : 3

   b Explain how you can tell that two numbers are in the ratio 1 : 3

2 Each of these ratios simplifies to 1 : 7
Copy these ratios and fill in the gaps.

   a 2 : __   **c** __ : 21   **e** a : __

   b 5 : __   **d** __ : 3500

3 James is making fruit juice, using fruit cordial and water.

The label on the cordial says "To make 1 litre of fruit juice, use 200 ml of cordial and 800 ml of water."

James uses 250 ml cordial and 850 ml water.

Is James using the correct proportions?

Show working to justify your answer.

4 A builder makes mortar by mixing cement and sand in the ratio 1 : 5

   a How many buckets of sand does he need to mix with 3 buckets of cement?

   b How many buckets of cement does he need to mix with 10 buckets of sand?

   c How many buckets of cement and sand does he need to make 30 buckets of mortar?

5 The numbers x and y are in the ratio $3:4$

    a If x is 12, what is y?

    b If y is 12, what is x?

    c If x is 1, what is y?

    d If y is 1, what is x?

    e If x and y add up to 35, what are x and y?

6 Here is a list of the ingredients you need to make 20 peanut cookies.

    a List the ingredients you would need to make:

        i 10 cookies

        ii 50 cookies.

    b Ewan wants to make some cookies.
He has bought a 200 g bag of peanuts.

        i How many peanut cookies can he make with this bag of peanuts?

        ii How much of each of the other ingredients will he need?

Recipe: Peanut Cookies (makes 20)
* 100 g Butter
* 50 g Sugar
* 150 g Flour
* 50 g Peanuts

7 A shop sells multi-packs of batteries.
A pack of 20 batteries costs £4.95. A pack of 32 batteries costs £6.28.
Which pack gives the best value for money?

8 Nina is paid £87.50 for 14 hours' work.

    a How much does she get paid for 20 hours' work?

    b She is paid £100. How many hours has she worked?

    c What assumption do you have to make to answer these questions?

9 Amy and Bianca go to Paris for the weekend.

    a They buy some euro at a bank. Amy gets 300 euro for £250.

        i What is the exchange rate in euro per £?

        ii How many euro does Bianca get for £275?

    b When they return, they go back to the bank to sell the euro they have left.
Amy gets £40 for 50 euro.

        i How much does Amy get for each euro?

        ii How much does Bianca get for 105 euro?

10 5 miles is approximately equal to 8 kilometres.

    a The distance from Southampton to Sheffield is 195 miles.
How far is this in kilometres?

    b The distance from Barcelona to Madrid is 624 kilometres.
How far is this in miles?

11 A box of chocolates contains milk chocolates, plain chocolates and white chocolates in the ratio $4:3:2$

    a What fraction of the chocolates is:

        i milk

        ii plain

        iii white?

    b Show how you can check your answers to part **a**.

D

C

12 The ratio of men to women on a holiday cruise is $3:5$

What percentage of the people on the cruise are women?

13 The weight of a pile of textbooks is proportional to the number of textbooks in the pile.

a Copy and complete this table.

Number of books	0	10	20	30
Weight (kg)		3.25		

b Plot the values in the table as points on a graph, using the number of books as the x-coordinates and their weight in kilograms as y-coordinates.

c The points should lie in a straight line through $(0, 0)$.

i Explain why.

ii Use the graph to find the weight of a pile of 24 books.

iii Mr Marks says he cannot lift anything heavier than 5 kilograms. How many books can he carry?

14 The cost of calls on a mobile phone is proportional to the length of the calls in minutes.

The cost per minute depends on whether calls are in peak or off-peak periods.

This graph shows the cost of calls made in peak periods.

a **i** Make a copy of the graph on graph paper.

ii In off-peak periods the cost of a call is 15 pence per minute.

iii Draw a line on your graph to show the cost of off-peak calls.

b **i** Tom makes a peak period call that lasts half an hour. How much does it cost?

ii How much would Tom have saved if he had made the call in an off-peak period?

iii Bill spends £12 on a peak period call. How much would the same length call have cost in an off-peak period?

c A contract phone costs £15 per month. You get 60 minutes of 'free' calls and pay for all other calls at 20 pence per minute.

i Draw a new graph to show this.

ii Bill uses a contract phone. Is the cost of calls proportional to the length of the calls? Give a reason for your answer.

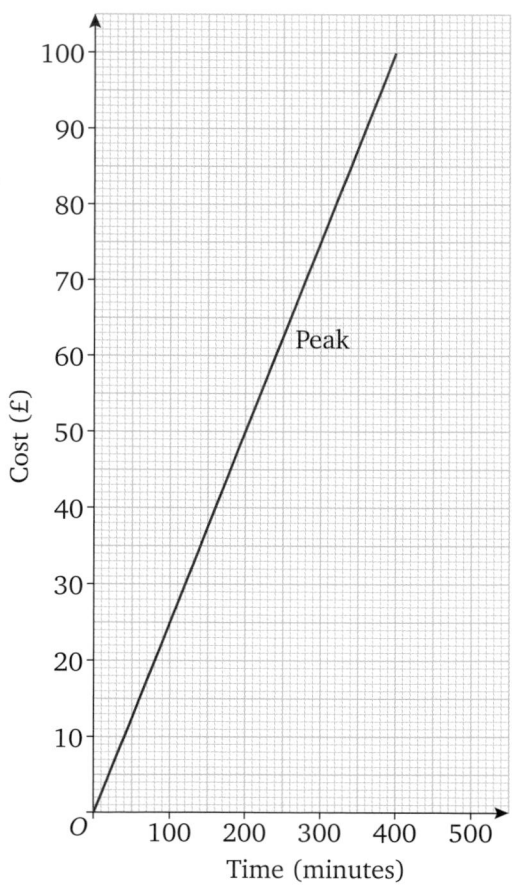

15 The scale on a map is $1:50\,000$

a The distance between two landmarks on the map is 12 centimetres. Find the actual distance.

b Kathy says the distance between these landmarks on a map with a scale of $1:25\,000$ will be 6 cm.

Is she correct? Give a reason for your answer.

16 Road signs use ratios or percentages to give the gradients of hills.

Ratio of vertical
distance : horizontal distance

Vertical distance as a
percentage of the horizontal distance

Which of the hills described by these road signs is steeper? Give a reason for your answer.

 17 When you enlarge a photograph, the ratio of the height to width must stay the same.
If the ratio is different the objects in the photograph will look stretched or squashed.

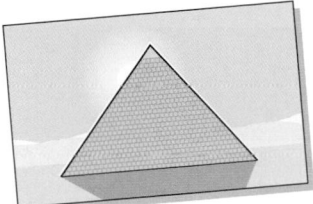 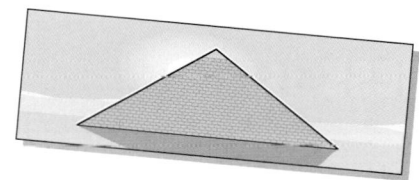

a Chloe has a photo of her favourite group that is 15 cm wide and 10 cm high.
What is the ratio of width to height in its simplest form?

b Chloe wants to put an enlarged copy of the photo
in a frame on her bedroom wall.

The table gives the sizes of the frames she can buy.

Which of these frames is most suitable?

Give a reason for your answer.

Frame	Width (cm)	Height (cm)
A	25	20
B	30	25
C	40	30
D	45	30
E	50	40

18 The table on the right gives the ages of the children
who are booked in to a nursery.

The nursery has three rooms: one for children under
2 years old, one for two-year-olds and one for children
aged 3 years and over.

The minimum adult : child ratios for nurseries are
given in the table below.

Age (years)	Number of children	
	morning	afternoon
0	2	1
1	4	2
2	6	9
3	5	8
4	2	1

Age	Minimum adult : child ratio
Children under 2 years	1 : 3
Children aged 2 years	1 : 4
Children aged 3–7 years	1 : 8

How many staff does the nursery need:

a in the morning **b** in the afternoon?

 **19 a** Which size of shampoo bottle gives
the best value for money?

You **must** show all your working and
give a reason for your answer.

b Why might someone buy a
different size?

£1.99
GLOSSY Shampoo
150 ml
Buy 1, get 1 free

£2.39
GLOSSY Shampoo
250 ml
20% extra free

£3.20
GLOSSY Shampoo
400 ml
10% off marked price

20 Students at a school can visit a theme park, a zoo or a safari park.
The table shows how many have chosen each place.

Choice	Number of students
Theme park	124
Zoo	76
Safari Park	98

The school's policy is to have a maximum child : adult ratio of 8 : 1 on school visits.

There are 20 teachers available and some parents have offered to go on the visits if they are needed.

How many parents are needed?

8   Assess 🄚

F

1 This diagram is made from equilateral triangles.

   a What percentage of the diagram is:

     i   shaded   **ii**   not shaded?

   b Another diagram has 65% shaded.

     What fraction of the diagram is shaded?

     Simplify your answer.

2 Molly got $\frac{5}{8}$ of the marks in a test. Rose got 65%.

Who did better in the test? Give a reason for your answer.

E

3 A painter has two tins of paint.

The 5 litre tin, *A*, is 35% full of paint.
The 2.5 litre tin, *B*, is two-thirds full of paint.

Which tin contains more paint? You **must** show your working.

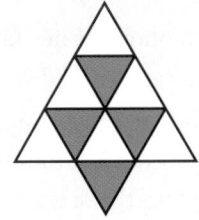

4 A Sat Nav usually costs £159.99.
It is reduced by 15% in a sale.

What is the cost of the Sat Nav in the sale?

D

5 A school buys 10 bottles of milk for drinks
at a parents' evening.
Each bottle holds enough for 25 drinks.
They make 235 drinks.

Calculate the percentage of milk used.

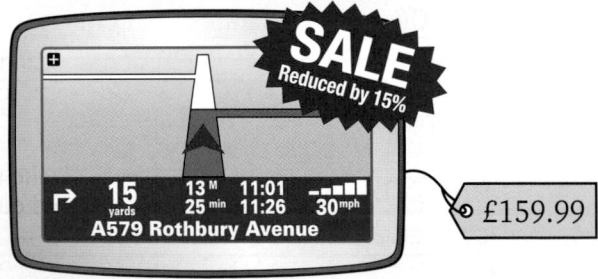

6 What percentage of this shape is shaded blue?

5 cm
2 cm
Not to scale
2 cm   4 cm

7 168 men and 210 women book a holiday cruise.

Write the ratio of the number of men to the number of women:

   a   in its simplest form   **b**   in the form 1 : *n*

8   The sizes of the interior angles of a quadrilateral are in the ratio 2 : 2 : 3 : 5
The equal angles are both 60°. Calculate the size of the other angles.

9   The table shows the amounts needed to make 24 fruit biscuits.

Ingredient	Amount for 24 biscuits (g)
Flour	300
Butter	150
Sugar	100
Fruit	120

Calculate the amounts needed to make 36 fruit biscuits.

10   In the 1908 Olympic Games, Reggie Walker won the 100 metres in a time of 10.8 seconds.
A century later, in the 2008 Olympics, Usain Bolt won the 100 metres in 9.69 seconds.
Calculate the percentage decrease in the winning time.

11   It costs £259.80 for 20 square metres of carpet.
How much does it cost for 36 square metres of the same carpet?

12   Sun tan lotion is sold in two different sizes: small and large.

  a   Which bottle gives the better value for money?

  b   Give one reason why you might prefer to buy the other bottle.

Practice questions ⓚ

1   **a**   Travelling 10 000 kilometres costs £800 for petrol.
How much does it cost to travel 12 500 kilometres?   *(1 mark)*

    b   Last year Mr Taylor travelled 15 000 km in his car and spent £1200 on petrol.
This year he expects to travel 20 000 km.
He estimates that the price of petrol has increased by 10% on what it was last year.
How much should Mr Taylor expect to pay for petrol this year?   *(4 marks)*

2   **a**   A water meter at a house records the volume of water used, in cubic metres.
The meter readings at the start and end of a 3-month period are as follows.

	Reading in cubic metres
End	4205
Start	4154

Water costs 104p per cubic metre.
Find the cost of the water used in this period.
Give your answer in pounds.   *(4 marks)*

    b   In this period the cost of water at another house is £62.
The sewage charge is 97% of the cost of the water.
Find the sewage charge.   *(2 marks)*

    c   A factory uses 34 cubic metres of water one week and 39 cubic metres in the
following week.
Calculate the percentage increase in the consumption of water.   *(3 marks)*

Objectives

Examiners would normally expect students who get these grades to be able to:

G

use a formula in words such as:
Total pay = rate per hour × no. of hours + bonus

F

substitute positive numbers into a simple formula such as $P = 2L + 2W$

derive simple expressions

E

use formulae such as $P = 2L + 2W$ to find W given P and L

substitute negative numbers into a simple formula

use formulae from mathematics and other subjects

derive expressions and formulae

D

substitute numbers into more complicated formulae such as $C = \dfrac{(A + 1)}{9}$

derive more complex expressions and formulae

distinguish between an expression, an equation and a formula

C

rearrange linear formulae such as $p = 3q + 5$

Key terms

expression
formula
symbol
substitute

values
equation
subject

I used the formula: cooking time = 20 per pound weight + 20 to work out how long the chicken needed. Perhaps the time should have been in minutes not hours!

Did you know?

Formulae can be very useful

Formulae are used in everyday life, for example in cooking instructions. Be careful to check that the units you are working with make sense!

You should already know:

✔ order of operations (BIDMAS)

✔ the four rules applied to negative numbers

✔ how to simplify expressions by collecting like terms

✔ how to solve linear equations.

 **Learn...** 9.1 **Writing formulae using letters and symbols**

An **expression** is a collection of algebraic terms such as $3x - 2y + z$.

A **formula** tells you how to work something out such as $A = l \times w$

This formula tells you to multiply l and w to obtain A.

A formula can be written using words or **symbols**.

When you write expressions and formulae using symbols you need to know:

- If a stands for a number, then $2 \times a$ can be written as $2a$.
  Always write the number in front of the letter.

- The expression $3x + 5$ means multiply x by 3 and then add 5.

- The expression $5(x - 2)$ means subtract 2 from x and then multiply the answer by 5.

Example: A rough rule for changing inches to centimetres is to multiply the number of inches by 2.5
Write a formula for this rule.

Solution: In words the formula would be:

'number of centimetres' = 'number of inches' $\times$ 2.5

Choose letters to stand for 'number of centimetres'
and 'number of inches'.

You could choose C for the 'number of centimetres'
and i for the 'number of inches'.

$C = i \times 2.5$

$C = 2.5i$ Remember to put the number in
front of the letter.

> **Study tip**
>
> Be careful when you choose
> your own letters in problems.
> Some letters are easily
> confused with numbers.
>
> Z and 2 can get confused.
>
> I and 1 can get confused.
>
> b and 6 can get confused.
>
> q and 9 can get confused.
>
> S and 5 can get confused.

Example: **1**   Write an expression for each of the following:

    a   Think of a number. Double it. Add 3.

    b   Think of a number. Add 1. Multiply by 2.

    2   Describe how the following expression is formed.

$$\frac{(x + 3)}{4} - 5$$

Solution: **1**   **a**   Think of a number, call it x x

        Double it $2x$ (*double* is the same as *multiply by 2*)

        Add 3 $2x + 3$

    b   Think of a number x

        Add 1 $x + 1$

        Multiply by 2 $2(x + 1)$

    2   Think of a number x

        Add 3 $x + 3$

        Divide by 4 $\dfrac{(x + 3)}{4}$

        Subtract 5 $\dfrac{(x + 3)}{4} - 5$

> **Study tip**
>
> Make sure you understand the
> difference between an equation
> (which can be solved) a formula
> (into which values are substituted)
> and an expression (which does not
> have an equals sign).

Example: Andy has *k* marbles.

a   Ben has five more marbles than Andy.
Write down an expression for the number of marbles Ben has.

b   Chris has one fewer marble than Andy.
Write down an expression for the number of marbles Chris has.

c   Dean has twice as many marbles as Andy.
Write down an expression for the number of marbles Dean has.

d   Enid has three times as many marbles as Ben.
Write down an expression for the number of marbles Enid has.

Solution: **a**   **Five more than** is the same as **add 5**.
Ben has $k + 5$ marbles.

b   **One fewer than** is the same as **subtract 1**.
Chris has $k - 1$ marbles.

c   **Twice as many** is the same as **multiply by 2**.
Dean has $2k$ marbles.

d   **Three times as many** is the same as **multiply by 3**.
Enid has $3(k + 5)$ marbles.

> **Study tip**
>
> Put brackets around expressions when you have to multiply them.
> $k + 5 \times 3$ would have given you the wrong number of marbles for Enid.

Example: Write a problem which leads to the expression $2x + 3$ as the answer.

Solution: There are *x* pencils in a pack.
Lee has two packs and three extra pencils.
Write an expression for the total number of pencils.
Answer: $2x + 3$

9.1 Writing formulae using letters and symbols

Practise...

F

1   Dermot has *x* books on his shelf.

a   Ewan has five more books than Dermot.
Write down an expression for the number of books Ewan has.

b   Fred has three times as many books as Dermot.
Write down an expression for the number of books Fred has.

2   Ranee earns £*y* per week.

a   Sue earns £4 less than Ranee.
Write down an expression for the amount Sue earns.

b   Tina earns twice as much as Ranee.
Write down an expression for the amount Tina earns.

3   Jon buys 12 bags of crisps.
The price of a bag of crisps is *z* pence.
Write down an expression for the total cost of the crisps.

4 Anna buys *m* apples.

Each apple costs 18p.

Write down an expression for the total cost of the apples.

5 A cookery book gives this rule for roast chicken:

40 minutes per kilogram plus 20 minutes

Write an expression for this rule.

Use *k* to stand for the number of kilograms.

6 Write an expression for each of these statements.

a Four times the number *x*

b Five times the number *z* plus six times the number *x*

c The sum of two times the number *x* and double the number *y*

d The product of the numbers *x*, *y* and *z*

e The sum of seven times the number *x* and double the number *y*

f Half the number *y* subtracted from six times the number *x*

7 Write an expression for each of these statements.

Let the unknown number be *x*.

a Think of a number. Add 3.   **d** Think of a number. Multiply by 3. Add 2.

b Think of a number. Double it.   **e** Think of a number. Add 1. Multiply by 2.

c Think of a number. Subtract 5.

8 The rule for finding out how far away thunderstorms are is:

'Count the number of seconds between the lightning and the thunder.

Divide the answer by 5. The answer gives the distance in miles.'

Write a formula for this rule.

Use *s* to stand for the number of seconds and *d* to stand for the distance in miles.

9 You can find out how many amps an electrical appliance will use by using this rule:

Number of amps equals the number of watts divided by 240.

Write a formula for this rule.

Use *a* to stand for the number of amps and *w* to stand for the number of watts.

10 Write a problem which leads to the expression $3x + 2$ as the answer.

11 In Gordon's takeaway a pizza costs £*m* and a pasta dish costs £*n*.

On Thursday evening, he sells 32 pizzas and 15 pasta dishes.

Write down an expression for his total takings from pizza and pasta dishes on Thursday evening.

12 Jan sells homemade cakes to raise funds for her son's school.

She charges £3 for each cake but has to pay £5 for her stall.

She sells *n* cakes.

Write down an expression in *n* for the profit she makes.

D

13 Write down a formula for the total cost (*T*) of:

    a   *x* lollies at 70p each and *y* lollies at 80p each

    b   *c* cakes at 90p each and *b* biscuits at 20p each.

14 Phil bought *x* cups of tea and *y* cups of coffee from his local cafe for himself and his friends. The tea cost 80p per cup, and the coffee cost 90p per cup.

Which one of the following could be a formula for the total cost in pence, *C*?

$C = 90x + 80y$

$C = 80x + 90y$

$C = 80x90y$

Explain your answer, and state why the other formulae are not correct.

C

15 Sean and Dee organise a quiz evening.

A quiz team is made up of four people.

Each team is charged £8 to enter the quiz.

Sean and Dee spend £20 on prizes and £25 on food and drink.

There are *x* teams at the quiz evening.

On average, each team member spends £3 on refreshments.

Write down an expression in *x* for the profit they make.

⚠ 16 Kate has £2 to spend. She buys *x* pens at *y* pence each.

    a   Write down an expression for the total amount she spends.

    b   Write down a formula for the amount of change she receives. Use *C* to stand for her change in pence.

> **Study tip**
>
> Make sure that units are consistent. If you are working in pounds then make sure all prices/costs are in pounds, if you are working in kilograms, then make sure that all weights are in kilograms, and so on.

⚠ 17 When Mrs Tyler does group work in her classroom, she arranges the tables and chairs in the following way.

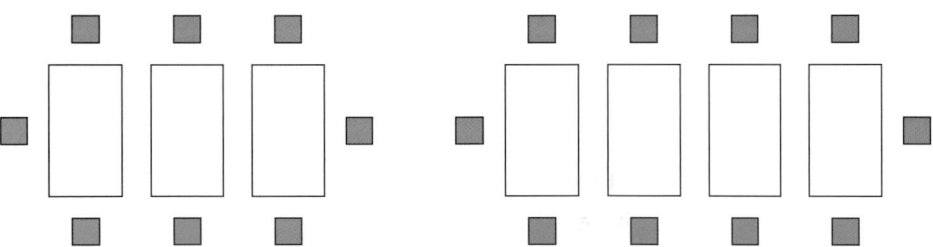

The first arrangement has three tables and eight chairs.

The second arrangement has four tables and ten chairs.

    a   How many chairs will there be if there are five tables arranged in this way?

    b   How many chairs will there be if there are ten tables arranged in this way?

    c   Copy and complete the following table for the number of tables and chairs.

Number of tables	1	2	3	4	5
Number of chairs					

    d   Write down a formula showing how to work out the number of chairs from the number of tables. Use the letter *T* for the number of tables and *C* for the number of chairs.

18 Natland Taxis use the formula $C = 3m + 4.5$ to work out the cost of journeys for customers.

C is the total charge in pounds and m is the number of the miles for the journey.
Every journey has a minimum charge and a charge for each mile.

a What is Natland Taxis' minimum charge?

b What is the cost per mile?

 19 Sedgwick Tool Hire charge £18 to hire a cement mixer for one day. They charge £9 for every day extra.

Harry says the formula for the total charge is $C = 18d + 9$.

He uses d for the number of days and C for the total charge.

a Explain why Harry's formula is not correct.

b Write down what Harry's formula should be.

c Use the internet to find some costs for tool hire. Write down some formulae for the cost of tool hire.

 Learn... ## 9.2 Substituting in formulae

When you use a formula you **substitute** the **values** you are given into it. This means you replace the letters with the numbers given to you.

Start by writing the expression or formula down, and then substitute the numbers given.

When you substitute numbers into a formula you get an equation.
This equation can then be solved to find the value of the unknown letter.

Example: If $a = 2$, $b = 3$, $c = -1$, find the value of y when

a $y = a + b + c$

b $y = ab$

c $y = 4a - 3b + 2c$

d $y = \dfrac{3a}{2b}$

Solution: **a** $y = a + b + c$ Write the expression down.
$y = 2 + 3 - 1$ Substitute the numbers given.
$y = 5 - 1$
$y = 4$

b $y = ab$ Write the expression down.
$y = 2 \times 3$ Substitute the numbers given (remember ab is the same as $a \times b$).
$y = 6$

c $y = 4a - 3b + 2c$ Write the expression down.
$y = (4 \times 2) - (3 \times 3) + (2 \times -1)$ Substitute the numbers given.
$y = 8 - 9 - 2$ Take care with signs (remember $2 \times -1 = -2$).
$y = -3$

d $y = \dfrac{3a}{2b}$ Write the expression down.
$y = \dfrac{3 \times 2}{2 \times 3}$ Substitute the numbers given.
$y = \dfrac{6}{6}$
$y = 1$

> **Study tip**
>
> You can use brackets to help you do calculations in the correct order.
>
> Remember, BIDMAS applies to algebra as well as arithmetic.

Example: This formula is used to work out the pay, P, for a plumber in pounds.

$P = 55 + 30h$ where h is the number of hours worked.

a What is the call-out charge?

b How much is the plumber paid for working:

i 2 hours   **ii** 3 hours 15 minutes   **iii** 20 minutes?

c How many hours does the plumber work in order to be paid £75?

Solution: **a** The formula is $P = 55 + 30h$

When $h = 0$, $P = 55$. The call-out charge is for turning up but not doing any work.

The call-out charge is £55.

> **Study tip**
>
> Remember to include the units in your answer.

b **i** For 2 hours work $h = 2$

$P = 55 + 30h$	Copy the formula.
$P = 55 + 30 \times 2$	Substitute (replace the letter with its value).
$P = 55 + 60$	Calculate carefully (use BIDMAS).
$P = 115$	

The plumber is paid £115.

ii 3 hours 15 minutes = 3.25 hours (remember there are 60 minutes in 1 hour.

15 minutes $= \frac{15}{60}$ hour $= \frac{1}{4}$ hour $= 0.25$ hour)

$P = 55 + 30h$	Copy the formula.
$P = 55 + 30 \times 3.25$	Substitute (replace the letter with its value).
$P = 55 + 97.5$	Calculate carefully (use BIDMAS).
$P = 152.5$	

The plumber is paid £152.50.

> **Study tip**
>
> When you work with money on your calculator it will often miss off the final zero. You must write money correctly in your exam. You will not gain the final mark for answers such as £152.5 so remember to write £152.50.

iii $h = 20$ minutes (remember there are 60 minutes in 1 hour.

20 minutes $= \frac{20}{60}$ hour $= \frac{1}{3}$ hour)

$P = 55 + 30h$	Copy the formula.
$P = 55 + 30 \times \frac{1}{3}$	Substitute (replace the letter with its value).
$P = 55 + 10$	Calculate carefully (use BIDMAS).
$P = 65$	

The plumber is paid £65.

c This time you are given the value of P.

$P = 55 + 30h$	Copy the formula.
$75 = 55 + 30h$	Substitute (replace the letter with its value).

This is an equation that you need to solve.

$20 = 30h$	Subtract 55 from both sides.
$\frac{20}{30} = h$	Divide both sides by 30.
$h = \frac{2}{3}$ hour	

$\frac{2}{3}$ of 60 minutes = 40 minutes

The plumber needs to work 40 minutes to be paid £75.

Example: Maxi is using the formula $p = 3x + 5xy$

He needs to find p when $x = 2$ and $y = 3$

Solution:
$p = 3x + 5xy$	Write the formula down.
$p = (3 \times 2) + (5 \times 2 \times 3)$	Substitute the numbers given.
$p = 6 + 30$	Take care to work this out in the correct order.
$p = 36$	

Study tip

Remember to show all stages of your working; you gain method marks for this in an examination.

Practise... 9.2 Substituting in formulae G F E D C

1 Tasty Pizzas works out its delivery charge with the formula:
Delivery Charge (£) = Number of pizzas × 0.50 + 1.25
Find the delivery charge for three pizzas.

2 Find the value of each y when $x = 10$

a $y = x + 4$ **d** $y = 2x + 3$ **g** $y = 5x - 12$

b $y = 3x$ **e** $y = 14 - x$ **h** $y = 2(x - 2)$

c $y = x - 3$ **f** $y = 40 + 3x$

3 Mrs Bujjit is working out the wages at the factory. She uses the formula:
Wages equal hours worked multiplied by rate per hour.

a How much does Ellen earn if she is paid £7 an hour and she works for 30 hours?

b How much does Francis earn if he works for 25 hours and is paid £8 an hour?

c Write out Mrs Bujjit's formula in algebra.

4 Find the value of r when $x = 3$, $y = 4$, $s = 6$ and $t = 0.5$

a $r = 2x$ **e** $r = \dfrac{s}{3} + 1$ **i** $r = xst$

b $r = 3y$ **f** $r = \dfrac{2s}{x}$ **j** $r = xy - st$

c $r = 3x + y$ **g** $r = yt$

d $r = 2y - t$ **h** $r = 2s - t + y$

5 Find the value of m when $y = -3$

a $m = 5 + y$ **c** $m = 4y + 6$ **e** $m = 8 - 2y$

b $m = 3y$ **d** $m = 6 - y$ **f** $m = 5y - 1$

6 In science, Andrea is using the formula $V = IR$
Find V if:

a $I = 3$ and $R = 42$ **b** $I = 2.5$ and $R = 96$

7 Here are two formulae:

$y = 2x + 6$ $y = 2(x + 6)$

If x is 5, work out which formula gives the larger value for y. Show your working.

D

8 Mary was working through question **2** in her maths lesson.
She said the answer to part **f** was 430.
She explained to her teacher that 40 + 3 = 43, and then 43 × 10 = 430.

What mistake did Mary make?

9 James is doing an experiment in science. He uses the formula

$$\text{Average speed} = \frac{\text{Total distance travelled}}{\text{Total time taken}}$$

He uses this formula to work out that if an object has an average speed of 20 m/s and travels for 10 seconds then it must have travelled 2 m.
What mistake has James made?

10 In geography, Ken is converting degrees Fahrenheit into degrees Celsius.

He uses the formula: $C = \dfrac{5(F - 32)}{9}$

Find C if:

a $F = 68$ **b** $F = 32$

11 In science, Brian is using the formula $S = ut + \frac{1}{2}at^2$

Find s if $u = 3$, $t = 2$ and $a = 4$.

12 Endmoor Cabs use the following formula to work out taxi fares.

> £3.50
> Plus
> £1.20 per mile

a Jack travels 2 miles. What is Jack's fare?

b Jane pays £7.10. How many miles has Jane travelled?

c Jim has £10. What is the maximum distance that he can travel?

Startmoor Cabs have a flat rate of £2 per mile.

d John needs to travel 10 miles. Which company should he choose?

e When does it become more expensive to choose Startmoor Cabs?

13 A gym has two schemes that people can choose from, to pay for using the facilities.
Scheme A: Pay £5 per session
Scheme B: Pay an annual fee of £120 and £2 per session.
When would scheme A be better than scheme B?

What if scheme B goes up to £150 and £2 per session while scheme A stays the same?
What if scheme A goes up to £6 per session while scheme B stays the same?

Learn... 9.3 Changing the subject of a formula (k)

Recognising algebraic statements

In this chapter you have used expressions and formulae. You have already solved equations in a previous chapter. You need to be able to identify whether an algebraic statement is an expression, a formula or an **equation**.

Remember the following about formulae, equations and expressions:

A formula tells you how to work something out. It can be written using words or symbols and will always have an equals sign. There will be at least two letters involved.

For example, here is a formula in words:

Area of a rectangle is equal to length multiplied by width

$A = L \times W$ is the same formula written in symbols, where A stands for area, L for length and W for width. From this formula, you can work out the area of any rectangle if you know its length and width.
You can tell this is a formula, since it tells you what to do with L and W to work out A. There is an equals sign, and there are more than two letters being used.

An equation is two expressions separated by an equals sign. You are often asked to solve an equation, in which case there will be only one letter, but it may appear more than once.

For example, here is an equation in x:

$x + 3 = 7$

In this equation, x is equal to 4. This is the only possible value of x, as any other number added to 3 does not equal 7.
You can tell this is an equation, as there is an expression on each side of the equals sign. There is only one letter involved. It can be solved to find a value of x.

An expression is just a collection of terms. An expression does not have an equals sign.
For example, here is an expression containing x and y terms:

$3x + 2y - 5$

You can tell this is an expression as it is just a collection of terms. There is no equals sign.

Formulae and equations can sometimes look very similar.

Changing the subject of a formula

The **subject** of a formula is the letter on the left-hand side of the equals sign.

P is the subject of the formula $P = 3L + 2$

You can change the subject of this formula to make L the subject.
You will then have a formula telling you what to do to P to work out L.

You use the same strategies that you learned when you solved equations.

Hint

Remember that what you do to one side of an equation, you must also do to the other side.

Example: Make L the subject of the formula $P = 3L + 2$

Solution:

$P = 3L + 2$	Write the formula down first.
$P - 2 = 3L + 2 - 2$	Subtract 2 from both sides.
$P - 2 = 3L$	
$\dfrac{P - 2}{3} = \dfrac{3L}{3}$	Divide both sides by 3.
$\dfrac{P - 2}{3} = L$	
$L = \dfrac{P - 2}{3}$	Rewrite the formula starting with L on the left-hand side.

Practise...

9.3 Changing the subject of a formula

1 In this chapter you have met these words: **expression**, **formula**, **equation**.
Choose the correct word to describe each of the following.

a $p = a + b + c + d$

b $2x + 5y - 4z$

c $7m + 3n$

d $3h = 6$

e $5 = 1 - 2q$

f $9k - 3$

g $c = 25h - 9$

2 Rearrange the formula $M = n + 42$ to make n the subject.

3 Rearrange each of these formulae to make y the subject.

a $a + y = c$

b $y - e = d$

c $e + 2y = f$

d $d = h + 3y$

e $j = 4y - 3k$

f $2m + 6y = n$

4 Rearrange each of these formulae to make x the subject.

a $y = x - 32$

b $y = bx$

c $d = 7x - 60$

d $kx - p = n$

e $p + sx = t$

f $y - x = 50$

5 Which of the following is a correct rearrangement of $m = 4x - 3$?

A $x = \dfrac{m - 3}{4}$

B $x = \dfrac{m + 3}{4}$

C $x = \dfrac{m - 4}{3}$

D $x = m + \dfrac{3}{4}$

E $x = \dfrac{3 - m}{4}$

F $x = \dfrac{m + 4}{3}$

6 The formula for finding the circumference of a circle is $C = \pi d$

Rearrange this formula to make d the subject.

7 Karen rearranges the formula $y = 4 + x$

She makes x the subject of the formula.

She thinks that the answer is $y + 4 = x$

Is she correct? Give a reason for your answer.

8 Sam rearranges the formula $y = \dfrac{3}{x}$ to make x the subject.

She gets the answer $x = \dfrac{y}{3}$

Is she correct? Give a reason for your answer.

9 Rajesh is using the formula $v = u + at$ in science.

Rearrange the formula to make a the subject of the formula.

10 The formula for finding the volume of a cylinder is

$V = \pi r^2 h$

where V = volume, r = radius and h = height. Write the formula for

finding the height of the cylinder if you know the volume and the radius.

11 Gary needs to change a temperature from °C to °F

He finds this formula: $F = \dfrac{9C}{5} + 32$

Rearrange this formula to make C the subject.

Remember, you must show your working.

12 A holiday is paid for by making a deposit of £300 and then paying instalments of £50 every month.

a How much has been paid after 4 months?

b Write down a formula for the total amount paid, £T, after m months of payments.

c Rearrange your formula to make m the subject.

d Use your rearranged formula to work out the number of months needed to pay for a holiday costing £700. How can you check that your answer is correct?

13 Drive Away car hire base their charges on a fixed daily rate plus an extra allowance for mileage.
Jane wants to hire a car for three days and spend no more than £160
What is the maximum mileage she can travel?

Study tip

Setting up a simple formula can help solve problems like these.

Assess

1 Strickland's corner shop work out their employees' total pay using the formula:

Total pay = Rate per hour × No. of hours + Bonus

Work out the total pay for Harry if he worked for 6 hours at £5 per hour and earned a bonus of £3.

G

2 The fast train from Birmingham to Coventry takes k minutes.
The slow train takes 15 minutes longer.
Write down an expression for the time the slow train takes.

F

3 Raj got q marks in his maths test.
Sam got three fewer marks than Raj.
Write down an expression for the number of marks Sam got.

4 Find the value of y when $x = 5$

a $y = x + 3$ **b** $y = x - 2$ **c** $y = 3x + 9$ **d** $y = 20 - 3x$

5 Write these word formulae using symbols:

E

a The perimeter of a rectangle is equal to twice the length plus twice the width.

b Kate's weekly wage is equal to £7 for every hour she works.

c Distance travelled is equal to speed multiplied by time.

d The volume of a cuboid is equal to the length multiplied by the width multiplied by the height.

e The length of a rectangle is equal to the area divided by the width.

f Joe delivers pies to customers' homes.
His charge is £5 per pie and he adds on a £2 delivery charge.

E

6 John uses the formula $P = 2L + 2W$ to find the perimeter of rectangles. The length is L and the width is W. Use John's formula to find the perimeter of a rectangle with

  a length 8 cm and width 5 cm.

  b width 11 m and length 4 m.

7 Mary uses the formula $v = u + at$ in science. Find v if $a = -5$, $u = 24$ and $t = 3$.

D

8 Jake is having a birthday party.

His Mum buys x packs of balloons and y tweeters.

Each pack of balloons costs 25p and one tweeter costs 14p.

Write down an expression for the total cost of the balloons and tweeters.

9 Which of the words **expression**, **equation**, **formula** best describes the following?

  a $m = 4n + p$

  b $3m = 2m + 5$

  c $m + 3n$

10 Karen is using the formula $C = \dfrac{(A + 1)}{9}$

Find C if $A = 26$

C

11 Make x the subject of the equation $y = 4x - 7$

12 Rearrange the formula $m = 3(C - 2)$ to make C the subject.

Practice questions (k)

1   A shopkeeper uses this formula to calculate the total cost when customers pay by monthly instalments.

$$C = d + 24 \times m$$

C is the total cost in pounds.
d is the deposit in pounds.
m is the monthly instalment in pounds.

a   The deposit for a wardrobe is £16.
The monthly payments are £10.
What is the total cost?   *(2 marks)*

b   How many years does it take to finish paying for goods using this formula?   *(1 mark)*

c   The total cost of a sofa is £600.
The deposit is £120.
Work out the value of the monthly instalment.   *(3 marks)*

AQA 2009

2   After exercise you can work out your fitness index, F.
You need to know:
    your exercise time in seconds (T)
    the number of your pulse beats in three 30-second intervals after you have stopped exercising (a, b and c).

Tony is working out his fitness index.

a   i   Tony exercises for 3 minutes 30 seconds.
Work out T.   *(1 mark)*

ii   After exercise he obtains $a = 70$, $b = 55$ and $c = 45$
Work out $a + b + c$.   *(1 mark)*

iii   Work out F, Terry's fitness index, using the formula:

$$F = \frac{50T}{a + b + c}$$ *(2 marks)*

b   Your fitness grade can be worked out from your fitness index, F, using this table.

Fitness index, F	less than 50	50 to 59	60 to 69	70 to 79	80 to 89	$\geqslant 90$
Fitness grade	Very poor	Poor	Fair	Good	Excellent	Superb

What is Terry's fitness grade?   *(1 mark)*

AQA 2009

10 Probability

Objectives

Examiners would normally expect students who get these grades to be able to:

G

understand and use the vocabulary of probability

F

understand and use a probability scale

express a probability as a fraction

display outcomes systematically

E

understand the differences between experimental and theoretical probability

D

use a two-way table to find a probability

understand mutually exclusive events

identify different mutually exclusive events and know, if they cover all possibilities, then the sum of their probabilities is 1

C

use probability to estimate outcomes for a population

understand and use relative frequency.

Key terms

probability	event
outcome	two-way table
impossible	sample space diagram
unlikely	mutually exclusive event
evens	theoretical probability
fair	trial
likely	experimental probability
certain	relative frequency
probability scale	biased

Did you know?

Insurance

Have you ever thought how insurance companies decide what to charge?

To insure a driver for accidents the insurance company needs to know or estimate:

- the probability a driver will have an accident
- the likely cost of an accident to the insurance company.

Think about the factors that affect the answers to these points.

These include the:

- age of driver (younger drivers have more accidents)
- size and type of car.

Can you think of other factors?
You can see that insurance is a complicated business and is full of statistics!

You should already know:

✔ how to cancel a fraction to its simplest form using a calculator

✔ how to add and subtract fractions using a calculator

✔ how to add and subtract decimals using a calculator

✔ how to convert between fractions, decimals and percentages.

Learn... 10.1 Describing probability

Probability words

Probability is all about how likely a particular **outcome** is.

Words can be used to describe probability.

The words you need to know are:

Impossible an outcome that could not happen
e.g. a cow passes GCSE English

Unlikely an outcome that most of the time would not happen
e.g. it snows in May in London

Evens an outcome that has an equal chance of happening or not
e.g. a **fair** coin lands showing heads

Likely an outcome that most of the time would happen
e.g. you have a hot meal during the day

Certain an outcome that will always happen
e.g. you will be older next year than you are now.

Other words can sometimes be added to these such as very unlikely and very likely.

A very unlikely outcome is one which is hardly ever going to happen but is not actually impossible, e.g. it will not rain in England for a whole month.

> **Study tip**
>
> If a question in the exam requires the use of words to describe probability, then you will be specifically asked to use words such as impossible and unlikely.

Probability scales

Numerical values for probability give more information than the probability words.

- An outcome that is impossible has a probability of 0.
- An outcome that is certain has a probability of 1.
- All other probability values lie between 0 and 1.

Fractions or decimals are the best way of showing probabilities.

Percentages are also sometimes used.

> **Study tip**
>
> Never use words such as 3 out of 10, or ratios such as 3 : 10, to describe probability. This always scores no marks. You must use fractions ($\frac{3}{10}$), decimals (0.3) or percentages (30%).

A **probability scale** can be used to show probability words and values.

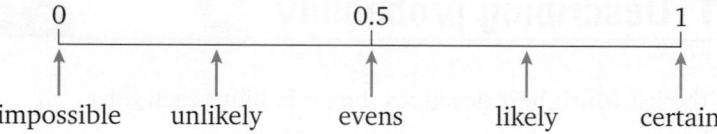

Example: On a probability scale, place an arrow to indicate the probability of each **event**.

W you get an even number when you roll an ordinary fair dice

X you get wet the next time you have a shower

Y you write a book when you are asleep

Z your teacher's birthday is in a month beginning with J

> **Study tip**
>
> The words ordinary fair dice are used in exams to indicate it is a six-sided dice numbered 1, 2, 3, 4, 5, 6 with each score equally likely.

Solution:

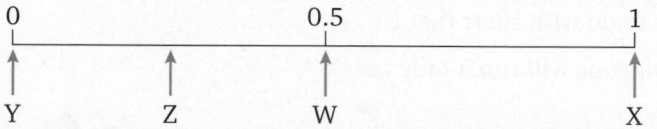

W when you roll an ordinary fair dice there is an equal chance of getting an even number or not getting an even number so the probability is 0.5

X you will always get wet when you have a shower so the probability is 1

Y it is impossible to write a book when you are asleep so the probability is 0

Z there are only three months in the year which begin with J so your teacher's birthday is unlikely to be in a month beginning with J

Calculating probabilities

The probability of an event happening = $\dfrac{\text{number of outcomes for that event}}{\text{total number of possible outcomes}}$

Example: A letter is chosen at random from the word RANDOMNESS.

What is the probability that the letter is:

a   an S

b   a vowel?

Note that 'P(S)' can be used as a quick way of writing 'the probability of an S'. You don't need this for the exam, but it can save you time.

Solution: When a letter is chosen at random, each one of the 10 letters has an equal chance of being chosen.

a   Probability of an event happening = $\dfrac{\text{number of outcomes for that event}}{\text{total number of possible outcomes}}$

Probability of an S = $\dfrac{2}{10}$ ⟶ there are 2 Ss in the word 'randomness'
⟶ there are 10 letters in the word 'randomness'

Study tip

You might be asked to give your answer in its simplest form. Otherwise, you do not need to cancel fractions down.

b   Probability of an event happening = $\dfrac{\text{number of outcomes for that event}}{\text{total number of possible outcomes}}$

Probability of a vowel = $\dfrac{3}{10}$ ⟶ there are 3 vowels in the word randomness (a, o and e)
⟶ there are 10 letters in the word randomness

Practise...   10.1 Describing probability

G

1   Choose the word from the list which best describes the probability each time.

IMPOSSIBLE   UNLIKELY   EVENS   LIKELY   CERTAIN

a   You will be younger on your next birthday.

b   It will be sunny on Christmas Day this year.

c   A black counter is taken out of a bag with 10 black and 10 white counters.

d   You will marry an earwig when you are older.

2   Write down a statement to do with sport that is:

a   impossible (e.g. someone will run a mile in under a minute)

b   unlikely

c   likely

d   certain.

3 Make a copy of this probability scale.

0   0.5   1

Put arrows on the scale with letters a, b, c, and d for the events in Question 1.

4 An ordinary fair dice is rolled.

Find the probability of rolling each of the following.

> **Study tip**
>
> Use fractions for answers on questions like these (Q4 and Q5). Decimals or percentages will make it far harder to score marks for accuracy.

a A five   **c** A number less than 4

b A one   **d** An odd number

5 A card is picked at random from a standard pack of 52 cards.

Find the probability of picking the following.

a A red card

b A black nine

> **Hint**
>
> A pack of cards has two red suits, hearts and diamonds, and two black suits, clubs and spades. Every suit has an ace, 2, 3, 4, 5, 6, 7, 8, 9, 10, jack, queen and king.

c An ace

d The six of clubs

6 Quinlan has a set of cards numbered 1 to 100.

He picks one of these cards at random.

Find the probability of picking the following.

a A card with 34 on it   **c** A card with a 9 on it

b A card with a number greater than 80 on it   **d** A card without a 9 on it

7 Ross has 5 red marbles and 11 white marbles in a bag.

a If he picks a marble at random, what is the probability that it is red?

b What is the probability that it is not red?

c Jamie adds 4 black marbles to the bag and says 'The probability of getting a black marble is $\frac{4}{16}$'
Explain why he is wrong.

d What is the probability of picking a black marble from the bag?
Give your answer in its simplest form.

8 Jack has 30 marbles. Some are blue, some are yellow and some are grey.

He picks a marble at random.

The probability that he will pick a blue marble is 0.4
The probability that he will pick a yellow marble is 0.1

a How many blue marbles does he have?

b How many yellow marbles does he have?

c What is the probability that he will pick a grey marble?

9 There are some discs in a large bag.

There are three times as many black discs as blue.

There are twice as many blue discs as red.

A disc is taken from the bag at random.

What is the probability of picking a red disc at random?

Learn... 10.2 Combining events

Sometimes more than one event can happen at the same time.

You can use lists or **two-way tables** to help you work out these probabilities.

A table showing all possible outcomes is known as a **sample space diagram**. In the exam this sort of diagram will always be referred to as a two-way table.

> **Study tip**
>
> In the exam this sort of diagram will always be referred to as a two-way table.

Example: Tracey buys a drink and an ice cream from a shop.

The drinks available are Orange juice (O), Lemonade (L) and Water (W).

The ice creams available are Vanilla (V), Strawberry (S) and Chocolate (C).

a   Make a list of the possible combinations of drink and ice cream.

b   Show the same information in a table.

c   Find the probability of Tracey buying:

    i   lemonade and strawberry ice cream

    ii   orange juice and an ice cream other than vanilla.

d   What assumptions do you make for these probabilities?

Solution: **a**   Be systematic (this means try to use an organised method) and list the options by letter.

    OV   OS   OC   LV   LS   LC   WV   WS   WC

b   Using a two-way table reduces the chances of missing one out.

> **Study tip**
>
> Remember to be systematic when you complete a two-way table in an exam. This will help you to avoid making mistakes and to work out the correct probabilities.

	Vanilla	Strawberry	Chocolate
Orange juice	OV	OS	OC
Lemonade	LV	LS	LC
Water	WV	WS	WC

c   **i**   The table shows there are nine possible combinations of drink and ice cream.

Lemonade and strawberry ice cream is one of these nine.

Probability $= \dfrac{1}{9}$

ii   The options are OS or OC.

This is two out of the nine options.

Probability $= \dfrac{2}{9}$

d   You have to assume that all the options are equally likely to be chosen.

This means that Tracey must like all the options and not have a favourite.

In real life this is unlikely.

Tracey does not like vanilla ice cream.

Vanilla ice cream now has no chance of being picked and is not an equally likely choice.

Practise... 10.2 Combining events

D

1   Trevor is having lunch at his office restaurant. He chooses a sandwich and a piece of fruit.

The sandwich choice is ham (H), beef (B), cheese (C) or egg (E).

The fruit choice is apple (A), orange (O) or pear (P).

a   Make a list of the combinations of sandwich and fruit Trevor could choose.

b   Show this information in a table.

c   What is the probability that Trevor chooses the following?

   i   a ham sandwich and an apple

   ii   an egg sandwich

d   What assumption did you make in answering part **c**?

e   Do you think this assumption is valid? Explain your answer.

> **Hint**
>
> Remember to be systematic. First list all combinations where ham is the sandwich choice, then all when beef is the sandwich choice, and so on.

2   Two ordinary fair dice are rolled.

The scores on each dice are added together.

a   Copy and complete the two-way table.

b   Use the table to find the probability that the total is:

   i   2   **iii**   more than 9

   ii   4   **iv**   even.

	1	2	3	4	5	6
1	2	3	4	5		
2	3	4	5			
3	4	5				
4	5					
5						
6						

3   Two ordinary fair dice are rolled.

The scores on each dice are multiplied together.

a   Construct a two-way table to show all the possible totals.

b   Use the table to find the probability that the total is:

   i   1   **iii**   less than 10

   ii   12   **iv**   odd.

C

4   Lucy says that if you flip two coins, the possible outcomes are two heads, two tails or one of each. She therefore decides that the probability of getting two heads is $\frac{1}{3}$

Explain why Lucy is wrong.

5   Use your answer to Question 4 to help in this question.

Three coins are flipped.

What is the probability of getting two heads and a tail in any order?

6   Amy is trying to persuade her parents to double her pocket money if, when she rolls two dice, the total is a prime number.

Her parents suggest the money is doubled when the total is a square number.

Should Amy accept her parents' suggestion?

7   Two dice are rolled and their scores added to give a total.

The probability of a total of X is $\frac{1}{9}$

What are the two possible values for X?

> **Hint**
>
> You may find your answer to Q2 helpful in answering this.

Learn... 10.3 Mutually exclusive events

Mutually exclusive events are events that cannot happen at the same time.

For example, the following events are mutually exclusive.

- Getting a head and getting a tail when a coin is flipped once.
- Getting a three and getting an even number when a dice is rolled once.
- Sleeping and running the marathon at the same time.
- Flying a plane and swimming the English Channel at the same time.

Other events are not mutually exclusive and can happen at the same time.

For example, the following events are not mutually exclusive.

- Getting a four and getting an even number when a dice is rolled.
- Getting a red card and getting an Ace when a card is taken from a pack.
- Driving a car and listening to the radio.
- Eating a meal and watching TV.

> **Study tip**
>
> In the examination the words 'mutually exclusive' will not be used.
>
> However, you need to understand how events happening at the same time affect probabilities.

In any given probability situation, the total probability is always 1.

More accurately, you can say that if mutually exclusive events cover all the possibilities the sum of their probabilities total 1.

Example: 10 discs are placed in a bag.

They are labelled X1, X2, X3, X4, Y1, Y2, Y3, Y4, Z1 and Z2.

One disc is picked at random.

Work out the probability of picking the following.

a   A disc with an X on it

b   A disc without an X on it

c   A disc with a 3 on it

d   A disc without a 3 on it

e   A disc with an X or a 3 on it

Solution: **a**   Probability of an event happening = $\dfrac{\text{number of outcomes for that event}}{\text{total number of possible outcomes}}$

Probability of picking an X = $\dfrac{4}{10}$ → there are 4 discs with an X on
→ there are 10 discs altogether

b   Probability of an event happening = $\dfrac{\text{number of outcomes for that event}}{\text{total number of possible outcomes}}$

Probability of not picking an X = $\dfrac{6}{10}$ → there are 6 discs without an X on
→ there are 10 discs altogether

Alternatively, if mutually exclusive events cover all the possibilities, their probabilities total 1.

Here every disc has to be either an X or not an X.

The probability of picking an X + the probability of not picking an X = 1.

So, the probability of not picking an X = 1 − the probability of picking an X.

Probability of not picking an X = $1 - \dfrac{4}{10} = \dfrac{6}{10}$

c   Probability of an event happening = $\dfrac{\text{number of outcomes for that event}}{\text{total number of possible outcomes}}$

Probability of a 3 = $\dfrac{2}{10}$ → there are 2 discs with a 3 on
→ there are 10 discs altogether

d $1 - \dfrac{2}{10} = \dfrac{8}{10}$ (probability of not picking a 3 is $1 -$ probability of picking a 3)

e   The probability of picking a disc with an X or a 3 on is not $\dfrac{4}{10} + \dfrac{2}{10}$

This would count the X3 disc twice!

This confirms that only mutually exclusive probabilities can be added.

Here you must use the list. Out of the ten possible outcomes, there are five discs with either an X or a 3 on them.

X1, X2, X3, X4, Y3

So the probability is $\dfrac{5}{10}$

> **Study tip**
>
> None of the answers in the example are simplified, as simplest form was not asked for.
> If the question in the exam does not ask you to provide an answer in its simplest form, then there is no need to cancel.

Practise... 10.3 Mutually exclusive events   G F E D C

1   Which of these pairs of dice events could not happen at the same time?

   a   Roll a 1 and roll a number less than 5

   b   Roll a 2 and roll an odd number

   c   Roll an even number and roll an odd number

   d   Roll a number more than 3 and a number less than 4

2   The probability that Georgina will wear black on a Saturday is 0.95

   What is the probability that Georgina will not wear black on a Saturday?

3   The probability that Mike will have fish and chips for dinner is 0.07

   What is the probability that Mike will not have fish and chips for dinner?

4   The probability that Toni will not drink tea at work is 0.001

   What is the probability that Toni will drink tea at work?

5   Losalot Town are playing in a football tournament.

   Here are some probabilities for the outcome of their opening match.

   Complete the table.

Probability of winning	Probability of drawing	Probability of losing
$\dfrac{1}{10}$	$\dfrac{1}{5}$	

> **Study tip**
>
> Remember that you can use a calculator in this unit.
> There is no point trying to answer these questions without one!

C

6   A bag contains coloured discs.

Each disc also has a letter on it.

There are 5 red discs D, E, F, G and H.

There are 8 blue discs D, E, F, G, H, I, J and K.

There are 2 yellow discs D and E.

Work out the probability of picking a disc that:

a   is red   **d**   is red or has an E on it

b   has an E on it   **e**   is yellow or has an F on it

c   does not have an E on it   **f**   is blue or has an H on it.

7   Errol goes out to buy a new sweatshirt.

The probability that he buys it from Supershirts is $\dfrac{9}{20}$

The probability that he buys it from BestSweats is $\dfrac{2}{5}$

What is the probability that he buys it from either one of these stores?

8   A local council is looking at traffic flow at a busy junction.

The approach to the junction has three lanes.

The table shows the probability of a car being in a given lane.

Lane	Probability
Left	0.39
Centre	0.06
Right	

a   Work out the probability of a car being in the right hand lane.

The probability of a car containing a single person is 0.77

b   Explain why the probability of a car with a single person being in the centre is **not** 0.83

c   Complete this table.

Lane	Single person	More than one person
Left	0.33	
Centre	0.05	
Right		

> **Hint**
>
> The events 'a car with a single person in' and 'a car with more than one person in' are mutually exclusive.

9   Of the people attending a festival, one is chosen at random to win a prize.

The probability the chosen person is male is 0.515

The probability the chosen person is married is 0.048

The probability the chosen person is a married male is 0.029

What is the probability the chosen person is an unmarried female?

10   A bag contains shapes which are coloured.

The probability of a red square is 0.2

The probability of a red shape is 0.2

Write down one fact about the shapes in the bag.

 **Learn...   10.4 Relative frequency**

The probabilities so far have all been theoretical probabilities.

Theoretical probability is the probability of an event based on expectation (or theory).

A probability experiment is a test in which a number of **trials** are performed.

Experimental probability is the probability of an event based on testing (or experiment). The experimental probability is also called the **relative frequency**.

Example: Niles rolls an ordinary dice 120 times.

His results are shown in the table.

Score	1	2	3	4	5	6
Frequency	17	18	24	22	25	14

a   Work out the relative frequency for each score.

b   How many of each score would you expect if the dice was fair?

c   Do you think the dice is fair? Explain your answer.

d   Estimate the probability of scoring a two on this dice.

Solution: a   Relative frequency of an event $= \dfrac{\text{number of times an event has happened}}{\text{total number of trials}}$

The score of 1 happened 17 times out of 120.

This means the relative frequency of a 1 is $\dfrac{17}{120}$

The remaining relative frequencies are shown in the extended table.

Score	1	2	3	4	5	6
Frequency	17	18	24	22	25	14
Relative Frequency	$\dfrac{17}{120}$	$\dfrac{18}{120}$	$\dfrac{24}{120}$	$\dfrac{22}{120}$	$\dfrac{25}{120}$	$\dfrac{14}{120}$

b   You would expect **about** 20 of each number if the dice is fair $\left(120 \times \frac{1}{6}\right)$.

(You can rarely get exactly what you expect in an actual experiment.)

c   The dice looks like it is **not** fair.

The values are reasonably close to the expected value of 20.

It is highly unlikely it would be exactly 20.

Indeed if the same experiment is repeated it would probably give different results even if the dice was fair.

d   The experimental results give an estimate of the probability of rolling a 2 as $\dfrac{18}{120}$

Since these results are close to the expected outcome, the dice appears to be fair.

On a fair dice the theoretical probability of rolling a 2 is actually $\dfrac{1}{6}$

> *Study tip*
>
> Relative frequencies should always be given as fractions or decimals. Giving the frequencies will often score zero.

The more times you carry out an experiment, the more reliable the results will be.

What if Niles had only rolled the dice 20 times?

It would be impossible to tell if the dice was **biased** or to use the results for estimating.

This idea can be shown on a relative frequency graph.

Example: When Niles rolled the dice, he kept a record of the number of 2s every 10 throws.

Here are his results.

Number of throws	10	20	30	40	50	60	70	80	90	100	110	120
Number of 2s	1	5	8	10	10	12	13	13	15	15	16	18

a   Find the relative frequency after every 10 throws.

b   Draw a line graph to show these results.

c   What can you see from the graph?

Solution: **a**   After 10 throws there had been one 2 giving a relative frequency of $\frac{1}{10} = 0.1$

After 20 throws there had been five 2s giving a relative frequency of $\frac{5}{20} = 0.25 \ldots$

Number of throws	10	20	30	40	50	60	70	80	90	100	110	120
Number of 2s	1	5	8	10	10	12	13	13	15	15	16	18
Relative frequency	0.1	0.25	0.27	0.25	0.2	0.2	0.19	0.16	0.17	0.15	0.15	0.15

b

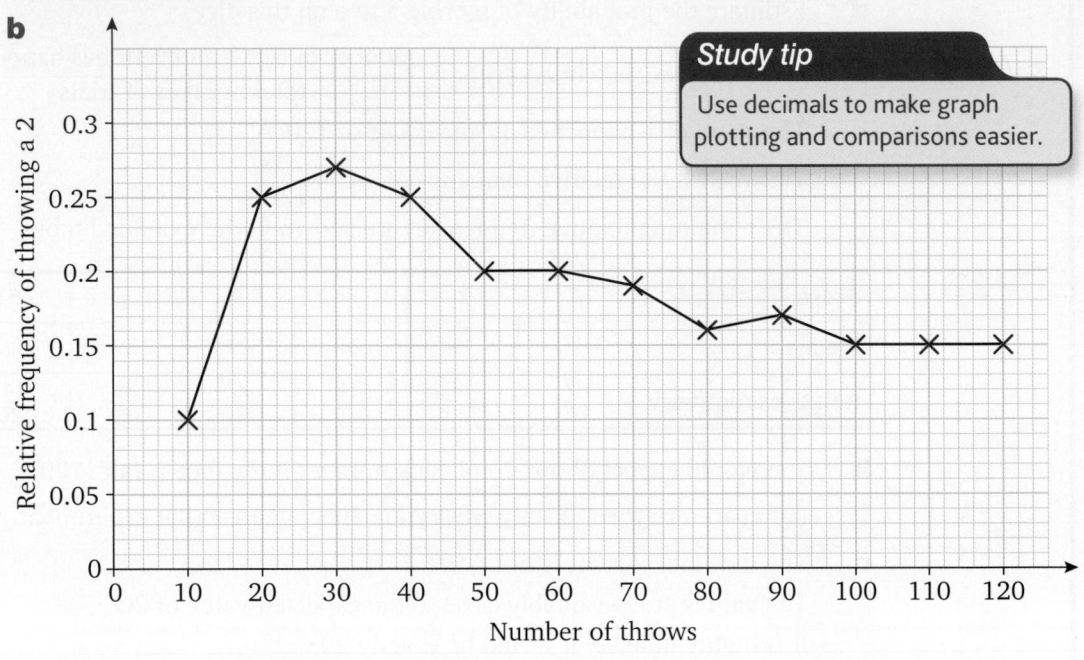

> **Study tip**
>
> Use decimals to make graph plotting and comparisons easier.

c   Early on in the experiment the line is unpredictable (it seems to vary a lot).

Any relative frequency used to estimate theoretical probability would be unreliable (you could not be sure it was a good estimate).

After a while the graph settles down.

This shows that more results leads to better estimates of theoretical probability.

Practise...   10.4 Relative frequency   G F E D C

E

1   A dice is rolled 100 times. A six appears on one quarter of these rolls.

What is the relative frequency of a six?

2   A spinner is spun 200 times. 'Red' appears 25 times.

What is the relative frequency of 'red'?

3 Alan rolls an ordinary fair dice 600 times.

a How many times would he expect to get a five?

b Would you expect to see exactly this number occurring?
Give a reason for your answer.

4 Ruth flips a coin 240 times.

a How many times would she expect to get a tail?

b She actually gets 109 tails.
Do you think the coin is biased?
Give a reason for your answer.

5 A fair spinner with five equal divisions labelled A, B, C, D, E is spun 100 times.

a How many times would you expect it to land on A?

b How many times would you expect it to land on D?

c Julie spins the spinner 10 times and gets 2 As, 3 Bs, no Cs and 5 Ds.
She says this shows the spinner is biased. Is she correct?
Explain your answer.

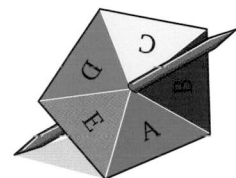

6 Over a long period of time it is found that the probability of a faulty light bulb is 0.01

a How many light bulbs would you expect to be faulty in a batch of 500?

b One day, a light bulb checker finds 17 faulty bulbs.
Estimate how many bulbs she has checked that day.

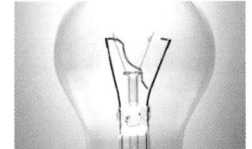

7 The table shows the frequency distribution after drawing a card from a pack 40 times. The card is put back after each draw.

Results from 40 draws			
	Club	Heart	Diamond	Spade
Frequency	9	9	12	10

a What is the relative frequency of getting a heart?

b What is the relative frequency of getting a red card?

c What is the theoretical probability of getting a club?

d Ciaron says 'If you drew a card out 80 times you would probably get twice as many of each suit.' Explain why Ciaron is wrong.

8 Kali has a spinner with coloured sections of equal size.

She wants to know the probability that her spinner lands on pink.

She spins it 100 times and calculates the relative frequency of pink after every 10 spins.

Her results are shown on the graph.

a Use the graph to calculate the number of times the spinner landed on pink:

  i after the first 10 spins

  ii after the first 50 spins.

b From the graph, estimate the probability of the spinner landing on pink.

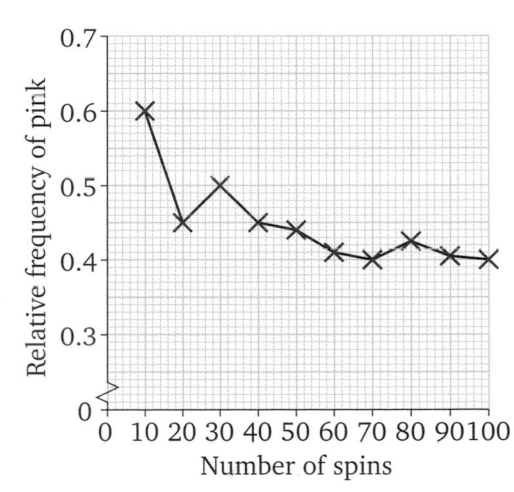

9   Izzy is rolling a dice.

After every 10 throws she works out the relative frequency of a score of 1.

The diagram shows the relative frequency throughout the experiment.

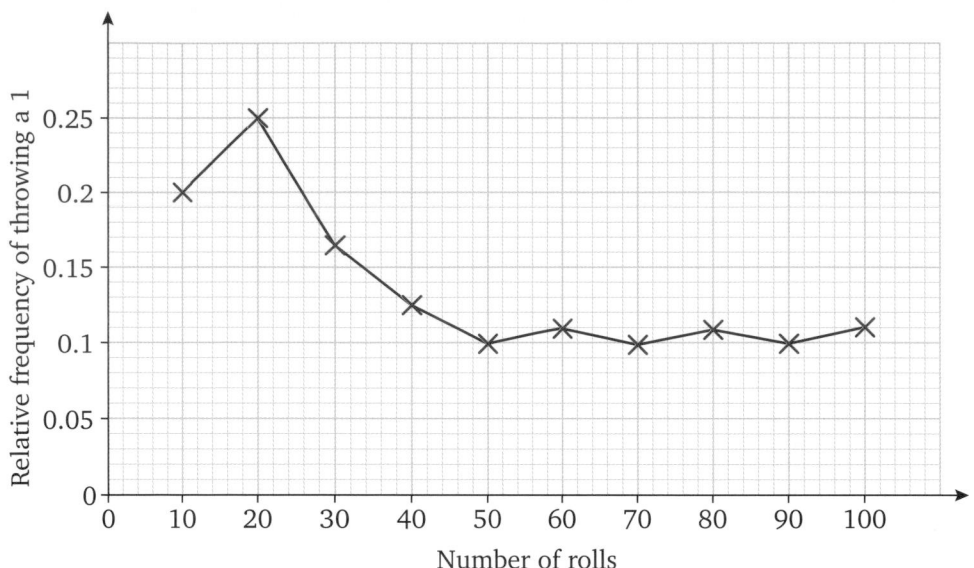

a   After 20 throws, how many 1s had there been?

b   How many 1s were there between the 21st and 50th throws?

c   Do you think this dice is biased? Explain your answer.

10   The table shows the frequency distribution after throwing a dice 270 times.

Results from 270 throws of dice					
1	**2**	**3**	**4**	**5**	**6**
52	56	41	37	45	39

(Frequency row label: **Frequency**)

a   What is the relative frequency of getting a 2?

b   What is the relative frequency of getting a score greater than 4?

c   What is the relative frequency of getting an even number?

d   Ellie says the relative frequency of getting a score less than 3 is $\frac{149}{270}$
Is this correct? Explain your answer.

e   Which one of the frequencies is the same as the result you would expect from theoretical probability?

11   A fair spinner is made from a regular octagon.

Each of the eight sections of the spinner has one of the letters P, Q, R, S.

It is spun 240 times and the results are shown in the table.

Results from 240 spins			
P	**Q**	**R**	**S**
34	62	88	56

(Frequency row label: **Frequency**)

How many times does each letter appear on the spinner?

10 Assess

1 Mark the probabilities of the events shown below on a probability scale like this one.

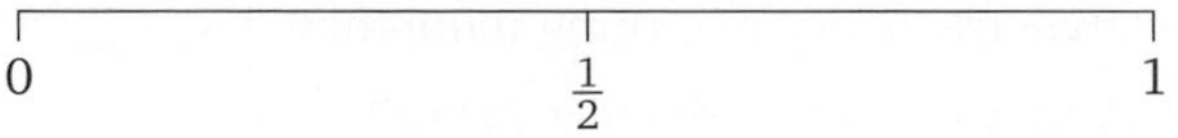

```
┌─────────────────┬─────────────────┐
0                 ½                 1
```

a The probability of obtaining a tail when a fair coin is flipped.

b The probability of scoring more than four when a fair six-sided dice is rolled.

c The probability of taking a green ball out of a bag containing 9 green and 3 red balls.

d The probability that you will need to breathe tomorrow.

e The probability that a card picked from a standard pack will be a heart.

f The probability that a number picked at random from the list: 1, 3, 5, 7, 9 will be even.

2 Work out the probability of:

a obtaining a 5 when an ordinary fair dice is rolled

b selecting an 8 from a standard pack of cards

c picking an even number from a bag containing the first 21 whole numbers

d picking an M from a bag containing the letters of the word ALUMINIUM.

3 Here are three of the longest words in the English language.

ANTIDISESTABLISHMENTARIANISM

FLOCCINUACINIHILIPILIFICATION

PNEUMONOULTRAMICROSCOPICSILICOVOLCANOCONIOSIS

A letter is picked at random from each of these words.
Which word has the greatest probabilty of having a letter I picked at random?

> **Hint**
> Use your calculator to convert to decimals.

4 In the UK the probability of being left handed is about 0.11

How many left-handed people would you expect to find in the following?

a A class of 33 children.

b A street of 132 people.

c A town of 55 000 people.

5 Two pentagonal spinners, each with the numbers 1 to 5, are spun and their outcomes added together to give a score.

a Draw a two-way table for the two spinners.

b Use your diagram to find:

   i the probability of a score of 4

   ii the probability of a score of 5

   iii the probability of a score of 9

   iv the most likely score.

c Repeat parts **a** and **b** for a score that is the outcomes **multiplied** together.

C

6 A fair six-sided dice is thrown 250 times and the following results obtained.

Score	1	2	3	4	5	6
Frequency	45	48	43	40	38	36

a What is the relative frequency of a score of 1?

b What is the relative frequency of a score of 6?

c What is the relative frequency of scoring more than 3?

d How do these data confirm that the dice is fair?

e Draw a new table with possible frequencies if this dice was thrown 6000 times.

7 The table below shows the probabilities of selecting tickets from a bag.

The tickets are coloured yellow, black or green and numbered 1, 2, 3 or 4.

	1	2	3	4
Yellow	$\frac{1}{20}$	$\frac{1}{16}$	$\frac{3}{40}$	$\frac{1}{8}$
Black	$\frac{1}{10}$	$\frac{3}{40}$	0	$\frac{3}{40}$
Green	0	$\frac{1}{8}$	$\frac{3}{16}$	$\frac{1}{8}$

A ticket is taken at random from the bag.

Calculate the probability that:

a it is green and numbered 2

b it is black

c it is not green

d it is yellow or numbered 4.

8 A bag contains red, white, blue and green counters.
A counter is picked at random from the bag.
The probability of picking a red counter is 0.5
The probability of picking a white counter is 0.1
The probability of picking a red or blue counter is 0.7

What is the probability of picking a green counter?

9 In a game a play can choose to roll one dice or two dice.
The player needs to score 5 to win.

Should the player choose to throw one dice or two?

Practice questions **k**

1 The spinner has eight equal sections.

Each section of this spinner has the number 1, 2, 3 or 4 in it.

All the numbers appear on the spinner.

Copy the diagram and write the numbers in the sections so that:
1 is the most likely score
4 is the least likely score
2 and 3 are equally likely scores.

(3 marks)

AQA 2008

Objectives

Examiners would normally expect students who get these grades to be able to:

G

select congruent shapes

measure a line accurately to the nearest millimetre

F

use simple scale drawings

measure and draw an angle to the nearest degree

E

understand congruence and similarity

use scales, such as a scale on a map

draw scale drawings

draw a triangle given three sides, or two sides and the included angle, or two angles and a side

D

draw a quadrilateral such as a kite, parallelogram or rhombus with given measurements

understand that giving the lengths of two sides and a non-included angle may not produce a unique triangle

C

construct perpendicular bisectors and angle bisectors.

Did you know?

This type of mathematics is part of geometry and is very old

The ancient Greek mathematician Euclid is the inventor of geometry. He did this over 2000 years ago, and his book 'Elements' is still the ultimate geometry reference. He used construction techniques extensively. They give us a method of drawing things when simple measurement is not appropriate.

Key terms

arc
construction (construct)
equilateral triangle
perpendicular
bisector
vertex
scale
similar
congruent

You should already know:

✔ how to draw and measure a line

✔ how to measure an angle

✔ how to use a pair of compasses to draw arcs and circles

✔ how to write ratios and reduce them to their simplest form

✔ how to convert between metric units

✔ how to recognise and draw enlargements of shapes

✔ the names of common quadrilaterals

✔ facts about common quadrilaterals

✔ the names of different types of triangle

✔ facts about right-angled triangles.

Learn... 11.1 Drawing triangles accurately

There are different ways to draw a triangle accurately. The method you use depends on what you know about the triangle.

Drawing a triangle when all three sides are known

The following example shows how to draw a triangle when all three sides are known.

Example: Draw a triangle with sides 4.2 cm, 5.3 cm and 6 cm.

Solution: First draw a sketch to see what the triangle looks like.

This gives you an idea of what the finished triangle will look like and where to start on your page.

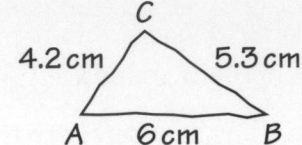

Draw and measure the line *AB* using a ruler and pencil. You should clearly mark end points on the line. Make sure you have enough space to draw the rest of the triangle.

Use your compasses to draw an **arc** of radius 5.3 cm with centre *B*.

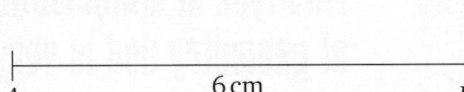

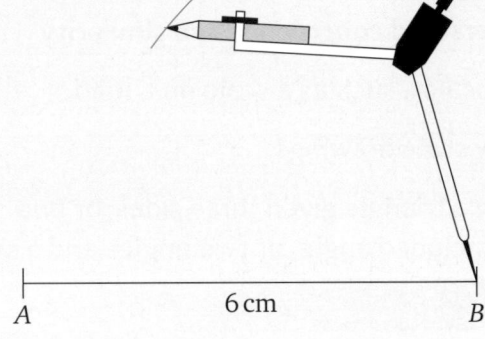

Use your compasses to draw an *arc* of radius 4.2 cm with centre *A*. Make sure your arcs cross each other.

Point *C* is where the two arcs cross. Join *C* to *A* and *C* to *B*. Label the sides with their lengths.

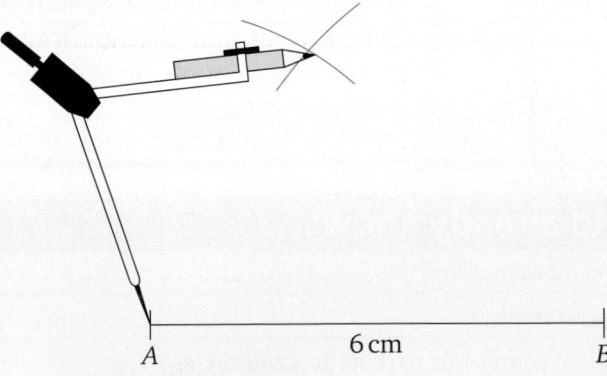

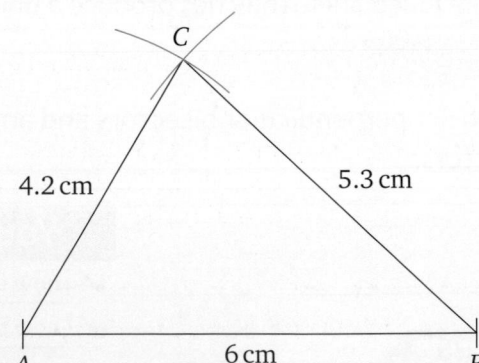

Drawing a triangle when one side and two angles are known

The following example shows how to draw a triangle when one side and two angles are known.

Example: Draw the following triangle accurately.

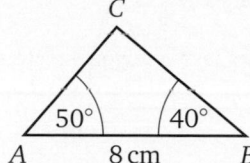

Solution: A diagram has been provided as part of the question, so there is no need to sketch a diagram.

Start by measuring and drawing the line *AB*.

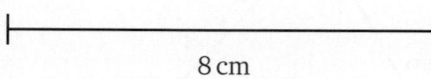

8 cm

Use a protractor to measure an angle of 50° at point *A*. Mark the point and then join it to point *A*. Extend the line beyond the point you have marked. It is much better to have a line that is too long than too short.

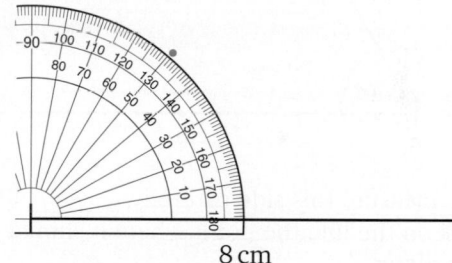

8 cm

> **Study tip**
>
> It is best to draw the two angles from either end of the given side. If one of these angles is the angle not given, then you can work out its size using the fact that angles of a triangle add up to 180°.

Repeat for the other angle (40°).

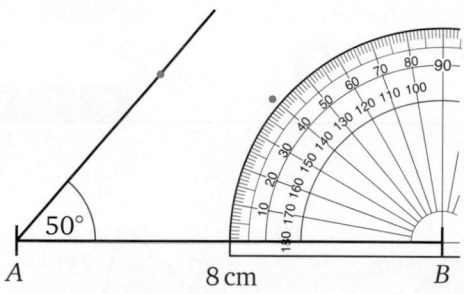

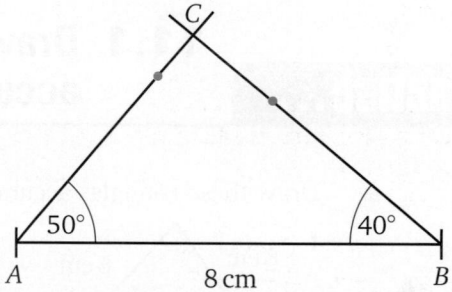

Now draw a line from *B*, so that angle *CBA* is 40°. Draw this line long enough so that it crosses the line drawn from *A*. Where these lines cross is point *C*.

Label the triangle with two known angles and one known side.

Drawing a triangle when one angle and two sides are known

The following example shows how to draw a triangle when one angle and two sides are known.

Example: Draw the following triangle accurately.

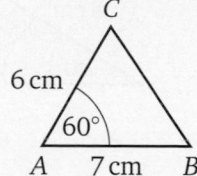

Solution:

Start with the longest side, *AB*.

Measure the angle given, using a protractor.

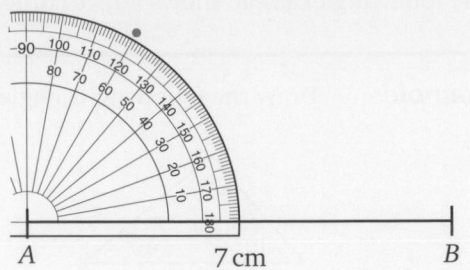

Draw in the side and remember to make it long enough. As before, it is better too long than too short.

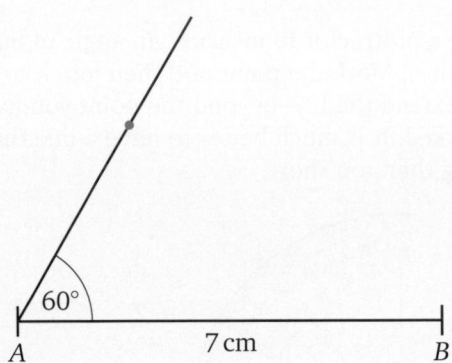

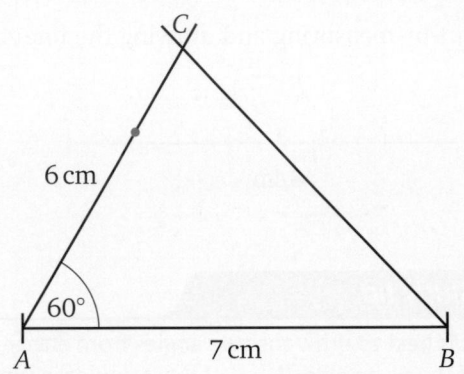

Now measure this side carefully.
Mark on the line the point where it should end 6 cm along.

Draw a line from this point to *B*. Label the triangle with the sides and angles you know.

11.1 Drawing triangles accurately

G F E D C

Practise...

1 **a** Draw these triangles accurately.

i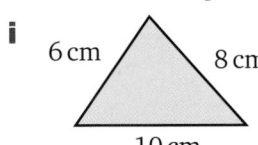

ii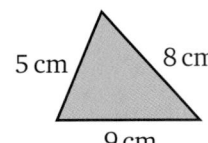

iii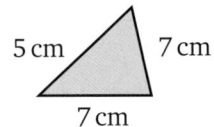

b Measure the angles in your diagrams and check they add up to 180°.

2 Jack and Jill are asked to draw a triangle with sides of length 4 cm, 5 cm and 10 cm.
Jack says that he can draw this triangle. Jill says the triangle cannot be drawn.

Who is correct? Give a reason for your answer.

3 **a** Draw these triangles accurately.

i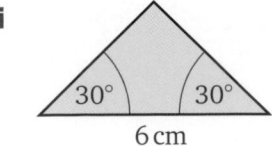

ii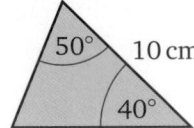

iii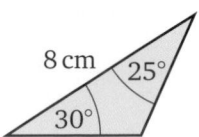

b Measure the third angle in each triangle.
Check the angles in each triangle add up to 180°.

4 Draw this triangle accurately.

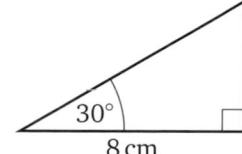

5 Draw this shape accurately.

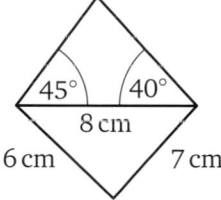

6 Bill and Ben have been asked to draw this triangle accurately.

• The triangle has sides of 8 cm, 5 cm and a non-included angle of 30°.

They both draw it correctly, but their drawings look different.

Can you draw both Bill and Ben's diagrams?

7 Draw a rhombus accurately which has all sides equal to 6 cm and a shorter diagonal of 7 cm.

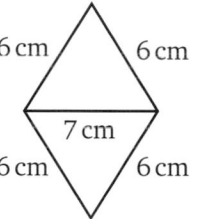

8 John is making a triangular prism from card.

Draw an accurate net for his prism.

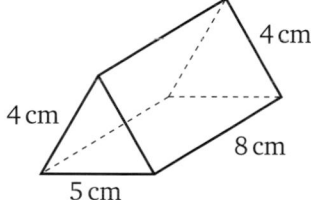

9 Jackie has a large packet of sweets. It weighs 1 kg. She is going to divide the sweets equally between four of her friends. She wants to make four identical gift boxes from cardboard to contain the sweets.

Design a suitable gift box that she could use for the sweets. Show clearly how she can make the gift box from a flat sheet of card.

Learn... 11.2 Constructions

Constructions are drawn using only a straight edge and a pair of compasses. You need to be able to construct **equilateral triangles**, the **perpendicular** bisector of a line, and angle bisectors.

A **bisector** is a line which cuts something into two equal parts. A line bisector cuts a line into two equal parts. An angle bisector cuts an angle into two equal parts.

Equilateral triangles

The following example shows how to construct an equilateral triangle.

Example: Construct an equilateral triangle.

Solution: Start with a line which will become one of the sides in your triangle, with a point *P*, where one **vertex** will be.

Open your compasses to the length of one side. With the point of your compasses on *P* draw a large arc that intersects the line at *Q*.

Keep the radius of your compasses the same. Put the point of the compasses on *Q* and draw an arc that passes through *P* and cuts the first arc at *R*.

Join *P* to *R*, and *Q* to *R*. You have now finished your construction.

You can use this technique to construct an angle of 60°. Follow the first two steps above, and then just join *P* to *R* (or *R* to *Q*).

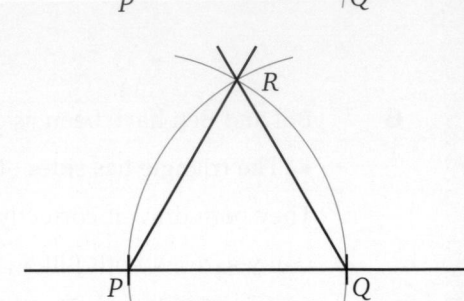

> ### Study tip
> Remember to leave your arcs. They show your method and will score you marks.

Line bisectors

The following example shows how to construct the bisector of a line.

Example: Construct the bisector of line *AB*.

A —————————— B

Solution: Open your compasses to more than half of *AB*. Put the point on *A* and draw arcs above and below *AB*.

Keep the radius of your compasses the same. Put the point of your compasses on *B* and draw two new arcs to cut the first two at *C* and *D*.

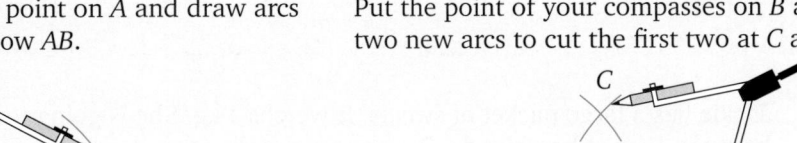

Join *CD*.

X is the midpoint of *AB*. *CD* not only bisects *AB*, it is called the perpendicular bisector of *AB*. This is because it meets *AB* at 90°.

Angle bisectors

The following example shows how to construct the bisector of an angle.

Example: Construct the bisector of angle *BAC*.

Solution:

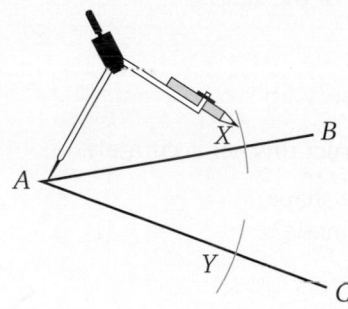 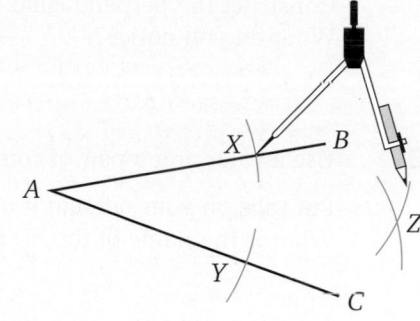

Open your compasses to less than the length of the shorter line. Put the point on *A* and draw arcs to cut *AB* at *X* and *AC* at *Y*.

Keep the radius of your compasses the same. Put the point of your compasses on *X* and *Y* in turn and draw arcs that intersect at *Z*.

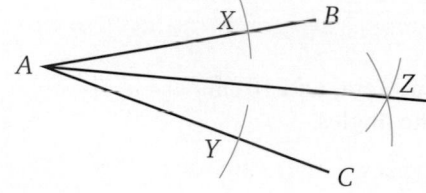

Join *AZ*.
AZ is the angle bisector of angle *BAC*.

To construct an angle of 30° you first construct an angle of 60° (as part of an equilateral triangle) then bisect it.
To construct an angle of 45° you construct an angle of 90°, and then bisect it.
There are lots of other possible angles that can be constructed in a similar way.

Practise...   11.2 Constructions (k)   G F E D C

1   Construct the perpendicular bisector of a line 8 cm long.

2   Draw this rectangle accurately.

Using only a ruler and compasses construct the perpendicular bisector of the diagonal *BD*.

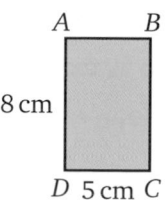

3   Construct an equilateral triangle of side 6 cm.

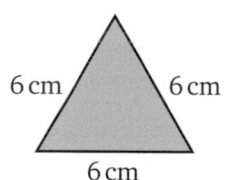

C

4 Draw a line 10 cm long.

    a Construct the perpendicular bisector of your line.

    b Your diagram shows four right angles. Bisect one of them to show an angle of 45°.

5 Accurately draw a triangle with sides 8 cm, 9 cm and 10 cm.
Construct the perpendicular bisector of each of the sides.
What do you notice?

6 Use a ruler and a pair of compasses to construct this net accurately.

Put tabs on your net, cut it out and make the shape.
What is the name of the 3D shape you have made?

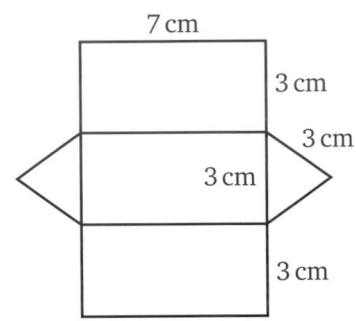

7 Accurately draw a triangle with sides 8 cm, 9 cm, and 10 cm.
Construct the angle bisector for each of the angles.
What do you notice?

⚠ 8 Construct an angle of 60°. Bisect your angle to show an angle of 30°.

⚠ 9 Harvey is asked to construct a perpendicular from a point, *P*, on a line, *l*.

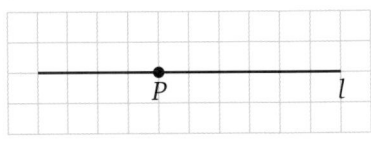

He starts by opening his compasses, and drawing arcs on *l* with the point of the compasses on *P*.

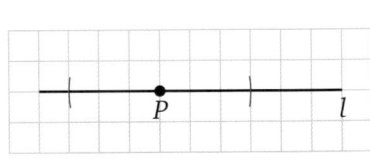

This gives him two points on *l* which are the same distance from *P*. He then opens his compasses a little more and draws arcs above *l*, as shown.

    a What does Harvey need to do next to complete his diagram?

    b Why did Harvey only draw arcs above *l*?

    c Copy and complete Harvey's diagram.

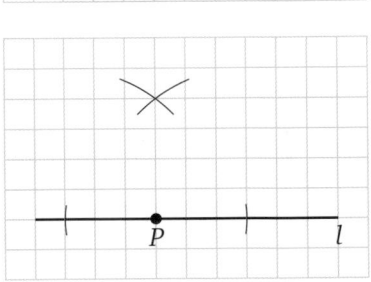

⚠ 10   **a** Construct this rectangle.

    b Label your diagram carefully and draw in the diagonal *AC*.

    c Construct the perpendicular from vertex *B* to the diagonal *AC*.

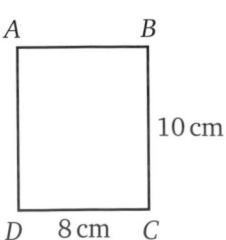

11 Harriet is asked to construct a perpendicular from a point, P, to a line, l.

She opens her compasses and draws an arc crossing l with her compass point on P.

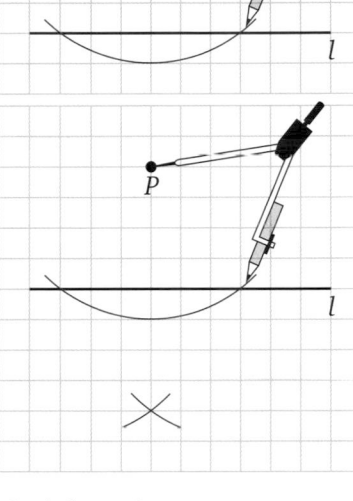

This gives Harriet two points on the line.
She now starts to construct the perpendicular bisector of the line between these points.

a Why does Harriet only need to draw arcs below the line for this last step?

b What does Harriet need to do to complete her diagram?

c Copy and complete Harriet's diagram.

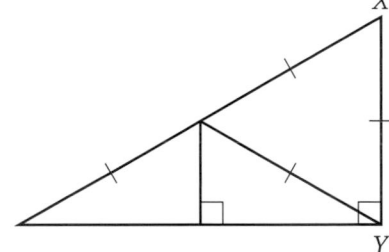

12 Using a ruler and compasses only, construct a right-angled triangle which has a hypotenuse 10 cm long and a shorter side 8 cm long. Measure the third side. You may find it helpful to draw a sketch of the triangle first.

 13 The diagram shows the roof design for a house.

Alan needs an accurate drawing of this roof to order wood from a supplier.

Construct the diagram $XY = 5$ cm.
Measure the width of the base of the roof to the nearest millimetre.

Learn... 11.3 Using scales

If something in real life is too large to draw you can use a **scale** to draw a smaller version.

Scales are used in models, plans and maps.

There are two ways to describe a scale:

- A scale of 1 centimetre to 1 kilometre means that 1 centimetre in the small version represents 1 kilometre in real life.
- A scale of 1 : 1000 means that every centimetre in the smaller version represents 1000 centimetres in real life.

Example: **a** A plan has a scale of 1 centimetre to 5 kilometres. Write the scale as a ratio in its simplest form.

b A map has a scale of 1 : 200 000. What distance is represented by 1 centimetre on the map?

c The distance between two crossroads on a map is 12 centimetres. The distance between the crossroads in real life is 6 kilometres. What is the scale of the map?

d The scale on a map is 1 : 10 000. The distance between a church and a pub on the map is 5.3 centimetres. How far is it from the church to the pub in real life?

Solution:

a 1 centimetre on the plan represents 5 kilometres in real life.

First change the units so they are the same. Change the units from large (km) to small (cm).

5 kilometres = 5 × 1000 = 5000 metres (as there are 1000 metres in 1 kilometre).

5000 metres = 5000 × 100 = 500 000 centimetres (as there are 100 centimetres in 1 metre).

1 centimetre represents 500 000 centimetres in real life.

The scale is 1 : 500 000

b 1 : 200 000 means 1 centimetre on the map represents 200 000 centimetres in real life.

200 000 centimetres = 200 000 ÷ 100 = 2000 metres (as there are 100 centimetres in 1 metre).

2000 metres = 2000 ÷ 1000 = 2 kilometres (as there are 1000 metres in 1 kilometre).

1 centimetre represents 2 kilometres.

c The information in the question tells you that 12 centimetres on the map represents 6 kilometres in real life.

Change the units from large (km) to small (cm).

6 kilometres = 6 × 1000 = 6000 metres (as there are 1000 metres in 1 kilometre).

6000 metres = 6000 × 100 = 600 000 centimetres (as there are 100 centimetres in 1 metre).

12 centimetres represent 600 000 centimetres.

The ratio is 12 : 600 000

This simplifies to 1 : 50 000 (by dividing both parts of the ratio by 12).

d 1 : 10 000 means 1 centimetre on the map represents 10 000 centimetres in real life.

5.3 centimetres on the map represents 5.3 times as far as 1 centimetre.

5.3 × 10 000 = 53 000 centimetres

53 000 centimetres is not a sensible choice of unit, so change to a more sensible one.

53 000 centimetres = 530 metres

Either 530 metres or 0.53 kilometres are sensible choices here.

Practise... 11.3 Using scales

E

1 How many kilometres do these lengths represent on a map that uses a scale of 1 : 70 000?

a 8 cm   **b** 2.8 cm   **c** 8 mm

2 A map uses a scale of 1 : 25 000

Calculate the length on the map that represents a distance of:

a 20 km   **b** 65.2 km   **c** 400 m.

3 A plan is drawn using a scale of 1 : 400

a A path on the plan has a length of 4.5 centimetres.
How long is the actual path?

b A garden is 80 metres long in real life.
What is the length of the garden on the plan?

4 A map has a scale of 1 : 20 000

a How long is a road which measures 7.5 centimetres on the map?

b A field is 400 metres long. How long is this field on the map?

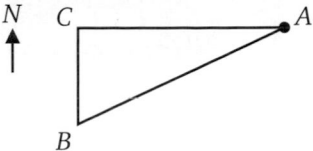

5 A, B, C, are three points. B is 3 kilometres due south of C, and A is 4 kilometres due east of C.

a Draw an accurate scale drawing showing the positions of A, B, and C. Use a scale of 1 : 50 000

b Measure the distance from A to B on the plan.

c What is the actual distance from A to B?

6 A ladder leans against a wall. The ladder reaches 5.5 metres up the wall and its base is 3.1 metres from the wall.

a Use a scale of 2 centimetres to 1 metre to make an accurate drawing showing the position of the ladder.

b Use your diagram to find the actual length of the ladder.

7 Molly draws a plan of her classroom using a scale of 1 : 40. The classroom is 8 metres long. Molly says her scale drawing will be 5 centimetres long. Is she correct? Give a reason for your answer.

8 Paul is a keen model maker. He makes the following models.

a **A Spitfire**. The scale of the model is 1 : 72 and the model is 12.2 centimetres long. How long is the actual Spitfire?

b **HMS Bounty**. The model is 37.2 centimetres long. The actual ship is 40.92 metres long. What is the scale of the model?

9 This is a sketch of Hilary's bedroom.

She plans to reorganise her room. She uses a scale drawing to help decide where to put her furniture.

She uses an A4 sheet of graph paper.

Draw an accurate plan of her bedroom using an appropriate scale.

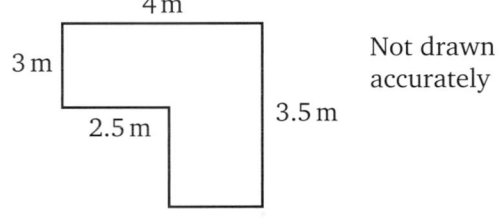

10 The diagram shows the front elevation of a garage.

The manufacturer claims the height of the garage at its highest point is 4.4 metres. Is this claim correct?

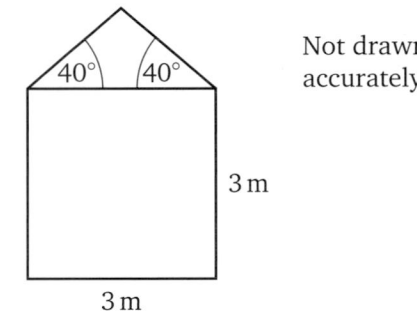

11 This diagram shows the space under the stairs in a house.

Jack wants to put a cupboard under the stairs. The cupboard is 1.6 metres high, 60 centimetres deep and 1.2 metres wide. It has two doors on the front, each is 60 centimetres wide.

Does this cupboard fit under the stairs? If so, can the doors open? Show working to justify your answers.

Scale: 1 cm = 0.2 m (20 cm)

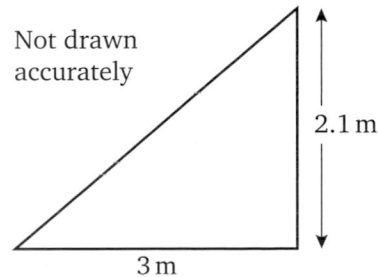

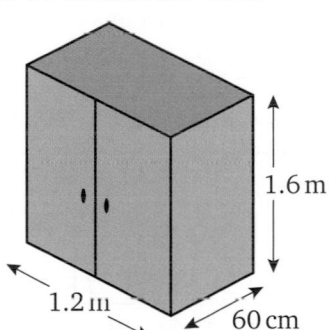

Learn... 11.4 Similarity and congruence

Two shapes are mathematically **similar** if they have the same shape but different sizes. So one shape is an enlargement of the other with an associated scale factor.

Two shapes are **congruent** if they have both the same shape and the same size. That is, the two shapes are identical. If you cut one of the shapes out then it will fit on top of the other. You may need to turn it around or 'flip' it over to do this.

Example: Look at the shapes in the diagrams below.

The two shapes labelled **a** and **b** are **similar**. They have the same shape but different sizes. Shape **b** is an enlargement of shape **a**. Here the scale factor is two, since all the lengths in shape **b** are twice as long as the lengths in shape **a**.

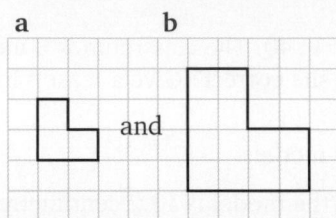

The two shapes labelled **c** and **d** are **congruent**. They have the same shape and size. They are identical.

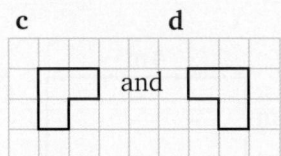

The two shapes labelled **e** and **f** are neither congruent nor similar. They are different shapes. Although it may look as though shape **f** is an enlargement of shape **e**, in fact the lengths have not all been increased by the same factor.

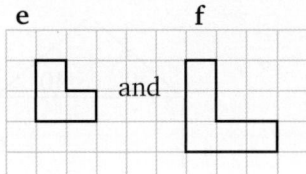

> **Study tip**
>
> In an enlargement all the sides are multiplied by the same factor.

Practise... 15.4 Similarity and congruence Ⓚ G F E D C

1   Name the pairs of congruent shapes in this diagram.

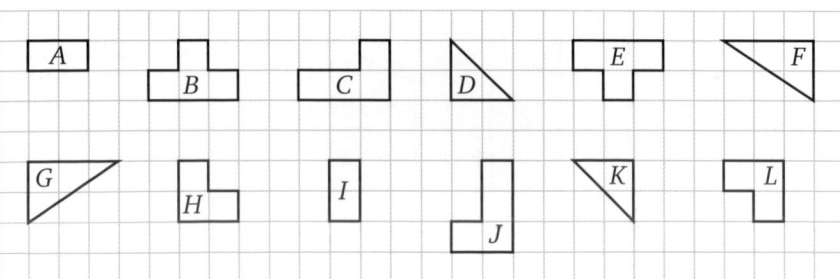

2

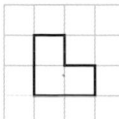

Which of the following shapes are similar to the shape above?

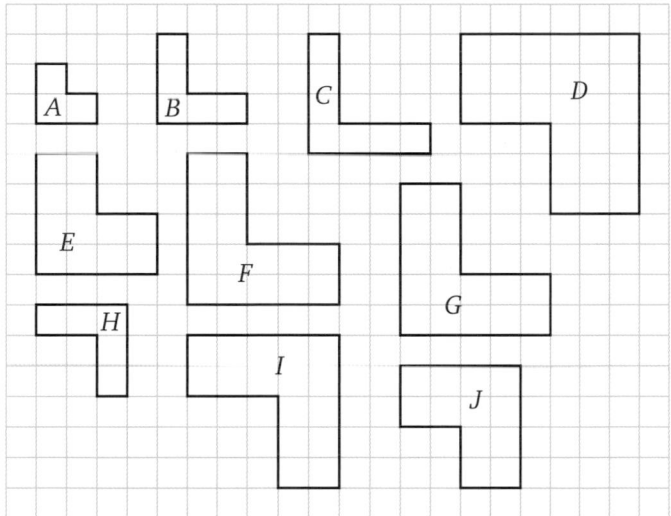

3   Group these shapes into sets of congruent shapes.

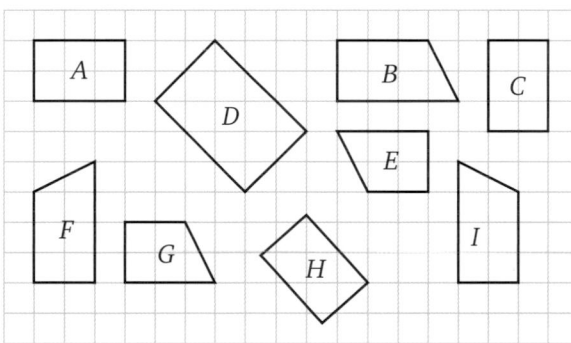

4   Which of the following shapes are similar to the red triangle?

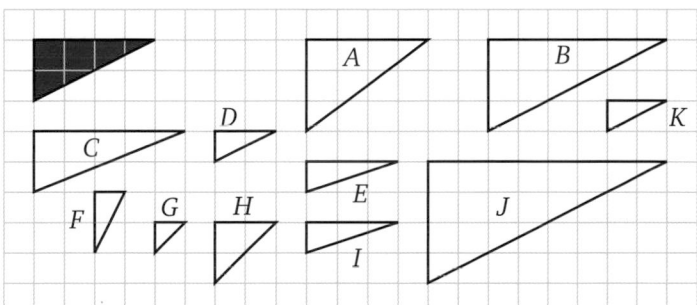

5   Group these shapes into sets of similar shapes.

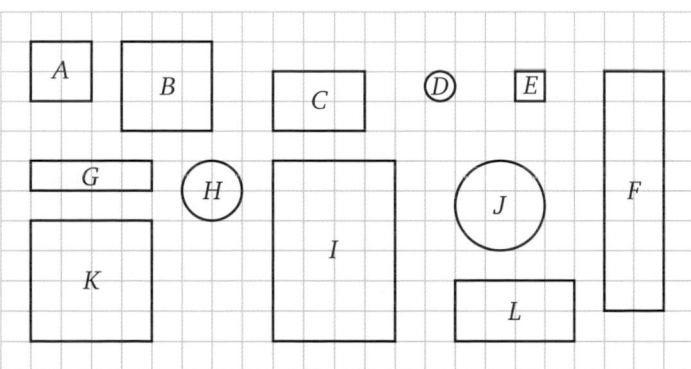

F

6

a Tim says, 'Any two squares are similar to each other.' Is Tim correct?
Give a reason for your answer.

b Jim says, 'Any two rectangles are similar to each other.' Is Jim correct?
Give a reason for your answer.

c Pam says, 'Any two circles are similar to each other.' Is Pam correct?
Give a reason for your answer.

d Sam says, 'Any two triangles are similar to each other.' Is Sam correct?
Give a reason for your answer.

? **7** Join the dots on a copy of the grid to make a triangle.

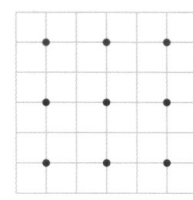

a Find as many **different** triangles as you can. Similar
triangles are allowed, but not congruent triangles.
How can you check you have found all the possible
triangles?

Write down as many facts about each triangle as you can.
Sort them into groups which have facts in common.

b Using the same 3 × 3 dotted grid, find as many different quadrilaterals as you
can. Similar quadrilaterals are allowed, but not congruent quadrilaterals.
How can you check you have found them all?

Write down as many facts about each quadrilateral as you can.
Sort them into groups which have facts in common.

11 Assess ⓚ

F

1 Which of these shapes are similar and which are congruent?

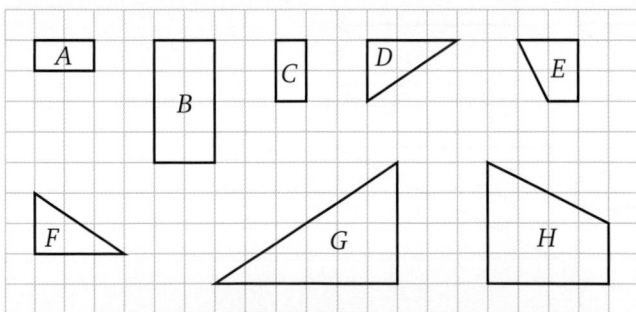

E

2 Draw these triangles accurately.

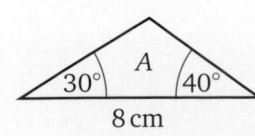
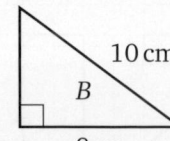
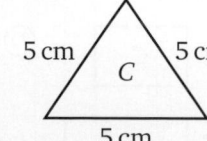
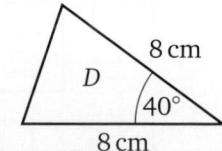

Not drawn
accurately

3 The scale on a map is 1 : 50 000. How many kilometres do each of these lengths
on the map represent in real life?

a 8 cm   **b** 2.8 cm   **c** 8 mm

4   A map uses a scale of 1:25 000. Calculate the length on the map that represents a distance of:

   a   10 km   **b**   24.8 km.

5   A maths class is asked to draw this triangle accurately.

   Explain why they may not all agree on the answer.

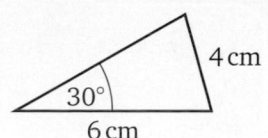

6   Draw this kite accurately.

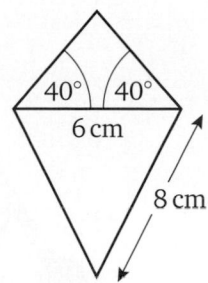

7   **a**   Draw this rectangle accurately.

   b   Bisect angle *ABC*.

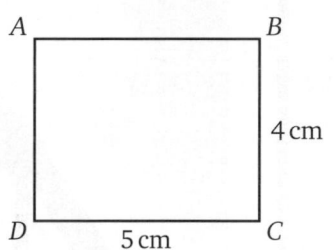

Not drawn accurately

8   **a**   Draw this diagram accurately.

   b   Construct the perpendicular bisector of *AB*.

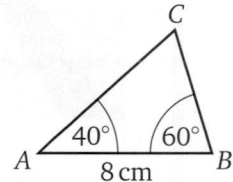

Not drawn accurately

9   This diagram shows the sails on Rob's boat.

   Draw an accurate diagram of the sail.

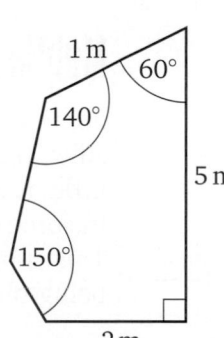

Not drawn accurately

Practice questions ⓚ

1   The side of a rhombus is 7 cm.
The length of the shorter diagonal is 5 cm.

Make an accurate drawing of the rhombus.

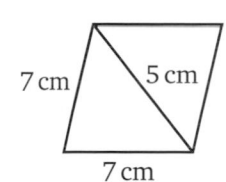

Not drawn accurately

(4 marks)

AQA 2007

12 Loci

Objectives

Examiners would normally expect students who get these grades to be able to:

G
measure and draw lines accurately

F
measure and draw angles accurately

E
use map scales to find a distance

D
understand the idea of a locus

C
construct the locus of points equidistant from two fixed points

construct the locus of points equidistant from two fixed lines

solve loci problems, for example the locus of points less than 3 cm from a point *P*.

Did you know?

Mobile phone masts

Some mobile phone masts have a range of 40 km.
Hills, trees and buildings can all reduce this distance to as little as 5 km.
In some places, mobile phone masts are only 1 or 2 km apart.
This is because they could not cope with the number of calls being made in the area on their own.

Key terms

locus, loci
perpendicular
bisect, bisector
equidistant

You should already know:

✔ how to measure a line accurately

✔ how to measure and draw an angle accurately

✔ how to construct the perpendicular bisector of a line

✔ how to construct the bisector of an angle

✔ how to construct and interpret a scale drawing.

12.1 Drawing and measuring lines, angles and circles

When drawing or measuring a line, take care to be as accurate as possible.

Start measuring from 0 on the ruler. This line is 7.6 cm long.

When drawing or measuring an angle, put the central mark on the vertex.

Make sure you use the scale that starts at 0. This angle is 103°. The inner scale starts at 0.

To draw a circle, measure the distance between your compass point and pencil point carefully against a ruler.

Example: The diagram shows a parallelogram *ABCD*, with *CD* = *BA* = 8 cm, *AD* = *BC* = 6 cm

Angle *ADC* = 68° and *DAB* = 112°

A semicircle is drawn on *AB*.

Make an accurate drawing of this figure.

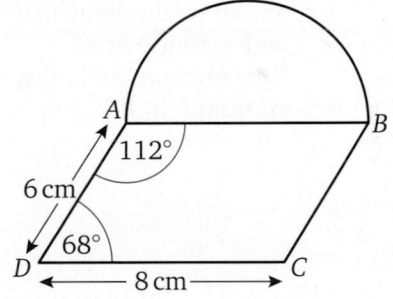

Solution: Draw and label a line, *DC*, 8 cm long.

Angle *ADC* is the angle between *AD* and *DC*, so it is at *D*.

At *D*, draw an angle of 68° from *DC*.

Measure 6 cm along this line, and label the point *A*.

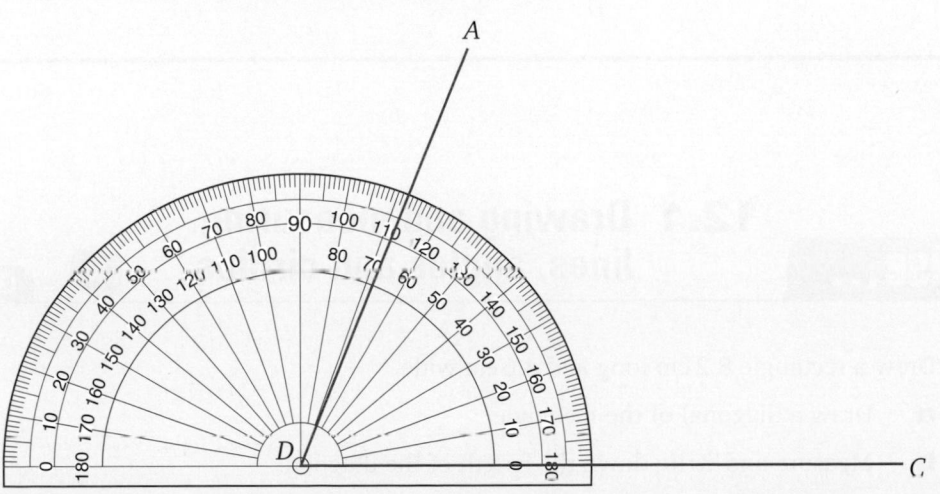

At *A*, draw an angle of 112° from *DA*.

Measure 8 cm along this line, and label the point *B*.

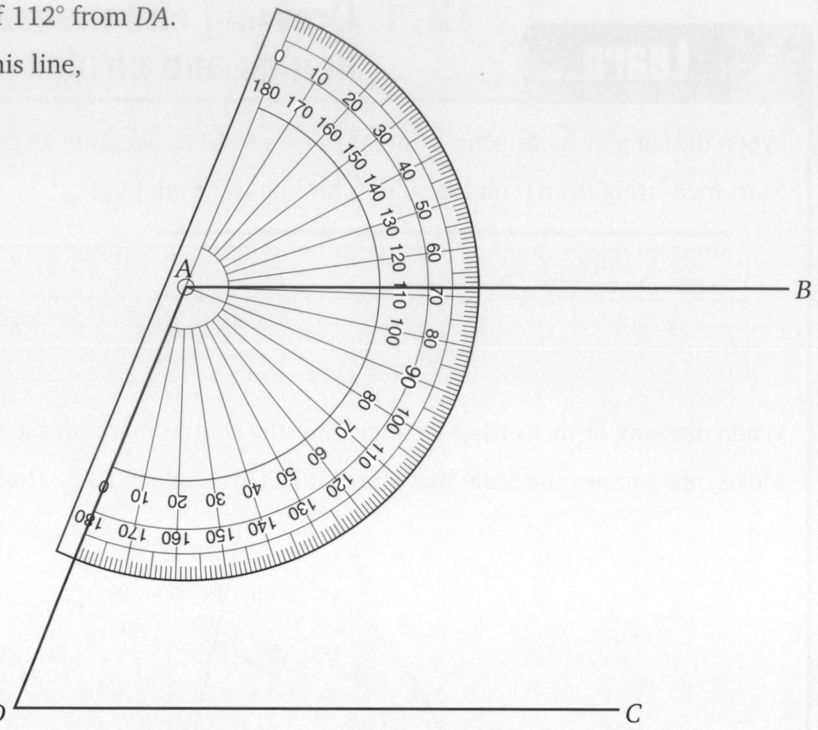

Draw the line *BC*. Measure it to check it is 6 cm long.

Measure 4 cm along *AB* to find the centre of the line. Label this point *M*.

Open your compasses to 4 cm and draw the semicircle with a centre at *M*. Your semicircle should go from *A* to *B*.

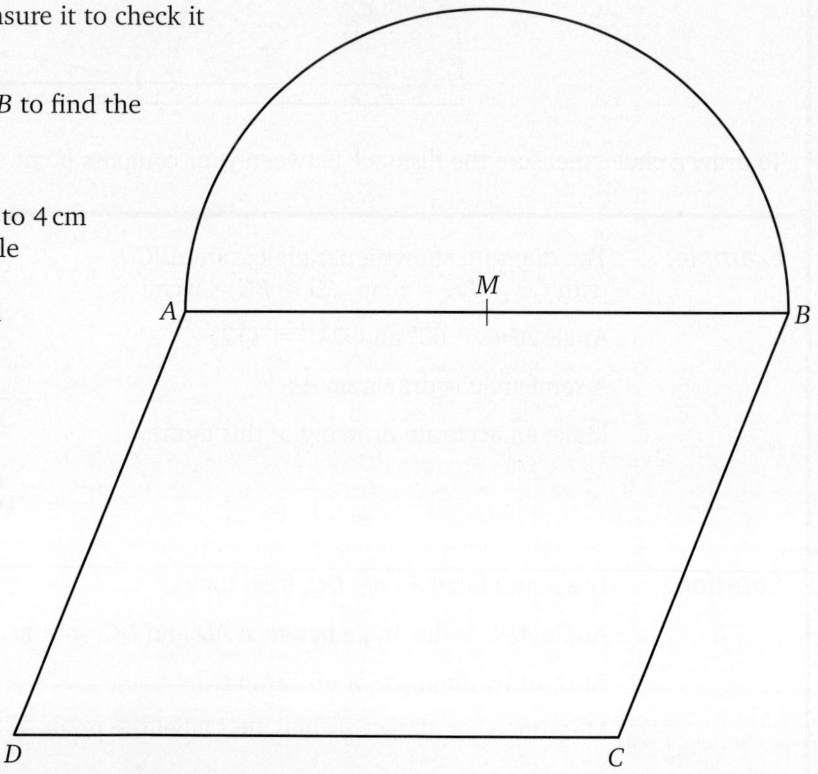

12.1 Drawing and measuring lines, angles and circles

Practise...

1   Draw a rectangle 8.2 cm long and 4.6 cm wide.

     a   Draw a diagonal of the rectangle.

     b   Measure and write down the length of the diagonal.

F

2 Triangle ABC has side AB = 7.4 cm, and BC = 5.2 cm
Angle ABC (the angle at B) is a right angle.

   a Make an accurate drawing of the triangle.

   b Measure and write down the length of AC.

   c Measure and write down the size of angles BAC and ACB.

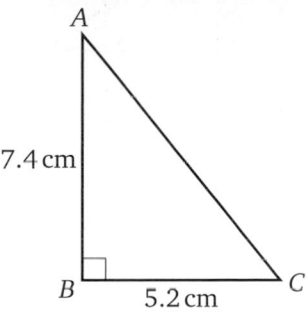

3 In trapezium ABCD, AB and DC are parallel.
Make an accurate drawing of the trapezium.

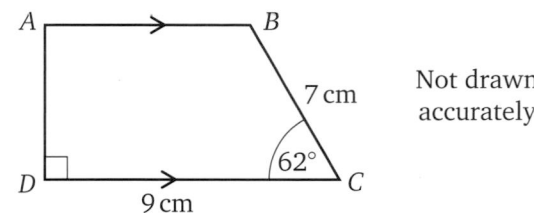

Not drawn accurately

4 Triangle XYZ has XY = 7.2 cm, YZ = 8.4 cm and angle XYZ = 54° as shown.

Make an accurate drawing of the triangle.

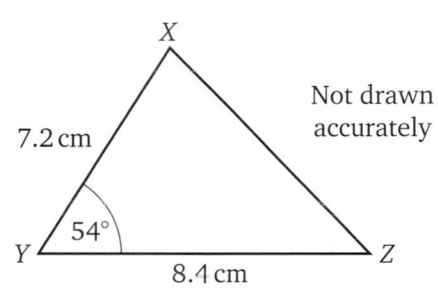

Not drawn accurately

! 5 A rhombus has sides of 8 cm and angles of 72° and 108°.

   a Make an accurate drawing of the rhombus.

   b Draw a circle that just touches the four sides
of the rhombus.
Show clearly how you found the centre
of the circle.

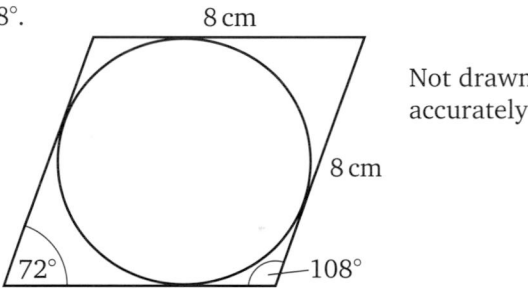

Not drawn accurately

6 A hockey pitch has these markings and dimensions.
Make a scale drawing of the pitch, using 1 cm to represent 10 m.

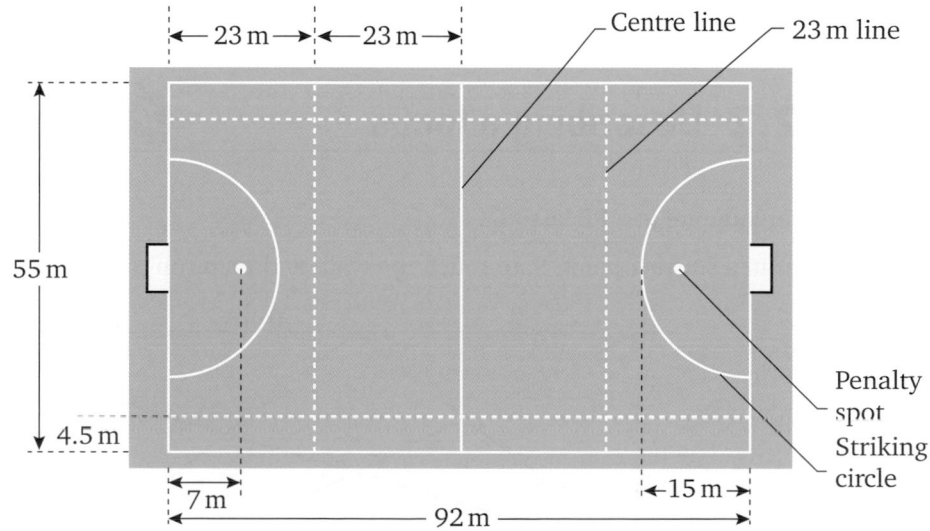

7 **a** Draw a rectangle, ABCD, with AB = 8.2 cm and AD = 5.7 cm

   b A circle passes through A, B, C and D.
Draw this circle, showing clearly on your diagram
how you found its centre.

Not drawn accurately

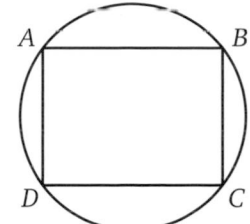

Learn... 12.2 Describing a locus

A **locus** can be thought of in two different ways.

It is the path that a moving point follows, or a set of points that follow a rule.

For example, a circle with a radius of 10 cm, centre C, can be thought of as all the points 10 cm from C, or as the path of a moving point which is always 10 cm from a fixed point, C.

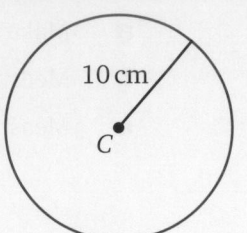

Example: Find the locus of a point on a train moving on a straight track.

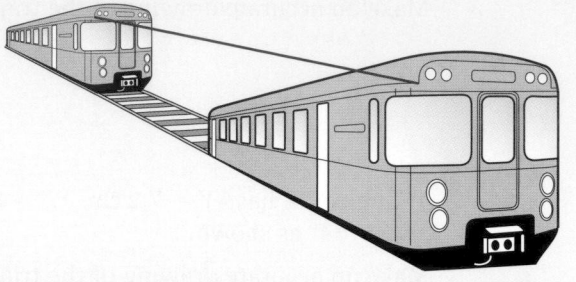

Solution: It follows a path that is a straight-line segment, shown here in red.

Example: Sketch the locus of the vertex A of the triangle ABC, as it rotates clockwise about C until CB is horizontal.

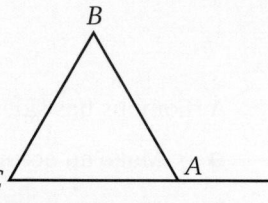

Solution: The diagram shows how the point A (marked in red) moves in an arc (or part of a circle.)

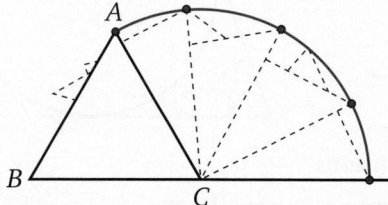

> **Study tip**
>
> As well as visualising the locus, always look for any fixed points in the situation, in this example, point C.

Practise... 12.2 Describing a locus   ⓚ Ⓖ Ⓕ Ⓔ Ⓓ Ⓒ

G

1 Alan, Nicky and Margaret are in a PE lesson.

They have to run from a starting point, S, to touch the wall, and then run to the finishing point F.

The diagram shows their paths.

Use the diagram to find out who runs the shortest distance.

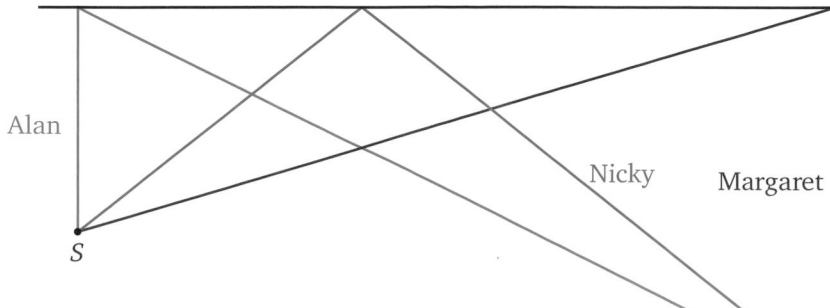

2 Gill goes to a park to play.

She goes on two slides, a swing and a roundabout.

 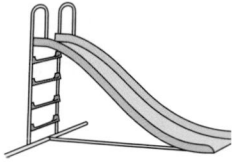  

a Sketch the side view of the locus of her head as she goes down the slides.

b Sketch the side view of the locus of her head as she plays on the swing.

c Sketch the plan view of the locus of her head as she rides on the roundabout when viewed from above.

3 Mark a point, X, on a piece of paper.

Place some counters so that their centres are exactly 5 cm from the point.

Draw the shape that your counters would make if you had an unlimited supply.

4 Draw a line 10 cm long.

Place some counters so that their centres are exactly 5 cm from the line.

Draw the shape that your counters would make if you had an unlimited supply.

5 Bill throws a ball from his window.

Harry, Hope and Oli try to sketch the locus of the ball.

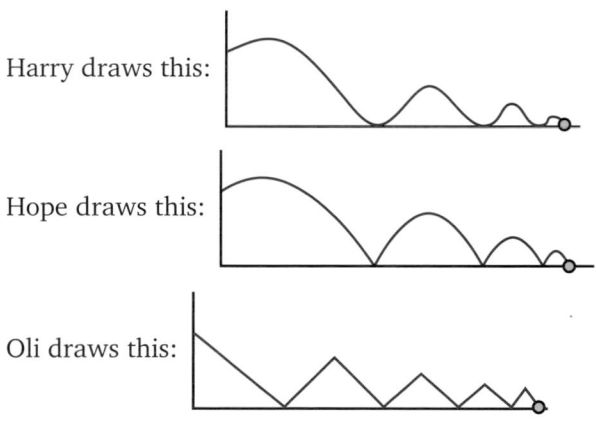

Harry draws this:

Hope draws this:

Oli draws this:

Who is correct?

Give a reason for your answer.

6 Most cars have one of the three arrangements of windscreen wipers shown below.

      a   **b**   **c**

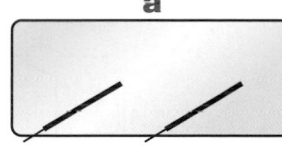 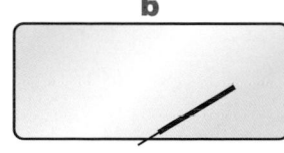 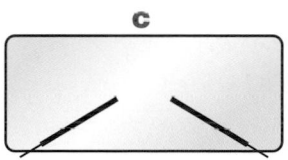

For each arrangement, sketch the area of windscreen that the wipers will clear.

Which is the best arrangement? Give a reason for your answer.

7 A square is rolled along a straight line. Sketch the locus of a vertex of the square as it is rolled.

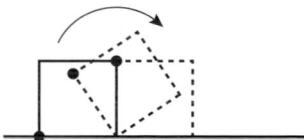

Check your answer by cutting a square from card, and rolling it along a ruler.

D

8   On a separate diagram, sketch the locus of:

    a   the end of the minute hand of the clock

    b   the end of the pendulum on a grandfather clock

    c   a mouse running up the pendulum of the clock.

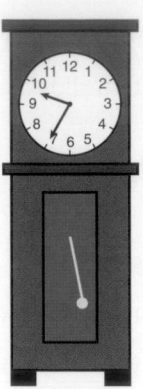

9   Sketch the locus of a piece of chewing gum stuck to a car wheel as the car moves.

> **Hint**
>
> Mark a point on the edge of a coin and roll it along a ruler (without letting it slip) to see how the point moves.

10   Describe the locus of:

    a   all the points 5 cm from a fixed point, *P*

    b   all the points 2 cm from the circumference of a circle of radius 6 cm.

11   Describe the loci shown with red lines in the diagrams below.

a

c

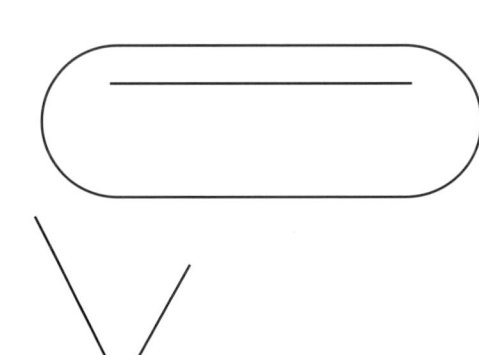

b

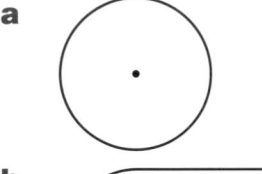

d

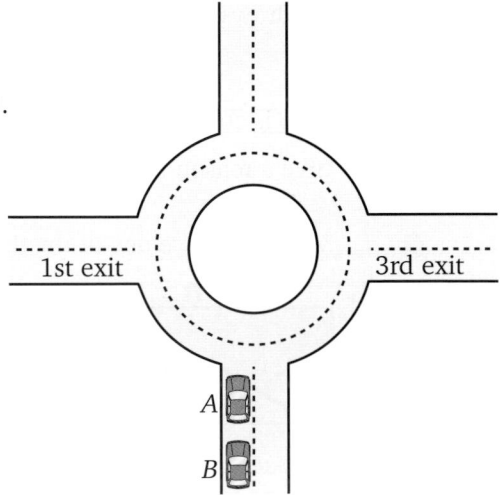

12   Two cars are waiting at a roundabout.

Car *A* is going to take the first exit (the one on the left).

Car *B* is going to take the third exit (the one on the right).

Draw the loci of the two cars.

13   Place two 5p coins together as shown.

    a   Hold one still and roll the other one all the way round it.
How many times does the coin rotate as it goes round the stationary one?
Use two coins, counters or discs to find the answer.

    b   Find the locus of a point on the moving coin as it goes round.
What would happen if one coin had a diameter twice the size of the other?

 **Learn...   12.3 Constructing loci**

You need to remember your constructions from Chapter 15.

It is always useful to draw a sketch first before tackling any locus question.

A **perpendicular bisector** of the line *AB* joins all the points **equidistant** from (the same distance from) *A* and *B*.

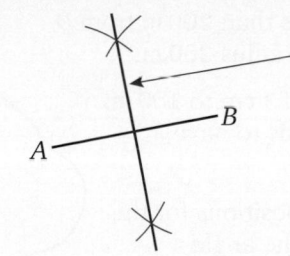

Locus of points equidistant from *A* and *B*: perpendicular bisector

Draw four arcs of the same radius, two with centre at *A*, two with centre at *B*. Join the points of intersection.

An angle bisector joins all points equidistant from two lines that meet at the angle.

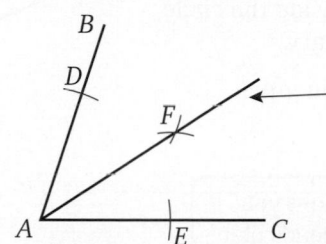

Locus of points equidistant from *AB* and *AC*: angle bisector

Draw two arcs of equal radius, centre *A*, to cut *AB* and *AC* at *D* and *E*. Draw equal arcs from *D* and *E* to intersect at *F*.

This circle joins all the points that are 1 cm from point *A*.

Inside the circle are all points less than 1 cm from *A*.

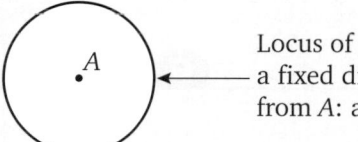

Locus of points a fixed distance from *A*: a circle

The circle is made up of all points 1 cm from *A*.

> **Study tip**
>
> The locus of a point equidistant from two fixed points and the locus of points equidistant from two fixed lines are the only constructions you need to know.

The locus of all points 1 cm from a line *AB* is shown below.

The parallel lines are joined by semicircles.

All the points less than 1 cm from *AB* are inside the closed shape.

All the points more than 1 cm from *AB* are outside the closed shape.

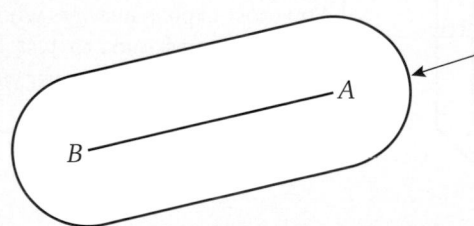

Locus of points a fixed distance from *AB*: parallel lines with semicircular ends

> **Study tip**
>
> To get full marks, make sure you leave your construction lines showing.

Example: An electricity pylon has to be placed so that it is equidistant from *AB* and *AC*, and no more than 200 m from *D*.
It must be within the boundary.

Mark the points where the pylon could be placed.

Scale: 1 cm = 100 m

Solution: Draw *AB* and *AC*.

Construct the angle bisector of *BAC*, as this marks the locus of points equidistant (the same distance) from *AB* and *AC*.

The points less than 200 m from *D* form a circle, radius 200 m.

With a scale of 1 cm to 100 m, this circle needs to have a radius of 2 cm.

The possible positions for the pylon are on the angle bisector and inside the circle and the boundary.

This is shown in green.

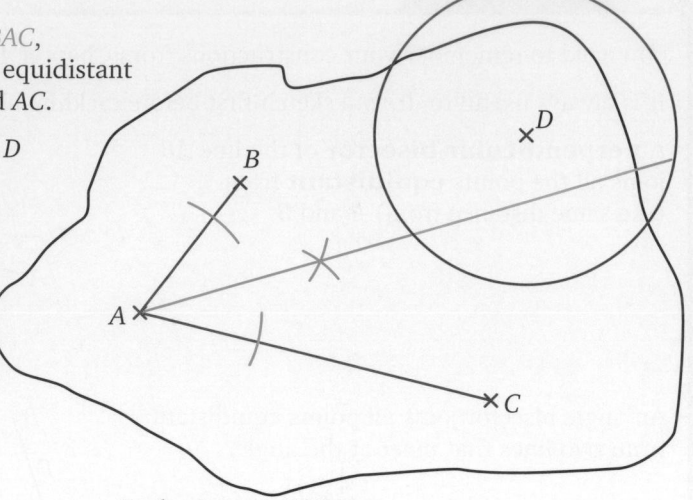

Scale: 1 cm = 100 m

Study tip

There are only two constructions you need to know how to do, perpendicular bisector and angle bisector.

Practise... 12.3 Constructing loci Ⓚ

G F E D C

1 Alice, Kat and Becky tried to draw the locus of points a distance of 1 cm outside a rectangle *ABCD*.

Here are their answers.

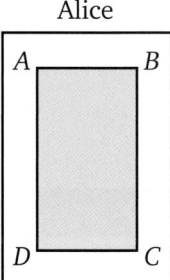   Alice   Kat   Becky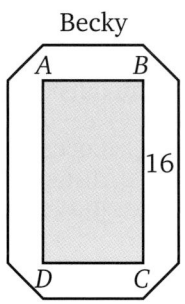

Study tip

You must explain answers when the question asks you to. Just choosing the correct answer will not gain you marks.

Who is correct: Alice, Kat or Becky?

Give a reason for your answer.

2   **a**   Draw a line, *AB*, 8 cm long.

     b   Use a ruler and compasses to construct the locus of points equidistant from *A* and *B*.

3   **a**   Draw an angle, *ABC*, of 70°.

     b   Use a ruler and compasses to construct the locus of points equidistant from *AB* and *BC*.

4   Draw a line, 8 cm long. Label it *AB*.

     a   Find the locus of points that are 6 cm from *A*.

     b   Find the locus of points that are 4 cm from *B*.

     c   Shade the area containing all the points that are less than 6 cm from *A* and less than 4 cm from *B*.

5 Before answering this question, draw a sketch first so you can be sure it will fit on your page.

ABC is a triangle.

Angle $ABC = 90°$, $AB = 8\,cm$ and $BC = 6\,cm$

a Make an accurate drawing of triangle ABC.

b Use a ruler and compasses to construct the locus of points equidistant from A and C.

c Construct the locus of points 6 cm from C.

d Mark the points that are equidistant from A and C and are also less than 6 cm from C.

6 Draw a triangle ABC with sides at least 10 cm long.

a Use a ruler and compasses to construct the locus of points equidistant from A and B.

b Use a ruler and compasses to construct the locus of points equidistant from A and C.

c Mark the point that is equidistant from A, B and C. Label it X.

7 Draw a triangle ABC with sides at least 10 cm long.

a Draw the locus of points equidistant from AB and BC.

b Draw the locus of points equidistant from AB and AC.

c Mark the point that is equidistant from AB, BC and AC. Label it X.

8 Tommy has a rectangular garden, ABCD, 12 m long by 8 m wide.

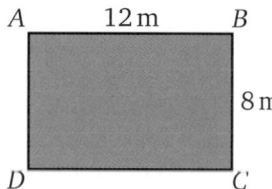

He wants to plant a tree in the garden.

He wants the tree to be at least 3 m from the edge CD of the garden.

It must be no more than 6 m from B.

Using a scale of 1 cm to 1 m, make a drawing of the garden, and shade the region where Tommy can plant the tree.

9 In Suffolk, there are two mobile phone masts, 40 km apart.

a Make a map showing the two masts, using a scale of 1 cm to 4 km. Label them A and B.

b Each mast has a range of 32 km if you are using a phone outside a building.

If you use a phone inside a building the range drops to 24 km.

i Shade the area where you can get a signal if you are outside.

ii Shade the area where you can get a signal inside a house.

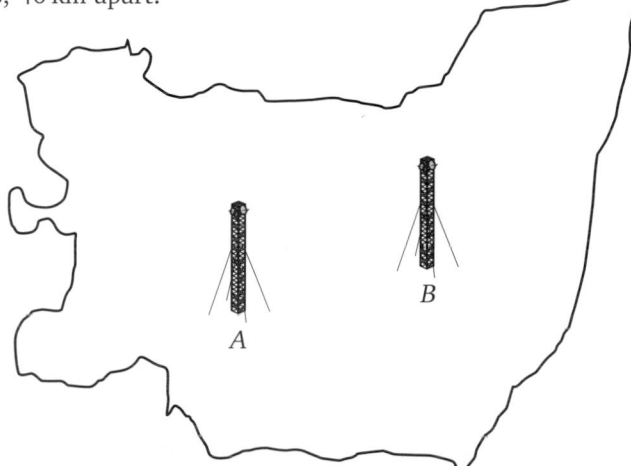

10 A rectangular lawn is 12 m long and 10 m wide.

A gardener waters the lawn with sprinklers, which spray water in a circle with a radius of 3 m.

Find the smallest number of sprinklers needed to water the entire lawn.

12 Assess (k)

F

1 Measure the sides and angles of this triangle.

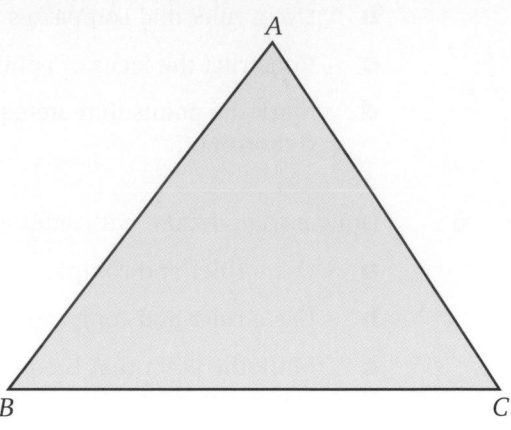

D

2 Draw a parallelogram, *ABCD*, with *AB* = 7.5 cm, *BC* = 6.8 cm and angle *ABC* = 66°

3 Make an accurate copy of the shape drawn below.

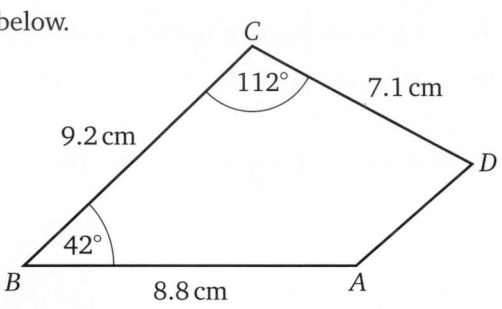

Not drawn accurately

4 Sketch the locus of point *A* on the key as it unlocks a door.

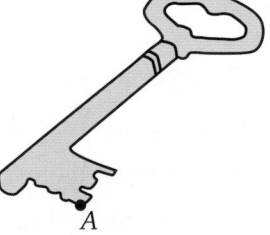

C

5 The diagram shows the plan, *ABCD*, of a garden. The scale is 1 cm to 2 m.

a A gnome, *G*, is to be placed 12 m from *C* and equidistant from *AB* and *AD*.

On a copy of the diagram, construct and mark the position of *G*.

b Find the real distance of the gnome from *D*.

6 A triangle *ABC* has *AB* = 8 cm, *BC* = 6.5 cm and angle *ABC* = 72°.

a Make an accurate drawing of the triangle.

b Use a ruler and compasses to construct the points that are the same distance from *BC* and *AC*.

7 Mark two points, *A* and *B*, 9 cm apart.

Shade the region that is no more than 6 cm from *A* and no more than 5 cm from *B*.

Practice questions ⓚ

1   *AB* and *AC* represents two walls.
A mast is to be erected that is:

- equidistant from *AB* and AC
- between 40 m and 70 m from *A*.

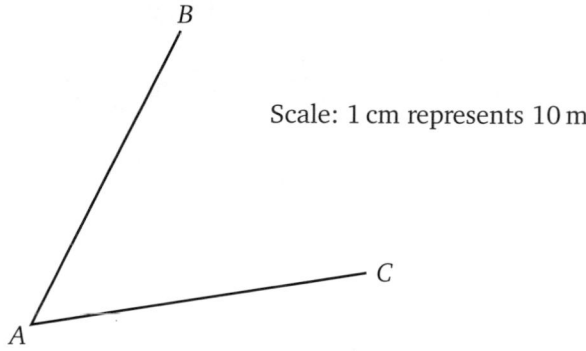

Scale: 1 cm represents 10 m

Show clearly all the possible positions of the mast.

(3 marks)

AQA 2006

2   Using a ruler and compasses construct the bisector of angle *ABC*.

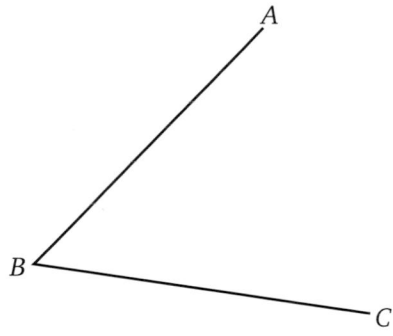

(2 marks)

AQA 2007

13 Quadratics

Objectives

Examiners would normally expect students who get these grades to be able to:

D

draw graphs of simple quadratics such as $y = x^2$, $y = x^2 - 4$ and $y = 3x^2$

C

draw graphs of harder quadratics such as $y = x^2 + 2x + 1$

use a quadratic graph to estimate x- and y-values, giving answers to an appropriate degree of accuracy.

Did you know?

Quadratic equations in action

Why are car headlights so bright?

The reflecting surface inside a car headlight is curved and the equation of its surface fits a quadratic equation.

When the light from the bulb is reflected from the surface, the light is brighter because all the rays are projected forward in a concentrated beam.

Key terms

quadratic expression
quadratic equation
parabola
symmetrical
line of symmetry

You should already know:

✔ how to plot coordinates in all four quadrants

✔ how to draw straight-line graphs

✔ how to substitute positive and negative numbers into an expression.

 **Learn...   13.1 Drawing graphs of simple quadratics**

A **quadratic expression** has x^2 as its highest power.

x^2, $x^2 + 3$, $2x^2 - 3x + 4$ and $3x^2 + 5x - 2$ are all examples of quadratic expressions.

The following expressions are **not** quadratics: $x + 7$, $x^3 - 3x^2$ and $x^2 + x^4$.

How to draw the graph of a quadratic

1. **Complete or construct a table of values.**

   This is the table for the **quadratic equation** $y = x^2$

x	-3	-2	-1	0	1	2	3
y	9	4	1	0	1	4	9

   When drawing the graphs of straight lines (linear graphs), you were taught to plot three points.

   The graphs of quadratics are all curves, so you need more than three values in the table.

   The y-values are found by substituting the x-values into the equation of the quadratic, e.g. for $y = x^2$

   when $x = 2$ $y = x^2 = 2^2 = 4$

   when $x = -3$ $y = x^2(-3)^2 = 9$

   Sometimes you are asked to construct the table for yourself.

   Make sure that you construct this table for the range of values given in the question.

2. **By looking at your table, find the smallest and largest y-values that you will need on the y-axis.**

3. **Draw a pair of axes for your graph and label them x and y.**

4. **From your table of values, plot the points on the graph as small crosses.**

   The points from this table would be $(-3, 9)$, $(-2, 4)$, $(-1, 1)$, $(0, 0)$, $(1, 1)$, $(2, 4)$, $(3, 9)$

5. **Join the points with a smooth curve.**

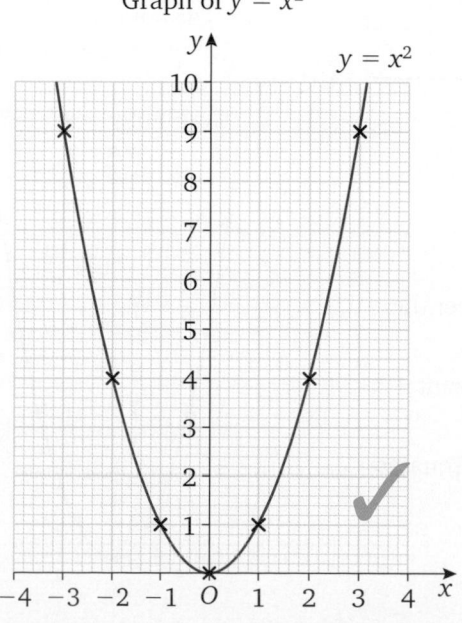

Graph of $y = x^2$

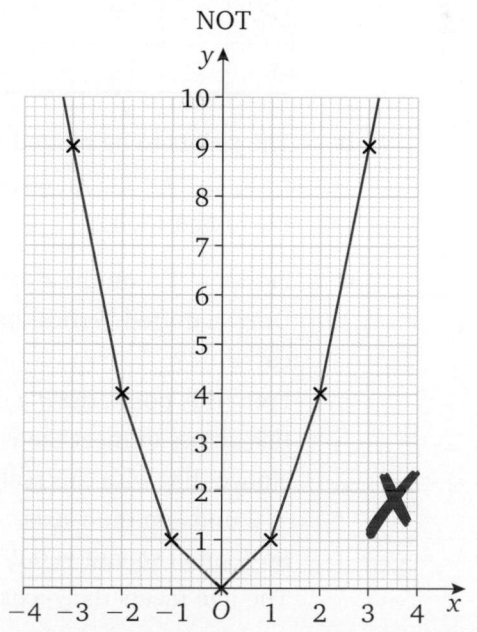

NOT

It should be smooth at the bottom.

Always draw your line with a sharp pencil, making sure that it passes clearly through the centre of the points plotted.

The graph obtained is a curve. This shaped curve is called a **parabola**.

$y = x^2$ is a U-shaped graph and has a minimum (lowest) point at (0, 0).

Note that the x^2 term is **positive** for a **U-shaped** curve.

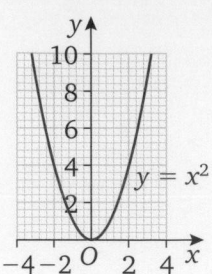

$y = x^2$

Other quadratics have maximum (highest) points and are hill-shaped graphs.

Note that the x^2 term is **negative** for a **hill-shaped** curve.

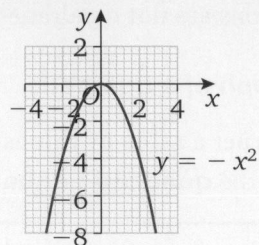

$y = -x^2$

All quadratics are parabolas. They are also **symmetrical**, having one **line of symmetry**.

You can sometimes see the pattern in the table of x- and y-values.

Example: **a** Copy and complete the table of values for the quadratic $y = x^2 + 3$

x	−3	−2	−1	0	1	2	3
y		7	4		4		12

b Draw the graph for the values of x shown in the table.

c From your graph, find the value of y when $x = 1.5$

d From your graph, find the values of x when $y = 7$

Solution: **a** When $x = -3$, $y = (-3)^2 + 3 = 12$
When $x = 0$, $y = 0^2 + 3 = 3$
When $x = 2$, $y = (2)^2 + 3 = 7$

x	−3	−2	−1	0	1	2	3
y	12	7	4	3	4	7	12

Notice that the graph is **symmetrical** about the y-axis.

You can see the symmetry in the table. The values for $x = -3$ and $x = 3$ give the same y-values.

b The points to be plotted are:
(−3, 12), (−2, 7), (−1, 4), (0, 3), (1, 4), (2, 7) and (3, 12)

c Find $x = 1.5$ on the x-axis.
Draw a dotted vertical line up to meet the curve.
From this point, draw a dotted horizontal line across to meet the y-axis.
Notice that with this scale 10 small squares = 2 units on the y-axis.
So 1 small square = 0.2
The line meets the y-axis at $y = 5.2$

Graph of $y = x^2 + 3$

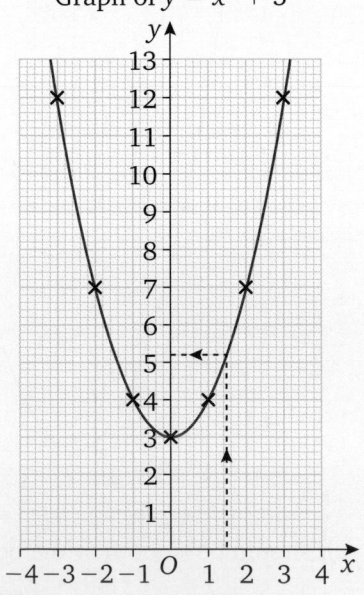

d   Find $y = 7$ on the y-axis.

Draw a dotted horizontal line to the left and the right to meet the curve in two places.

From each of these points, draw a dotted vertical line down to meet the x-axis.

These lines meet the x-axis at $x = -2$ and $x = 2$

With harder questions you can use an alternative method which has extra working in the table as shown in the second example below.

Graph of $y = x^2 + 3$

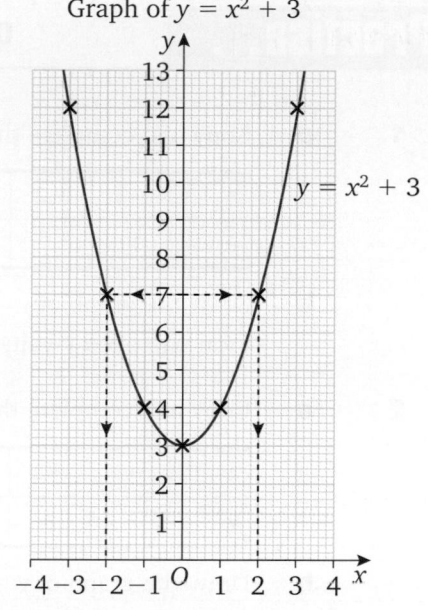

$y = x^2 + 3$

Example: **a**   Draw the graph of $y = x^2 + 2x$ for values of x from -3 to 2. Use the axes provided.

b   Identify the line of symmetry on your graph.

c   Write down the coordinates of the lowest (minimum) point.

Solution: **a**

Add these rows to get the y-values

x	-3	-2	-1	0	1	2
x^2	9	4	1	0	1	4
$+2x$	-6	-4	-2	0	2	4
y	3	0	-1	0	3	8

The coordinates of the points to be plotted are found in the top row (x) and the bottom row (y).

For example, $(-3, 3)$, $(-2, 0)$, $(-1, -1)$

b   This graph is symmetrical about a vertical line through $x = -1$

c   The minimum point is the lowest point on the graph, $(-1, -1)$. At this point, y has its smallest value.

Graph of $y = x^2 + 2x$

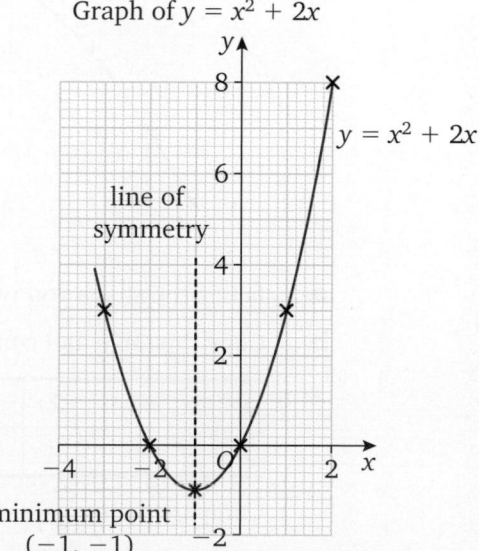

$y = x^2 + 2x$

line of symmetry

minimum point $(-1, -1)$

Study tip

All quadratic graphs should be smooth curves.

They are either U-shaped or hill-shaped.

If your graph is not either of these, check your working in the table.

A quadratic curve never has a flat base.

13.1 Drawing graphs of simple quadratics

Practise...

G F E D C

D

1 **a** Copy and complete the table of values for $y = x^2 + 1$

x	−3	−2	−1	0	1	2	3
y	10			1			10

b Draw the graph of $y = x^2 + 1$ for values of x from −3 to 3.
(You will need y-values from 0 to 10.)

2 **a** Copy and complete the table of values for $y = 2x^2$

x	−3	−2	−1	0	1	2	3
y		8		0	2		18

Hint

Remember that $2x^2$ means 2 times x^2. So square first then multiply the answer by 2.

b Draw the graph of $y = 2x^2$ for values of x from −3 to 3.
(You will need y-values from 0 to 18. Label the y-axis 0, 2, 4, ..., 18.)

c Write down the coordinates of the minimum point on the graph.

3 The graph shows the points that Susan has plotted for her graph of $y = 3x^2$

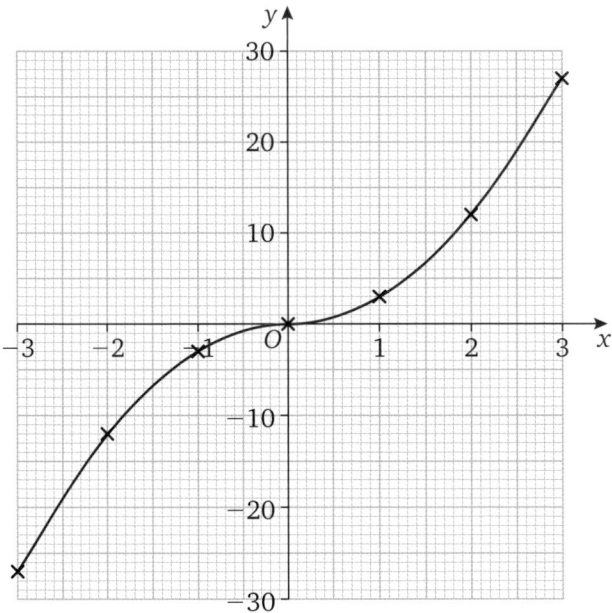

a Is this the shape you would expect? Give a reason for your answer.

b Copy the table and complete it for $y = 3x^2$.

x	−3	−2	−1	0	1	2	3
y							

Compare your y-values with those for Susan's graph.

c What mistake has Susan made in calculating the values?

4 **a** Draw the graph of $y = -x^2$ for values of x from −3 to 3.

b This graph has **no** minimum point. It has a maximum point.
How can you tell this from the equation?

c Write down the coordinates of the maximum point.

5 Here is the table for drawing the graph of $y = x^2 - 2x$

x	−3	−2	−1	0	1	2	3
x^2					1	4	9
$-2x$	6	4			−2		
y					−1		

} Add

Hint

You add the two middle rows to get the y-values.

Be careful with the signs.

a Compare this with the table in the second example in Learn 17.1.
What is the difference between the two tables?

b Copy and complete this table.

c Use your table to draw the graph of $y = x^2 - 2x$ for values of x from −3 to 3.

d What is the minimum point on this graph?

! 6 **a** Construct a table for $y = x^2 - x$ for values of x from −2 to 4.

b Plot the points from the table and join them up to make a smooth curve.

c By looking at the symmetry of the graph, what is the x-coordinate of the minimum point?

d Calculate the corresponding y-value and state the coordinates of the minimum point.

! 7 **a** Construct a table for $y = -x^2 + 2x$ taking values of x from −2 to 4.

b Plot the points from the table and join them up to make a smooth curve.

c Find the coordinates of the maximum point on the graph.

d From your graph, find the value of y when $x = 3.5$

e From your graph, find the values of x when $y = 2$

⚙ 8 The quadratic equation $d = \dfrac{s^2}{200} + 1$ gives the stopping distance, d (in car lengths), of a car moving at s mph.

According to this formula, at 20 mph the stopping distance is three car lengths.

When $s = 20$, $\quad d = \dfrac{20^2}{200} + 1 = 3$

According to this formula, at 40 mph the stopping distance is nine car lengths.

When $s = 40$, $\quad d = \dfrac{40^2}{200} + 1 = 9$

Copy and complete the table for the speeds shown.

s	20	30	40	50	60	70	80
d	3		9			25.5	

From this table, draw the graph showing how the stopping distance relates to the speed.

❓ 9 **a** Taking values of x from −4 to 4, draw tables of values for the quadratics
$y = x^2$, $y = x^2 + 3$ and $y = x^2 - 4$

b On the same grid and using the same axes and scales, draw the graphs of these quadratics.

c Compare your graphs. What effect does changing the number at the end of the quadratic have on the graph?

Learn... 13.2 Drawing graphs of harder quadratics

The quadratics already drawn have consisted of one or two terms.

For example, $y = \underline{x^2}$ and $y = \underline{x^2} + \underline{4x}$

        '1 term'   '2 terms'

For the exam you may be asked to draw the graph of a quadratic that contains three terms.

For example, $y = \underline{x^2} + \underline{2x} + \underline{3}$ or $y = \underline{5} + \underline{x} - \underline{x^2}$

          '3 terms'   '3 terms'

You may be asked to find the value of y for a given value of x or the value of x for a given value of y.

Example:

a Copy and complete the table for $y = 6 + x - x^2$

x	−3	−2	−1	0	1	2	3	4
y	−6	0			6			

b What are the coordinates of the maximum point?

c Using your table, draw the graph of $y = 6 + x - x^2$ for $-3 \leqslant x \leqslant 4$

d What is the value of y when:

  i $x = 2.8$ **ii** $x = -1.2$?

  Give your answers to 1 d.p.

> **Hint**
>
> For $-3 \leqslant x \leqslant 4$ means that you take x-values from -3 to 4 inclusive.

Solution:

a This table has only two rows, x and y. As some of the values are already given, complete the table by substitution.

So when

$x = -1,$ $y = 6 + x - x^2 = 6 + (-1) - (-1)^2 = 6 - 1 - 1 = 4$

$x = 0,$ $y = 6 + 0 - 0^2 = 6$

$x = 2,$ $y = 6 + 2 - 2^2 = 4$

$x = 3,$ $y = 6 + 3 - 3^2 = 0$

$x = 4,$ $y = 6 + 4 - 4^2 = -6$

x	−3	−2	−1	0	1	2	3	4
y	−6	0	4	6	6	4	0	−6

If you were forming the table yourself you could use either the extended table or the shortened form as used here.

The extended table would begin like this.

All the entries are the same on this line. The term does not contain an x term so the answers do not change.

x	−3	−2	−1	0	1	2	3	4
6	6	6	6					
$+x$	−3	−2						
$-x^2$	−9	−4						
y	−6	0						

The quadratic contained three terms. Add these three rows.

The sign is included with the term

b The table shows that the graph is symmetrical about a point halfway between $x = 0$ and $x = 1$. This means that there will be a maximum point when $x = \frac{1}{2}$ (or 0.5)

At $x = 0$ and $x = 1$, the y-value is 6, so the y-value of the maximum point will be slightly larger than 6.

To get an accurate value, the y-value is found by substituting into the equation.

When $x = 0.5$, $y = 6 + 0.5 - (0.5)^2 = 6 + 0.5 - 0.25 = 6.25$

There is a maximum at (0.5, 6.25).

c Graph of $y = 6 + x - x^2$

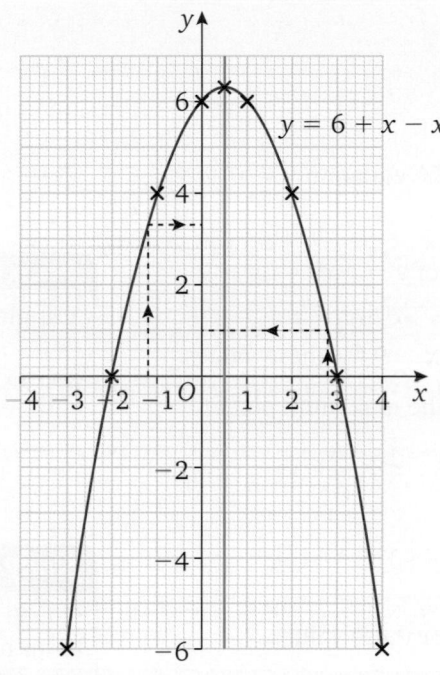

d **i** When $x = 2.8$, $y = 1.0$

ii When $x = -1.2$, $y = 3.3$

13.2 Drawing graphs of harder quadratics

Practise...

1 **a** Copy and complete this table for $y = x^2 - 2x - 8$

x	−2	−1	0	1	2	3	4	5
x^2	4	1	0		4		16	25
$-2x$	+4		0	−2	−4	−6	−8	−10
-8	−8		−8		−8			−8
y	0		−8		−8			7

b Draw the graph of $y = x^2 - 2x - 8$ for values of x from −2 to 5.

c When $x = 3$, what is the value of y?

d Work out the values of x for $y = 40$.

C

C

2   Julie constructed a table for $y = x^2 - x - 6$ for values of x from -2 to 4.

x	-2	-1	0	1	2	3	4
x^2	4	1	0	1	4	9	16
$-x$	-2	-1	0	-1	-2	-3	-4
-6	-6	-6	-6	-6	-6	-6	-6
y	-4	-6	-6	-6	-4	0	-6

The number -6 appeared four times in the bottom row.

The table was not symmetrical.

She had made some mistakes.

Five numbers in the table are incorrect.

Construct a new corrected table for the equation $y = x^2 - x - 6$

3   **a**   Construct a table for the graph of $y = -x^2 + 6x - 9$ for $0 \leqslant x \leqslant 6$

     b   Draw the graph of $y = -x^2 + 6x - 9$ for these values.

     c   Write down the coordinates of the maximum point.

     d   Work out the values of x for $y = -16$.

> **Hint**
>
> You may use an expanded table or a short table as in the first example in Learn 17.2.

4   **a**   Construct a table for the quadratic $y = x^2 + 1$ for $-3 \leqslant x \leqslant 3$

     b   Draw the graph of $y = x^2 + 1$ for these values.

     c   Write down the coordinates of the minimum point.

> *Study tip*
>
> Not all quadratics have three terms but the highest power will always be x^2.

! 5   **a**   Copy and complete this table for $y = 2x^2 - 7x + 5$

x	0	0.5	1	1.5	2	2.5	3
$2x^2$	0	0.5		4.5			18
$-7x$		-3.5	-7		-14		-21
$+5$	$+5$	$+5$	$+5$	$+5$	$+5$	$+5$	$+5$
y		2					2

     b   Draw the graph of $y = 2x^2 - 7x + 5$ for values of x from 0 to 3.

     c   Find the coordinates of the minimum point.

> **Hint**
>
> You should be able to see both from your graph and from the table at which x-value the minimum point will be.
>
> You might find it useful to add an extra column to your table. It can be placed at the end.

! 6   **a**   Copy and complete this table for $y = (x - 4)(x + 2)$

x	-3	-2	-1	0	1	2	3	4	5
$(x - 4)$	-7				-3				
$(x + 2)$	-1				3				
y	$+7$				-9				

b   Draw the graph of $y = (x - 4)(x + 2)$ for values of x from -3 to 5.

c   Write down the coordinates of the minimum point.

d   Use your graph to find the values of x when $y = 3$.

> **Hint**
>
> The equation is in bracket form.
> This will still give a quadratic.
> The two middle rows here have to be multiplied together.

7   A ball is thrown vertically upwards in the air.

After t seconds, its height above the ground, h metres, is given by the equation:

$$h = 39.2t - 4.9t^2$$

a   Copy and complete the table for values of t from 0 to 8.

t	0	2	4	6	8
39.2t	0	78.4	156.8		313.6
$-4.9t^2$	0	-19.6		-176.4	
h		58.8	78.4		

b   Draw the graph of $h = 39.2t - 4.9t^2$ for values of t from 0 to 8.

c   At what time is the ball at its maximum height above where it was thrown from?

d   What is this maximum value for h?

e   At what times is the ball 40 metres above where it was thrown?

> **Hint**
>
> You will need to take h-values between 0 and 80 using 10 squares to equal 10. The graph will not be very accurate due to the values containing decimals. Just plot these as accurately as you can.

8   A flower bed is in the shape of a semicircle as shown. The quadratic equation $A = \frac{1}{2}\pi r^2$ gives the area for the flower bed in metres^2, where r is the radius.

a   Copy and complete the following table giving values of A to one decimal place.

r (metres)	0	1	2	3	4	5
$A = \frac{1}{2}\pi r^2$			6.3		25.1	39.3

b   Draw the graph of $A = \frac{1}{2}\pi r^2$ using 2 cm to represent 1 m on the r-axis and 2 cm to represent 10 m^2 on the A-axis.

c   Use your graph to estimate the area, A, of the flower bed when the radius is:

   i   1.5 m   **ii**   3.8 m

d   Use your graph to estimate the radius, r, of the flower bed when the area is:

   i   30 m^2 **ii**   16 m^2

13 Assess ⓚ

D

1 Which of the following are quadratic equations?

   a $y = x^2 + 3$ **b** $y = -2x^2$ **c** $y = x + 2$

2 **a** Copy and complete the table of values for $y = x^2 + 3$

x	−3	−2	−1	0	1	2	3
y	12		4			7	12

   b Draw the graph of $y = x^2 + 3$ for values of x from −3 to 3.
   (You will need y-values from 0 to 12.)

C

3 A rectangular enclosure has dimensions $(x + 2)$ metres by $(3 − x)$ metres.

$(x + 2)$ metres

$(3 − x)$
metres

The area of the enclosure is given by the formula

   $A = -x^2 + x + 6$

   a Construct a table for the values of x from 1 to 5 inclusive.

   b Draw the graph of $A = -x^2 + x + 6$ for values of x from 1 to 5 inclusive.

   c What is the largest possible area this rectangle can have?

4 A designer was asked to include an arch of a particular shape in his plans for a building.

The equation he was given for the arch was $y = 4.5 − 0.5x^2$

This quadratic is symmetrical about the y-axis.

   a Copy and complete this table for values of x from 0 to 3.

x	0	0.5	1	1.5	2	2.5	3
4.5	4.5	4.5		4.5		4.5	
$-0.5x^2$	0	−0.125			−2	−3.125	−4.5
y	4.5	4.375				1.375	

   b Draw the graph of $y = 4.5 − 0.5x^2$ for values of x from −3 to 3.

   Use 2 cm to represent 1 unit on each axis. You will need to approximate your answers from the table.

   This will show you the whole arch.

   c From this graph, estimate the value of y when $x = 1.2$

   d Find the values of x for which $y = 4$

Practice questions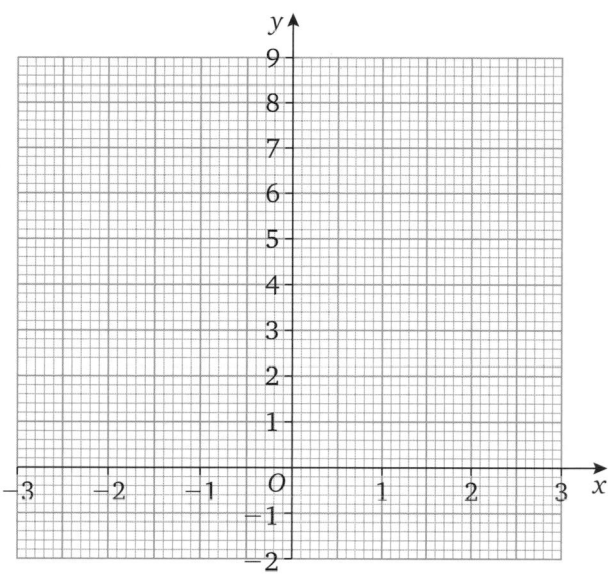

1   a   Explain why x^2 is never negative.   *(1 mark)*

    b   Copy the grid and draw the graph of $y = x^2$ for values of x from -3 to $+3$.

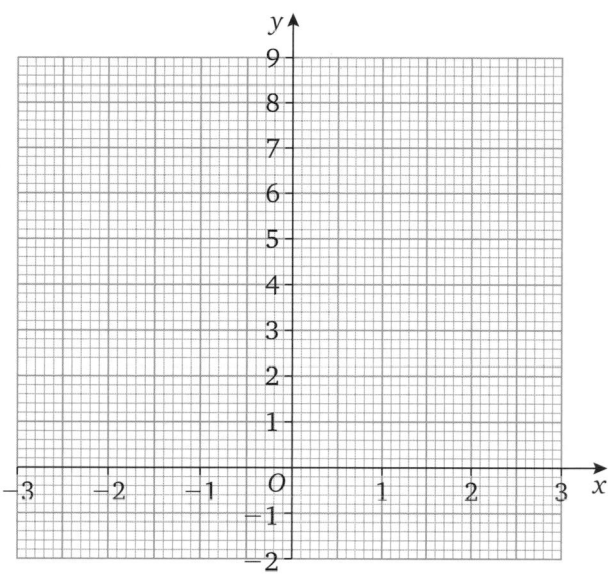

(2 marks)

AQA 2007

2   a   Copy and complete the table of values for $y = x^2 - x - 5$

x	-2	-1	0	1	2	3	4
y	1		-5	-5	-3	1	

(2 marks)

    b   Copy the grid below and draw the graph of $y = x^2 - x - 5$ for values of x from -2 to 4.

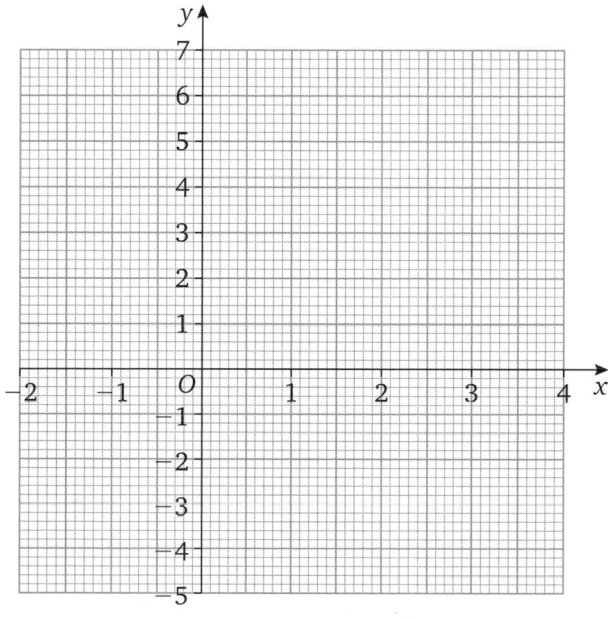

(2 marks)

AQA 2004

Pythagoras' theorem

You should already know:

✔ how to find squares and square roots using a calculator

✔ the properties of triangles and quadrilaterals.

Key terms

hypotenuse

Pythagoras' theorem

Did you know?

Pythagoras

Pythagoras lived in the 5th century BCE, and was one of the first Greek mathematical thinkers.

Pythagoras is known to students of mathematics because of the theorem that bears his name: 'The square on the hypotenuse is equal to the sum of the squares on the other two sides.'

The Egyptians knew that a triangle with sides 3, 4 and 5 has a 90° angle. They used a rope with 12 evenly spaced knots like this one, to make right angles.

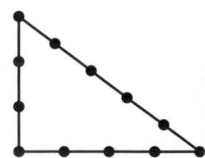

But they did not extend the idea to triangles with other dimensions.

Other people such as the Chinese and the Sumerians also already knew that it was generally true and used it in their measurements. However, it was Pythagoras who is said to have proved that it is always true.

 **Learn...   14.1 Pythagoras' theorem**

In any right-angled triangle the longest side is always opposite the right angle.

This side is called the **hypotenuse**.

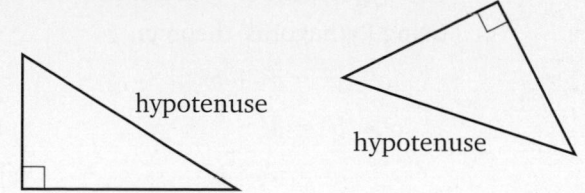

The diagram shows a right-angled triangle with sides of 3 cm, 4 cm and 5 cm.

Squares have been drawn on each side of the triangle and the area of each square is shown.

The area of the large square is equal to the sum of the areas of the two smaller squares.

$$25 = 9 + 16$$

This can be written as

$$5^2 = 3^2 + 4^2$$

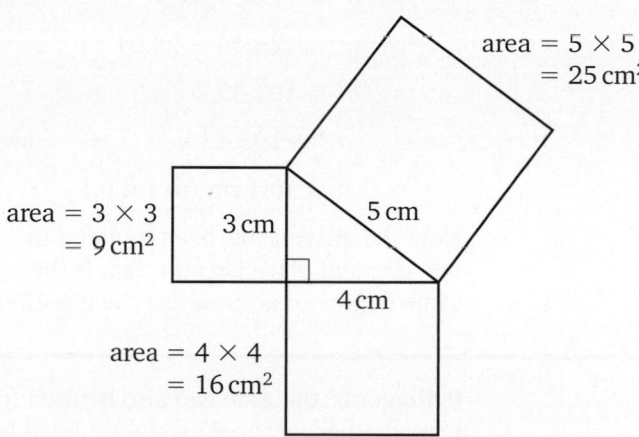

This relationship between the hypotenuse and the other two sides is true for any right-angled triangle. It is known as **Pythagoras' theorem**.

In general, in a right-angled triangle: $c^2 = a^2 + b^2$

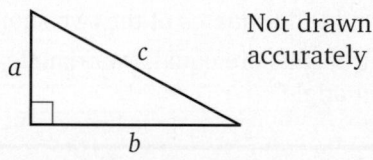

Not drawn accurately

Example: Calculate the length of the hypotenuse (labelled c) of this triangle.

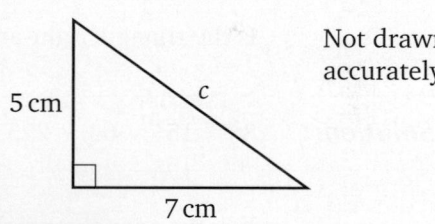

Not drawn accurately

Solution: Using Pythagoras' theorem,

$$c^2 = a^2 + b^2$$

$$c^2 = 5^2 + 7^2$$

$$= 25 + 49$$

$$= 74 \qquad \text{Take the square root of each side.}$$

$$c = \sqrt{74} = 8.6 \text{ cm (to 1 d.p.)}$$

> **Study tip**
>
> Check that your answers are sensible. If two sides are 5 cm and 7 cm then the third side cannot be 74 cm.
>
> This will help you to remember to take the square root.

Example: Work out the length of side a.

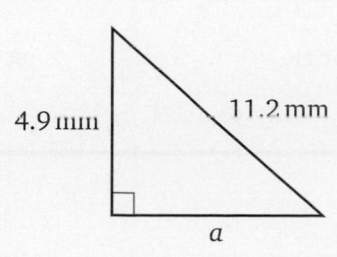

Not drawn accurately

Solution: This time you are trying to find a shorter side instead of the hypotenuse.

The hypotenuse is 11.2 cm.

Using Pythagoras' theorem,

$$c^2 = a^2 + b^2$$

$$c^2 - b^2 = a^2 \qquad \text{Subtract } b^2 \text{ from both sides.}$$

$$a^2 = c^2 - b^2 \qquad \text{Turn the equation round so that } a^2 \text{ is on the left.}$$

$$a^2 = 11.2^2 - 4.9^2 \qquad \text{Substitute in values for } c \text{ and } b.$$

$$a^2 = 125.44 - 24.01$$

$$a^2 = 101.43$$

$$a = \sqrt{101.43} \qquad \text{Take the square root of both sides.}$$

$$a = 10.1 \text{ cm (to 1 d.p.)}$$

Note the answer has been rounded to one decimal place because that is the same degree of accuracy as the question.

Pythagoras' theorem can also be used to test whether a triangle is right-angled by showing that the sides fit the theorem.

To test for a right angle, first square the longest side.

Then add the squares of the two shorter sides.

If your results are equal, the triangle contains a right angle.

> **Study tip**
>
> To find the hypotenuse, you must **add** the squares of the other two sides.
>
> To find a shorter side, you must **subtract** the squares of the other two sides.

Example: A triangle has sides of 8 cm, 15 cm and 17 cm.

Is the triangle right-angled?

Solution: $8^2 + 15^2 = 64 + 225 = 289$

$17^2 = 289$

Yes, the triangle is right-angled.

Right-angled triangles can be formed in other shapes. Some examples are shown below.

Wherever a right-angled triangle is formed, you can use Pythagoras' theorem to find the length of the third side.

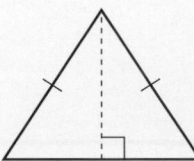

isosceles triangle

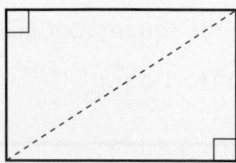

rectangle

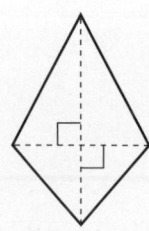

kite

Practise... 14.1 Pythagoras' theorem

1 Find the length of the hypotenuse in each of these triangles.

a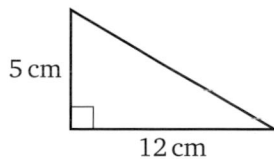
5 cm
12 cm

c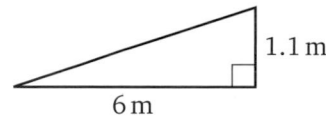
1.1 m
6 m

Not drawn accurately

b 6 cm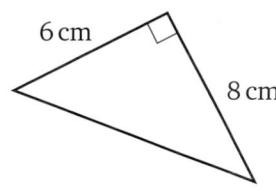
8 cm

d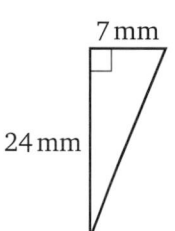
7 mm
24 mm

2 Find the length of the diagonal in each of these rectangles.

Give each answer correct to one decimal place.

a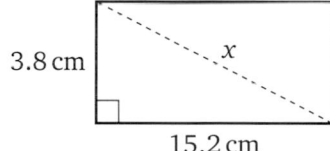
3.8 cm
x
15.2 cm

b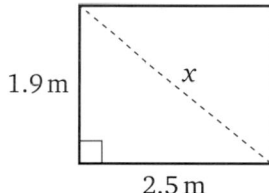
1.9 m
x
2.5 m

Not drawn accurately

c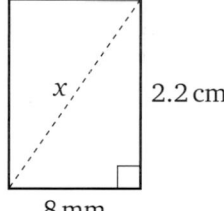
x
2.2 cm
8 mm

3 Find the length of the side marked x in each of these triangles.

Give each answer correct to one decimal place.

a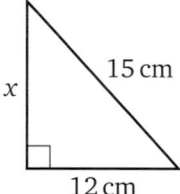
15 cm
x
12 cm

b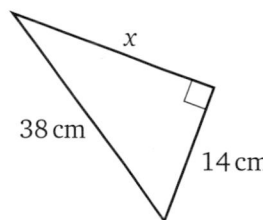
x
38 cm
14 cm

Not drawn accurately

c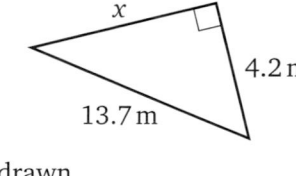
x
4.2 m
13.7 m

4 A triangle has sides 24 cm, 26 cm and 10 cm.

Beth says that this is a right-angled triangle. Amy does not agree.

Who is correct?

Show working to justify your answer.

5 Find the length of the side marked x in each of these triangles.

Give each answer to one decimal place.

a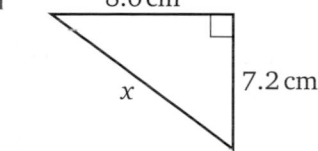
8.6 cm
7.2 cm
x

b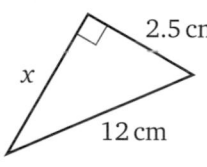
2.5 cm
x
12 cm

Not drawn accurately

c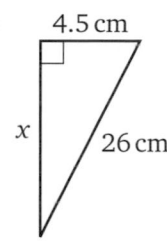
4.5 cm
x
26 cm

d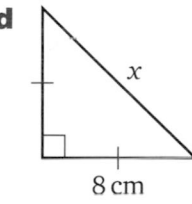
x
8 cm

C

6 Sarah and Ravi are working out the missing side in this triangle.

Sarah works out $7^2 + 22^2$ and says that $x = 23.1$ cm (to 1 d.p.)

Ravi works out $22^2 - 7^2$ and says that $x = 435$ cm

Both of these answers are incorrect.

Explain each person's mistake and work out the correct value of x.

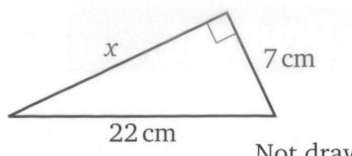

Not drawn accurately

7 An isosceles triangle has two sides of length 7.5 cm and one side of length 12 cm.

Calculate the height of the triangle.

Give your answer to one decimal place.

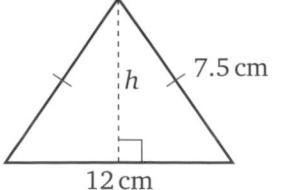

Not drawn accurately

8 Leon walks 1.5 km due north from his house.

He then turns and walks 2 km due east.

How far is he now from his house?

9 **a** A is the point (2, 3) and B is the point (5, 7) as shown in the diagram.

Use Pythagoras' theorem to find the distance between points A and B.

b Sketch a diagram and use Pythagoras' theorem to find the distance between each of the following sets of points.

i (3, 5) and (7, 8)

ii (0, 4) and (5, 10)

iii (−2, 3) and (1, 7)

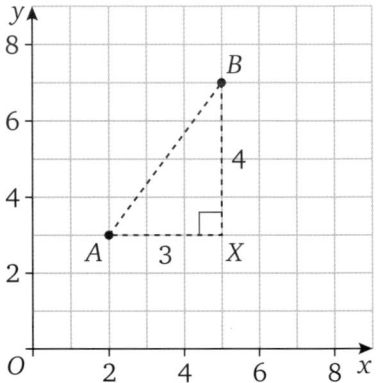

10 Find the length of the side marked x in each diagram.

a

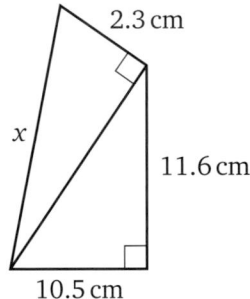

b

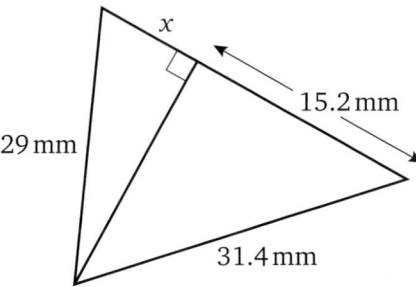

Not drawn accurately

11 A field is in the shape of a rectangle of length 45 metres and width 22 metres. A pipe runs diagonally from one corner of the field to the opposite corner.

How long is the pipe?

Not drawn accurately

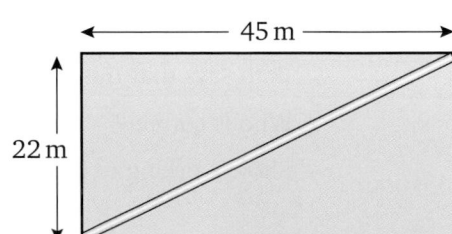

12 A ladder is 6.5 metres long.

The safety instructions say that for a ladder of this length:

- the maximum safe distance of the foot of the ladder from the wall is 1.7 metres

- the minimum safe distance of the foot of the ladder from the wall is 1.5 metres.

What is the maximum vertical height that the ladder can safely reach?

Give your answer to the nearest centimetre.

13 Cath has designed a pendant for a necklace in the shape of a kite.

Work out the length, x, of green line.

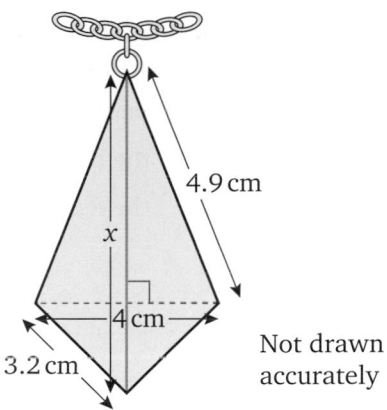

4.9 cm

x

4 cm

3.2 cm

Not drawn accurately

14 Pythagorean triples are sets of three integers that fit Pythagoras' theorem.

For example 3, 4, 5 is a Pythagorean triple as $3^2 + 4^2 = 5^2$. Similarly 5, 12, 13 and 7, 24, 25 are Pythagorean triples.

a Find other Pythagorean triples.

b What patterns can you see in the numbers?

c See if you can find a rule to generate other triples.

14 Assess ⓚ

1 Find the length of side x in each triangle.

Give each answer to one decimal place.

10 cm   26 cm x

4.3 cm   7.8 cm x

27 m   22 m x

Not drawn accurately

12.6 mm   9.1 mm x

2 Work out the perimeter of this quadrilateral.

Hint

Join B and D to form two right-angled triangles.

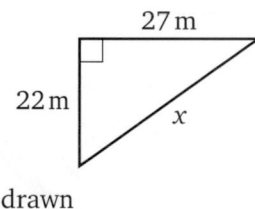

6 cm B
A
7 cm
9 cm
C
D

Not drawn accurately

3 An equilateral triangle has sides of length 15 cm.

Work out the perpendicular height of the triangle.

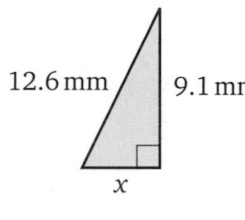

15 cm   15 cm

15 cm

Not drawn accurately

4 A field is in the shape of a rectangle of length 37 m and width 29 m.

A path runs diagonally from one corner of the field to the opposite corner.

What is the length of the path?

5 Rob walks from his house 3 km due south then 2 km due west.

How far is Rob now from his house?

6   A telegraph pole is kept in a vertical position by wires of length 10 metres and x metres that are fixed to the ground.

Calculate:

a   the height, h, of the telegraph pole

b   the length, x, of the second wire.

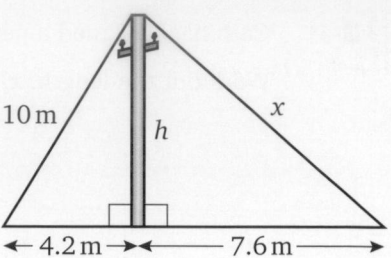

Practice questions

1   The diagram shows a right-angled triangle. Calculate the length x.

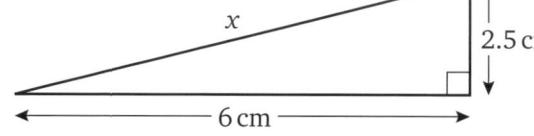

Not drawn accurately

(3 marks)

AQA 2009

2   A ladder of length 5 m rests against a wall. The foot of the ladder is 1.7 m from the base of the wall.

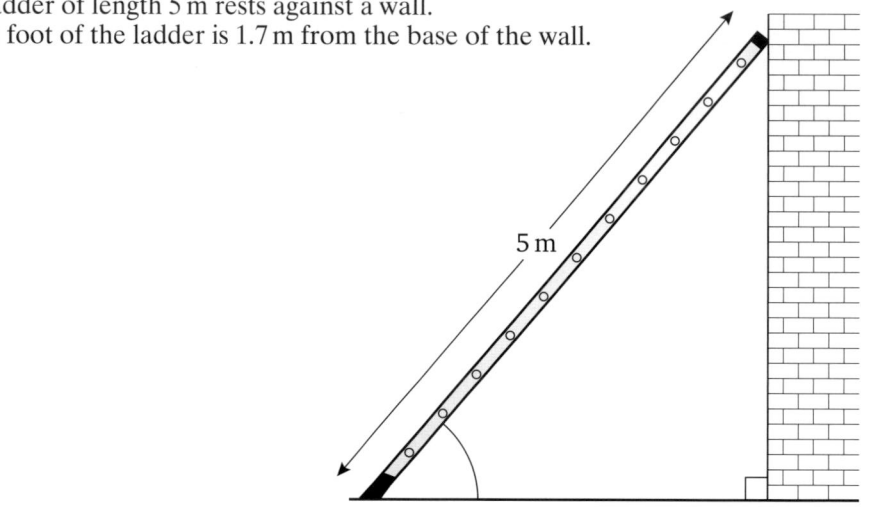

Not drawn accurately

How far up the wall does the ladder reach?   *(3 marks)*

AQA 2008

3   Calculate the length x.

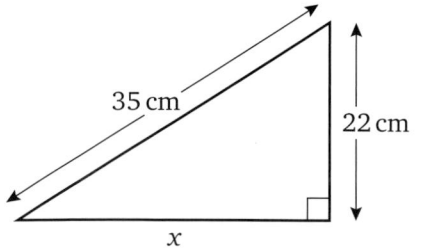

Not drawn accurately

(3 marks)

AQA 2007

Glossary

$<$ – this inequality sign is used to show that one value is **less than** another. For example, $3 < 8$ means '3 is less than 8'.

$>$ – this inequality sign is used to show that one value is **more than** another. For example, $3 > 1$ means '3 is more than 1'.

$\leqslant$ – this inequality sign is used to show that one value is **less than or equal to** another. For example, $x \leqslant 8$ means 'x is any number less than or equal to 8'. In this case x could be any negative number, zero, any positive number below 8 or 8 itself.

$\geqslant$ – this inequality sign is used to show that one value is **more than or equal to** another. For example, $x \geqslant -6$ means 'x is any number more than or equal to -6'. In this case x could be any positive number, zero, any negative number above -6 or -6 itself.

arc – a section of the circumference of a circle.

back-to-back stem-and-leaf diagram – a stem-and-leaf diagram where the stem is down the centre and the leaves from two distributions are either side for comparison.

bar chart – a frequency diagram where the height of a bar represents the frequency of an item.

biased – in the context of probability, not having the expected chance of happening.

bisect – to divide into two equal parts.

bisector – a line that cuts either an angle or a line into two equal parts.

brackets – these show that the terms inside should be treated alike, for example,
$2(3x + 5) = 2 \times 3x + 2 \times 5 = 6x + 10$

centre of enlargement – the point from which the enlargement is made.

certain – an outcome that has to happen.

composite bar chart – a frequency diagram for two or more sets of data with corresponding values from each set of data wholly contained within one bar.

congruent – exactly the same size and shape; the shape might be rotated or flipped over.

construction (construct) – this is the process of drawing a diagram accurately with a 'straight edge' and compasses only.

coordinates – a system used to identify a point; an x-coordinate and a y-coordinate give the horizontal and vertical positions.

correlation – a measure of the relationship between two sets of data; correlation is measured in terms of type and strength.

cross-section – a cut at right angles to a face, and usually at right angles to the length of a prism.

cube – a solid with six identical square faces.

cuboid – a solid with six rectangular faces (two or four of the faces can be squares).

decimal place – the digits to the right of a decimal point in a number.

denominator – the bottom number of a fraction, indicating how many fractional parts the unit has been split into. For example, in the fraction $\frac{4}{7}$ the denominator is 7 (indicating that the unit has been split into 7 parts).

dimension – the measurement between two points on the edge of a shape, for example, length.

dual bar chart – a multiple bar chart with specifically two sets of data.

enlargement – an enlargement changes the size of an object according to a certain scale factor.

equation – an equation is a statement showing that two expressions are equal, for example $2y - 17 = 15$

equidistant – to be equidistant from two points is to be the same distance from both points.

equilateral triangle – a triangle that has all three sides equal in length.

equivalent fractions – two or more fractions that have the same value. Equivalent fractions can be made by multiplying or dividing the numerator and denominator of any fraction by the same number.

evens – the chance of an outcome that is equally likely to happen or not happen.

event – something that takes place that we want to find the probability of. For example, for finding the probability of 'getting an even number with one throw of a dice', the event is 'getting an even number with one throw of a dice'.

experimental probability – the chance of a particular outcome based on results of experiments or previous data.

expression – an expression is a mathematical statement written in symbols, for example $3x + 1$ or $x^2 + 2x$

face – one of the flat surfaces of a solid. For example, a cube (such as a dice) has six flat faces.

fair – without bias; e.g. a fair coin has an equal chance of falling on head or tail.

formula – a formula shows the relationship between two or more variables. For example, in a rectangle, area = length $\times$ width, or $A = lw$

frequency diagram – any chart or diagram which compares the frequencies of objects.

frequency polygon – a frequency diagram for continuous data with a line joining the midpoints of the class intervals using the appropriate frequencies.

histogram – a diagram for continuous data with bars as rectangles whose areas represent the frequency.

hypotenuse – the longest side in a right-angled triangle. It is the side opposite the right angle.

impossible – an outcome that cannot happen.

improper fraction – a fraction with a numerator greater than its denominator.

inequality – statements such as a $c > b$, $a < b$ or $a \leqslant b$ are inequalities.

integer – any positive or negative whole number or zero, for example $-2, -1, 0, 1, 2, \ldots$

inverse operation – the opposite operation. For example, subtraction is the inverse of addition. Division is the inverse of multiplication.

key – an indication of how many items a symbol in a pictogram represents or which type of shading represents which data in other diagrams.

likely – an outcome that probably will happen.

line graph – a diagram for continuous data, usually over a period of time.

line of best fit – a line drawn to represent the relationship between two sets of data; ideally it should only be drawn where the correlation is strong, for example:

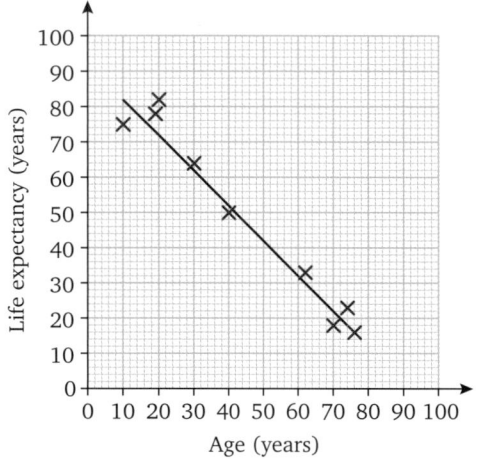

line of symmetry – a shape has reflection symmetry about a line through its centre if reflecting it in that line gives an identical-looking shape.

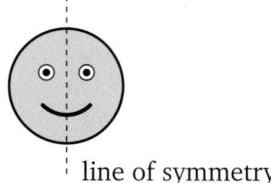

line of symmetry

locus (pl. loci) – a locus is the path followed by a moving point. It is also a set of points that meet a condition.

mixed number – a fraction that has both a whole number and a fraction part.

mutually exclusive events – events that are mutually exclusive cannot happen.

negative correlation – as one set of data increases, the other set of data decreases.

negative number – a number less than zero, expressed with a negative sign; examples: -5.3, -400

net – a net shows the faces and edges of an object. When the net is folded up it makes a 3-D object. For example, the net of a cube when folded up makes a cube.

numerator – the number on the top of a fraction.

operation – a rule for combining two numbers or variables, such as add, subtract, multiply or divide.

outcome – one of the possible results of an experiment or trial. For example, when rolling a dice there are six possible outcomes: 1, 2, 3, 4, 5, 6

outlier – a value that does not fit the general trend, for example:

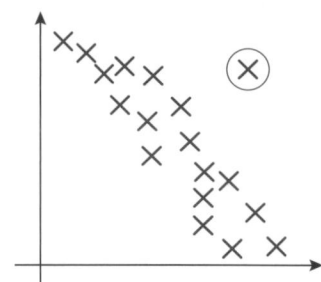

parabola – the curved graph of a quadratic equation is called a parabola.

percentage – the number of parts per hundred, for example, 15% means '15 out of a hundred' or $\frac{15}{100}$.

perpendicular – at right angles to; two lines at right angles to each other are perpendicular lines.

pictogram – a pictogram uses symbols to represent items of data.

pie chart – a frequency diagram where the angle of a sector represents the frequency of an item.

positive correlation – as one set of data increases, the other set of data increases.

positive number – a number greater than zero; sometimes expressed with a positive sign; examples: $+18.3$, 0.36

prism – a solid that has the same cross-section all the way through.

probability – a measure of how likely an event is to occur.

probability scale – a scale running from 0 to 1 on which events can be placed to indicate how likely they are to occur.

proportion – compares one part with the whole, whereas a ratio compares one part with another; if a class has 10 boys and 15 girls, the proportion of boys in the class is $\frac{10}{25}$ (which simplifies to $\frac{2}{5}$), the proportion of girls in the class is $\frac{15}{25}$ (which simplifies to $\frac{3}{5}$).

Pythagoras' theorem – in words 'the square on the hypotenuse is equal to the sum of the squares on the other two sides' or $c^2 = a^2 + b^2$

quadratic equation – a quadratic equation is one in which x^2 is its highest power. $y = x^2 + x - 2$ and $x^2 + x - 2 = 0$ are examples of quadratic equations.

quadratic expression – an expression containing terms where the highest power of the variable is 2

rate – the percentage at which interest is added.

ratio – a ratio is a means of comparing numbers or quantities. It shows how much bigger one number or quantity is than another. If two numbers or quantities are in the ratio $1:2$, the second is always twice as big as the first. If two numbers or quantities are in the ratio $2:5$, for every two parts of the first there are five parts of the second.

reciprocal – any number multiplied by its reciprocal equals 1. 1 divided by a number will give its reciprocal; for example, the reciprocal of 3 is $\frac{1}{3}$ because $3 \times \frac{1}{3} = 1$.

recurring decimal – a decimal number in which a number or group of numbers keeps repeating. You write a recurring decimal like this: $0.\dot{3}$ (the dot shows which number is recurring). If it is a group of numbers that repeats, you put the dot over the first and last digits.

relative frequency – the fraction or proportion of the number of times out of the total that a particular outcome occurs.

rounding – a number can be expressed in an approximate form rather than exactly; for example, it may be written to the nearest integer or to the nearest thousand. This process is called rounding. The number 36 754 rounded to the nearest thousand is 37 000

sample space diagram – a table or diagram showing all possible outcomes for an event.

scale – the units used to measure along an axis.

scale factor – the scale factor of an enlargement is the ratio of the corresponding sides on an object and its image.

scatter graph – a graph used to show the relationship between two sets of variables, for example, temperature and ice cream sales:

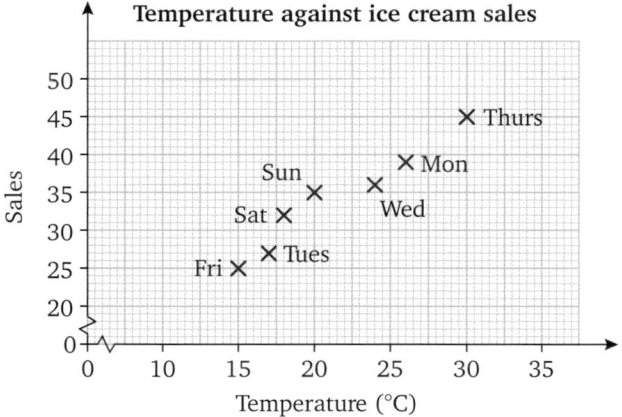

Temperature against ice cream sales

significant figures – the digits in a number; the closer a digit is to the beginning of a number then the more important or significant it is; for example, in the number 23.657, 2 is the most significant digit and is worth 20, 7 is the least significant digit and is worth 7 units; the number 23.657 has 5 significant digits.

similar – shapes are similar (mathematically similar) if they have the same shape but different sizes, that is, one is an enlargement of the other.

solid – a three-dimensional shape.

solve/solution – the value of the unknown quantity, for example, if the equation is $3y = 6$, the solution is $y = 2$

stem-and-leaf diagram – a frequency diagram which uses the actual values of the data split into a stem and leaves; the diagram needs a key.

strength of correlation – the strength of correlation is an indication of how close the points lie to a straight line (perfect correlation); correlation is usually described in terms of strong correlation, weak correlation or no correlation.

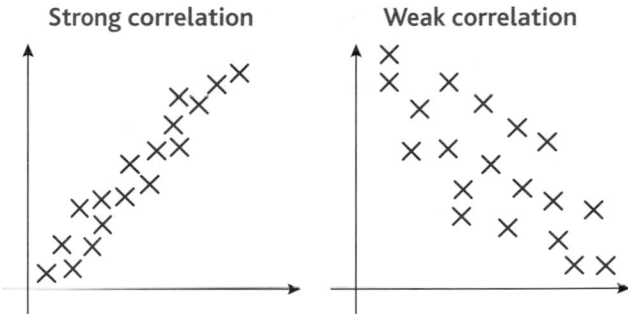

Strong correlation | Weak correlation

subject – the subject of the formula $P = 2(l + w)$ is P because the formula starts '$P = ...$'

substitute – in order to use a formula to work out the value of one of the variables, you replace the letters in the formula with numbers. This is called substitution.

surface area – the exposed area of a solid object, often measured in square centimetres (cm^2) or square metres (m^2).

symbol – when there is an unknown, a symbol, such as a letter, is used to represent it.

symmetrical – a shape or graph is said to be symmetrical if reflecting it about a line through its centre gives an identical-looking shape.

theoretical probability – the chance of a particular outcome based on equally likely outcomes.

time – is measured in years to work out interest (per annum means per year).

transformation – a transformation changes the position or size of an object. Examples of transformations include reflections, rotations, translations and enlargements.

trial and improvement – a method for solving algebraic equations by making an informed guess and then refining this to get closer and closer to the solution.

two-way table – a table showing information about two sets of data at the same time.

type of correlation –

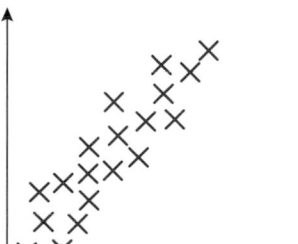

Positive correlation

in positive correlation an increase in one set of variables results in an increase in the other set of variables;

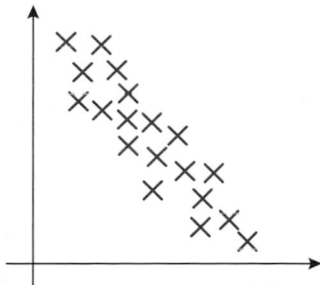

Negative correlation

in negative correlation an increase in one set of variables results in a decrease in the other set of variables;

Zero correlation

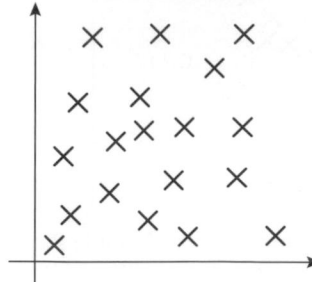

zero or no correlation is where there is no obvious relationship between the two sets of data.

unitary method – a method of calculating quantities that are in proportion by first finding one unit; for example, if 12 litres of petrol cost £11.76 you can find the cost of 10 litres:

12 litres cost   £11.76
1 litre costs   £11.76 ÷ 12 = £0.98
10 litres costs   £0.98 × 10 = £9.80

unitary ratio – a ratio in the form 1 : n or n : 1; this form of ratio is helpful for comparison, as it shows clearly how much of one quantity there is for one unit of the other.

unknown – the letter in an equation representing a quantity that is 'unknown'.

unlikely – an outcome that probably will not happen.

value – letters in a formula represent values. The given value of a letter is substituted into a formula to form an equation.

VAT (Value Added Tax) – this tax is added on to the price of some goods or services.

vertex (pl. vertices) – the point where two or more edges meet.

volume – the amount of space a solid takes up, often measured in cubic centimetres (cm^3) or cubic metres (m^3).

zero or no correlation – where there is no obvious relationship between the two sets of data.

Index

Key terms are given in **bold** and can be found in the glossary.